Bathhouses and Bodybags

And 98 Other Things You Need to Know About Japan

Anne Crescini

Bathhouses and Bodybags

Copyright 2013 by Anne Crescini. All rights reserved.

Printed in the United States of America

All rights reserved. No portion of this book may be reproduced, stored in a retrieval system, or transmitted by any form or by any means--electronic, mechanical, recording, or any other, except for brief quotations in printed reviews, without the prior written permission of the author.

ISBN-13: 978-1492217329

ISBN-10: 1492217328

Cover Design: Jim Xavier

Cover Art: Sophie Xavier

Back Cover Author Image: Riz Crescini

For my girls--

Mia, Abby and Emmy

My most important job is being your Mommy

Table of Contents

#1 My Kids English Not at All Can't Speak 13

#2 Because You're a Girl 17

#3 Gargling, Cold Tummies, and the Evil Air Conditioner 21

#4 Root Canal-Crazy Country 24

#5 Rice—A National Obsession 28

#6 What's a *Freeta*? 32

#7 Mind Your Manners 35

#8 No Debt, Please 41

#9 Swimming in a Sea of Gluten 44

#10 Where's the Soap? 47

#11 Skinny Girls 50

#12 Girly Guys 53

#13 Here Comes the Bride, There Goes My Money 55

#14 Death and Chopsticks 59

#15 Japanese Religion 101 62

#16 Show Me the Love! 66

#17 Smoking Gun 68

#18 The Happy Bag and Weird Food 70

#19 The Red and White Song Battle 74

#20 The Weather Bugs Me 76

#21 Traumatized Kids 78

#22 Cake, The Colonel and Love 81

#23 Land of Masks 84

#24 End of the Year Party 86

#25 Health Checkup Lottery, Part I 88

#26 Health Checkup Lottery, Part II 91

#27 Embarrassment and Culture 93

#28 Bonus Day 95

#29 Costco is Coming! Costco is Coming! 97

#30 Japanese English, Part I 101

#31 Funny Japanese Mistakes 104

#32 I am a Foreigner 106

#33 Funny Japanese Mistakes, Part II 108

#34 *Shaken* to the Core 111

#35 Key Money 113

#36 Driving School of Highway Robbery 118

#37 The *Gambaru* Spirit 123

#38 I Don't Eat Fish With Eyes 125

#39 When Japanese People Can't Use Japanese 130

#40 Japanese Food…Kind of 134

#41 Japanese Bakeries Kick Butt 138

#42 Booze 143

#43 My Kids Not at All English Cannot Speak, Part II 148

#44 What's in a Name? 153

#45 Naked 156

#46 Home Parties: Could You Spare an Hour or Seven? 160

#47 Cherry Blossom Crazy 165

#48 Karaoke-Dokie 168

#49 Killing Me Softly 172

#50 Dog Days 175

#51 Squatty Potties and Texas Toast 178

#52 Homeschooling in Japan 182

#53 Does It Really Cost More? 186

#54 Culture of No Moderation 191

#55 The Cuteness is Killing Me 196

#56 Volunteer--or ELSE!! 200

#57 IV, Please 206

#58 Election Noise 209

#59 The Westernization of Japan 212

#60 Say Cheese 216

#61 Crazy Rock Climbing Mama 221

#62 Excuse Me, Your Onion is Falling Out... 224

#63 Please Don't Call On Me 227

#64 Did You Know... 231

#65 Love Shack 234

#66 Slipper-y Slope 237

#67 Hee Hee Hee 240

#68 On the Radar 243

#69 Japanese English Quiz 246

#70 Country Girl 248

#71 Who Needs Disneyland? 250

#72 Caught Between Cultures 253

#73 Fattening Festival Food 258

#74 Baseball, Baby! 260

#75 Fat Americans 265

#76 Ruled by Rules 270

#77 Reflections on the Tohoku Disaster 273

#78 If I Only Had a Healthy Colon... 279

#79 What a Bunch of Garbage! 283

#80 Here Comes the Rain Again... 288

#81 The 240-Minute Load of Laundry 292

#82 Sports Day and the *Bento* Scheming Mommy 295

#83 Where's My Kid? 300

#84 No Fun in the Sun 304

#85 189 Pills 308

#86 School Lunch Gourmet 310

#87 Fill 'Er Up! 314

#88 A Better Anne Than I Am 316

#89 Hair You Go 322

#90 Above and Beyond 325

#91 Bad English 328

#92 It's Summertime...Now Do Your Homework! 330

#93 Seven 335

#94 You say fuu-TAAN, I say fu-TONE 341

#95 Peanut Butter Girl 345

#96 Socialize Me 349

#97 Your Phone is Smarter than You 352

#98 You Shoes, You Lose 356

#99 Costs an Arm and a Backpack 359

#100 I Love it Here But... 364

Introduction

In December 2012, I published my first book, *Driving Me Crazy About It: Reflections of an American in Japan*. Writing a book had been a lifelong dream of mine, but I found that after finishing it, the writing bug still had me firmly in its grasp. I just couldn't stop writing, and even though I thought I had covered Japan pretty thoroughly, I experienced something new almost everyday that I wanted to write about. It was like all of a sudden I was conscious of things around me, things--cultural differences, language usage, behavior--that I hadn't really noticed before.

My friend and personal graphic designer Jim Xavier encouraged me to start a blog to help promote my book. I had tried a blog before, but just couldn't keep it going. This time was different, however. I was so excited to write it that I was going blog crazy and writing more than once a day. My loving husband informed me that this was not the way to write a blog, and that I was going to overwhelm my readers at this rate. So, I calmed down on the blog, instead putting my thoughts into short, daily readings, and those readings have developed into this book. Many of the chapters in this book are blog posts, so those who follow my blog may already be familiar with some of them. Other chapters are new. My husband and I were joking that this is good bathroom reading material. We were joking, but this book *was* meant to be both humorous and informative at the same time. It is arranged for the busy person who wants to learn about Japan but doesn't have much time. My hope is that when you are finished with this book, you will have a greater understanding of not only the big things, but also the little things that make Japanese culture so wonderful and so complex.

Oh, in case you are wondering about why the term *body bags* is in the title, well, I can't tell you that. Keep reading and you will find out.

Anne Crescini

Kitakyushu, Japan

October 2013

"Hey Mommy! My English teacher is from England, but he still speaks English."--My 7-year old linguistically challenged daughter, Mia

"Mommy, who is the loudest person in China?"--My 5-year old daughter, Abby

"Mia, did you drink your medicine yet?"--Me

"Mommy, what is Jesus' middle name?"--Abby again

#1 My Kids English Not at All Can't Speak

Well, that is not exactly true. My kids can speak English, and most of the time we communicate fine, but every now and then it is a maze to maneuver the grammatical structure and vocabulary mixing that goes on in our house. Although we speak only English at home, they were born in Japan, and the time they spend at preschool or elementary school everyday is, unfortunately, much longer than the time they spend with us. So I guess it can be expected that their Japanese ability is higher than their English ability. That being said, because I am a native speaker, and worse yet, an English teacher, the fact that my own kids cannot communicate in English on occasion bothers me and makes me feel like I am doing something wrong. I know, you say, when they get a little older, they will work things out and be completely bilingual.

Most of my friends who have raised kids in a different culture tell me this, and I believe it, but it is still strange to me that my kids know certain words in Japanese way before they know them in English. For example, the word 'mole.' I will never forget the first time three-year old Mia pointed at my face and giggled, "*Hokuro!*" Because of my superior Japanese language skills, I, of course, know that means 'mole.' The kind on your skin, not the kind that crawls out of holes. That would be a *mogura*, another word my kids learned in Japanese first. Riz, on the other hand, because of his inferior language skills didn't know what a *hokuro* was. That was the first time we really thought that one day our kids are going to be making fun of our weird, flawed Japanese. By the way, I am just kidding about Riz's inferior language skills; he is an excellent Japanese speaker. But, he really didn't know the word for 'mole.' After all, it is not a word that comes up often in daily conversation…

The biggest problem we have is the mixing of Japanese and English vocabulary in one sentence. I am sure that anyone raising bilingual kids can relate. "Mommy, can you *musubu* (put up) my hair with this *gomu* (rubber band)." Another one is, "Mommy, today during *15-fun yasumi* (morning recess), I played *soto* (outside) with my friends and we did *nawa tobi* (jump rope)." This is just a small sampling of the colorful sentences that my kids produce everyday. Of course, I do the same thing, not only with them, but with any of my bilingual friends. I don't know why, but certain words just either sound better in Japanese, or there is no English equivalent that catches the nuance of what I want to say. Examples of Japanese words I almost always throw into my English sentences are *gaman* (suck it up), *eki* (train station), *keitai* (cell phone), *hoikuen* (preschool), *sensei* (teacher), *oyatsu* (snack), *ayashii* (sketchy), *bimyou* (hmm. I am not sure how to translate this one. Anybody know the best English? Maybe the best translation is actually, I'm not sure). So, with my train-wreck sentences, I guess that I can't really blame my kids, who are being raised here, for their weird linguistic creations. Sometimes I make Mia start over using only English. Maybe I should hold myself to the same standard.

Another interesting thing, and I have heard other parents say the same thing, is how my kids will put English inflection on Japanese words or vice versa. For example, the Japanese word for 'cut' is *kiru*. My kids will say, "Can you keet this?? For the longest time, I couldn't figure it out. Finally, I realized they were mixing 'cut' and '*kiru*.' A friend's child would take 'eat' and the Japanese equivalent *taberu*. She would say "eat-ta." This was so funny, because she put the past tense ending 'ta' (*tabeta*-I ate it) on the English word 'eat.'

Finally, there are times when they just don't have the vocabulary to tell me what they want to say. "Mommy, come here." "What?" "Just come here!" "Use words!" "I don't know how to say it! Come here." Another one is, "Can you fix my this?" Mia has gotten to the age where she is old enough to ask me how to say something in English. The younger two just say, "Can you fix my this?"

So, after all this exasperation (I'm not THAT exasperated; I laugh about their language use all the time!) about my kids' abuse of the English language, I must say this. They are going to be much better Japanese speakers than I will ever be, and in some ways, especially regarding pronunciation, they already are. Even my three-year old Emmy corrects me sometimes. I am so proud of how they can use Japanese, especially when I hear them speak in the rough local dialect. Mia loves Japanese class more than any other subject, and her writing is so beautiful. The kids sometimes talk in Japanese when playing together and sometimes, when fighting; some words just sound meaner in Japanese than English like, '*iyada!*' It sounds much more rebellious than the English 'no!' Another one, '*sen de!*' (stop it!) sounds particularly virulent in Japanese. As for their English, I am so proud of how good they are, despite the fact that Riz and I haven't really even started to formally teach them (just ordered home school curriculum yesterday!). Mia can read simple books even though we never taught her phonics, and Abby knows most of the alphabet. Emmy just wants to practice writing her 'E' all the time. To be honest, I am a very laid-back Mommy. I am about the farthest thing you will ever find from a Chinese Tiger Mother or Japanese Education Mother. I know that as long as we spend some time working with them, they will be fine. I know that if we ever go back to the U.S., they may be behind for a little while, but that they will catch up in no time. I also realize, though, that it is our responsibility to teach them, as they are not going to get formal English training until the fifth grade. I am troubled by kids with a Japanese mommy and an English-speaking Daddy who cannot speak a lick of English. I don't want my kids to be like that. Can you imagine the earful I would get from my Mom if my kids couldn't communicate with their grandparents? Anyone who knows my Mom can imagine it, and it is not pretty…

#2 Because You're a Girl

I grew up playing sports all the time with my two brothers, and I was super competitive and didn't want any special treatment because I was a girl. I didn't need it anyway. In basketball, I could outplay most of the boys in my neighborhood, school and even the State of Virginia. When I was in junior high, I took second place in the State Dribble and Shoot Basketball Championship, being one of the only girls in history ever to place. I was a huge tomboy growing up, played mostly with boys, and turned my chin up at dolls, makeup or other girly things. I was an athlete, and I could kick some butt.

So, when I came to Kitakyushu at the still pretty young age of 28, I decided that in my free time I would play basketball and other sports with the students as much as I could. I started playing with the girls' basketball team a couple times a week, and would play catch with students sometimes. Every year, my university has a sports festival in which students form their own teams and compete against each other in various ball sports such as basketball, volleyball, soccer, and my favorite, softball. I decided to join one of the student softball teams.

I was horrified by the rules. I learned that the rules for girls and boys were different. For example, if a girl even made contact when she was batting, she was safe. WHAT!!?? And, when in the field, if she fielded a ground ball, she didn't even have to throw it–the batter was automatically out. In basketball, a girl's 3-pointer was actually six points or something. These special girl rules insulted the competitive athlete in me, and annoyed my husband, Riz, too. You see, Riz is just as competitive as I am, and his very talented team got crushed by one female 6-point machine.

Like everything that gives special treatment to women here, these girl rules were made to protect and help the weaker sex. Everybody knows that Japan is a patriarchal society, and women are still seen as inferior in many ways, especially when it comes to physical activity. Whenever I talk about how much I love baseball, all the girls I know say, "Oh, me too! I love cheering for my favorite team!" Give me a break. Cheering is for wussies. I mean, I like playing – hitting, throwing, catching, sliding. I love being rough. My only two trips to the ER during my childhood were for baseball-related injuries. I love being physical – rock climbing, Billy's Boot Camp, running, going to batting cages. Most of my female friends just aren't that interested in exercise, and if they are, it's swimming or walking or something like that. Many Japanese women are thin, but it seems to me they don't have a whole lot of strength.

There are other ways, too, in which girls and boys are treated differently. There is Ladies' Day at movie theaters, a weekly event when women get to see the films for the reduced price of 1000 yen ($10) instead of the usual highway robbery price of 1800 yen ($18). Guys complained reverse discrimination, so recently many theaters are introducing Men's

Day as well. Many restaurants will have a Ladies' Set, a lighter menu for the thin female frame. There is a lot here about separating the sexes regarding food. When I first arrived in Japan, I ate a Pork Cutlet rice bowl, a pretty hearty meal, but hey, I was hungry. This girl told me, "Girls don't eat that kinda stuff." Come to think of it, most of the women around me don't eat all that much. Noodles and salads are popular female lunch fare. Once, I was shocked by my friend's *bento* lunch box. It was like, a teeny weeny bit of rice, a tomato, a bite size piece of fish or something, and some little veggie. It was a proper female lunchbox. Of course, I have female friends who eat more than some men I know, but in general, women are lighter eaters.

There is a car here specifically marketed to women, too, because of it's feminine rounded shape. It is small and cute, like women are supposed to be. There are snacks and foods given names like, "Men's Chocolate Crackers" or "Strong Man's Curry Bread." I guess I have never thought of products, especially food, as being for one specific gender. I think I am going to try that Strong Man's Curry Bread someday.

The Japanese language even has distinct words divided into female terms and male terms. The female terms are soft and feminine, while the male terms are manly and rough. While these days, the distinction between the sexes regarding language use is beginning to disappear, there are still words that are considered too rough for girls. My American friend has a Japanese husband and learned much of her Japanese from him. It cracks me up to hear this tall, pretty American girl talk in tough guy Japanese sometimes. "*Hara hetta! Meishi kuetai naa.*" (I am starving! I wanna eat.) A proper girl would say, "*Onaka ga suita. Gohan wo tabetai.*" As you can see, even if you cannot speak Japanese, those two sentences look nothing alike.

Sometimes the rules to protect and help females actually hurt me. Like when I was told that by law I had to take maternity leave after my second daughter was born, even though it was unpaid. Of course, the government made maternity leave mandatory to keep women from being pressured by families and bosses not to take it. It was a law intended to protect women, give them time to rest their delicate bodies after childbirth (many women don't leave the house for a month), and have a job to go back to later. Making it optional would leave the door open to outside pressure and a woman's rights would be compromised. I doubt they were thinking of women like me, who depend on their salary to pay the bills. For two months, we had to our pay bills out of savings.

I am not a feminist by the farthest stretch of the imagination. But I hate being treated differently, whether from good motives or bad, because I am a girl. I dislike both preferential treatment and discrimination. I am a human, a very competitive human, and my parents brought me up to believe I can do anything a boy can do. And I can. Just ask the boys at the State Dribble and Shoot Championship whom I crushed.

#3 Gargling, Cold Tummies and the Evil Air Conditioner

Every country has their share of ideas, passed down from generation to generation about how to stay healthy, and what to do when you do get sick. I remember when I was growing up, whenever I got sick, it was either oatmeal or chicken noodle soup. Of course, every effort was made to keep from getting sick in the first place. This started with hand washing before eating, and not going outside with a wet head, both of which are also preached to kids here in Japan. Interestingly enough, the wet head thing is actually not true; colds and flu are caused by viruses - not by going outside with a wet head. Of course, if you are already a little under the weather, going outside with a wet head can make it worse.

Regarding hand washing, Americans are pretty militant; every mom I know in the U.S. carries around hand sanitizing gel just in case there is no soap available. I was super careful about this during the Swine Flu epidemic a couple of years ago. Of course, my kids got the flu anyway. The Japanese also preach hand washing, but from the lack of soap in public toilets, I wonder if they think simple water will wash off those germs. Some stores do place hand sanitizer at the entrance, which I am thankful for. I have gotten a little lazy in recent days about the hand sanitizer. Maybe that is why my kids keep getting sick... hmm...

In Japan, there are three holy grails regarding preventing

sickness: gargle after returning home, keep your tummy from getting cold, and don't sleep with the air conditioner on, all three of which I had never heard before coming here. In the U.S., sometimes I was told to gargle with salt water AFTER getting sick to relieve the pain of a sore throat, but I had never heard about gargling as a preventative measure. I am not sure, but I think the Japanese believe that gargling, even with plain water, washes out some germs lurking in your throat, waiting for the opportune time to start wreaking havoc. I don't know if it works or not, but it can't seem to hurt. Still, I am a stubborn American on this one, and I never gargle, or have my kids gargle either.

The whole don't-let-your-tummy-get-cold admonition is fascinating to me. For some reason, letting your tummy get too cold is the cause of many sicknesses. As I wrote in my first book, there is this doctor in town who is famous for blaming many colds and fevers on cold tummies. He is always telling mothers not to let their kids eat ice cream or other cold stuff. At my kids' preschool, the teachers always tuck my daughters' shirts into their pants, sometimes pulling the pants up all the ways to their chest. They look so ridiculous, but again, the teachers are trying to keep their tummies from getting cold. Interestingly enough, Onesies are discouraged because they interfere with potty training. Seems to me there is no better article of clothing to keep the tummy from getting cold to me. Lastly, while keeping the tummy warm is crucial, keeping the feet cold is equally important to a healthy body. Once I asked a Japanese mommy friend why she didn't dress her baby in a footed sleeper like American moms do, and she said that the feet need to be uncovered to regulate body temperature or something like that. Maybe that is another reason my kids aren't allowed to wear socks at school, even in winter.

Then there is the evil air conditioner and heater. Many sore throats and sinus problems are blamed on them. The Japanese believe that sleeping at night with the air conditioner or heater on dries out the air, causing sickness. Of course, just like the wet head example, the air conditioner is not capable or evil enough to make someone sick. To be sure, it may dry the air and give someone a sore throat, but it cannot make someone sick. Every time I tell a friend that I keep the air on at night, they always say, "It doesn't make your throat hurt?" So, despite being incredibly cold or hot, most of my friends try not to keep the air or heater on all night, partly to prevent sickness, and probably partly to save money. Maybe that is why my electricity bill is so much higher than that of my friends….

So, who is to say which countries' beliefs about all this are right? I, personally, don't make an effort to have my kids gargle, keep their tummies warm, or turn off the air, but I have friends who do. When my kids have a fever, I might put them in a lukewarm bath, which my Mom always told me was a good thing to do for a fever. A Japanese person would never think of giving a kid with a fever a bath (Probably the only time in that kid's life they can get away with not getting a bath!)

In case, you are wondering what Japanese kids eat when they are sick, just last Sunday my middle daughter Abby had the stomach flu. I went to the store to buy her some salmon *okayu*, which is this soupy rice dish. I think it is gross, except when flavored with egg or soy sauce or something. My husband, Riz, loves it, and sometimes even eats it when he is healthy. I bet it is a good diet food…

So during winter, stay healthy, gargle, and no matter what you do, don't let your tummy get cold!

#4 Root Canal-Crazy Country

My seven-year old daughter Mia is undergoing her fifth root canal. Maybe you are thinking, "What??!! A seven-year old having one root canal, let alone five?? I have never heard of such a thing in my life!" To be honest, before coming to Japan, I had never heard of a child having a root canal either. When I went back to the U.S. last summer, I talked to a dental hygienist who assured me that even in the U.S. kids sometimes undergo root canals. That being said, I have a hard time believing root canals in the U.S. are nearly as common as they are here.

I experienced my first root canal when I was living in Kobe in 1998. At that time, my Japanese was poor, and I didn't even know the dentist was going to do a root canal until he was finished. He was like, "Oh yeah, I took the root out." I was shocked because I had heard from so many people how painful root canals are, and I couldn't believe that I had just had one without knowing it. Of course, I can't really say, "I had just had one" because, in fact, I was still in the process of having one. For some reason, whether it is due to the insurance system or belief that it needs to be done slowly to be done right, I had to go 8 or 9 times to get that first root canal done. Taking forever to treat cavities, sinus infections or other medical problems is so common in Japan that they even have a phrase in Japanese that means, "to commute to the hospital." I cannot really complain, because, even though I had to go 8 or 9 times, the whole deal cost just over 50 bucks. Can't beat that.

During pregnancy and my postpartum days, the extra nutrition required by my fetus and newborn seemed to suck the life out of my teeth. All of a sudden, no matter what I ate or how well I brushed, my teeth seem to be a magnet for cavities. I don't even know for sure how many root canals I had in those days, but I think it was three or four. And while, Japanese dentists use anesthesia to numb the tooth, there were a couple times that the pain was right up there with the pain of childbirth. The dentist kept telling me that the anesthesia should be working, but it wasn't, so he kept shooting me up with more. Things have calmed down for me a little lately; just a couple weeks ago I went in for a regular cleaning, and for the first time since I came to Japan, my dental hygiene was praised!! No cavities and very little plaque! It's a miracle!

Unfortunately, my kids are not so lucky. Mia has had five roots canals, and Abby, two. So far, little Emmy still has undefiled teeth, except for the back molar that came out a few years too early in a bathtub accident a couple of years ago. I used to beat myself up about my kids' poor teeth, blaming myself for not brushing them well enough or feeding the kids too much sugar. But now, I am starting to wonder if it may be something else. Maybe they just have weak teeth like me. I mean, they eat sugar, but all kids eat sugar, right?

Recently, they are eating much less than before. Tap water in Japan doesn't have fluoride, which may be another factor. But my husband and I have been brushing their teeth for them, and they have been getting fluoride treatments at the dentist. Yet, the cavities keep coming. I take that back, I would absolutely LOVE it if my kids would have a normal cavity. But, NO! It is always a root canal. Every time, it seems, we take them in for tooth pain or even a black spot we notice, it seems like the dentist is shouting, "Oh my goodness what a deep cavity! It needs a root canal!" Sometimes, the tooth isn't even hurting and they get root canals. Kids cannot bear the pain like adults, though, so they have to do a slower, kid-friendly version, killing the root with some silver-looking powdery stuff and then extracting it. Sometimes it feels like going to the dentist is a weekly event like swimming school or drum lessons. At least we don't have to pay anything for Abby...

Yesterday, Mia came home from school crying her tooth

hurt so bad. Apparently, a cavity that had been filled weeks ago got infected, and since it was filled, there was nowhere for the inflammation to escape, causing excruciating pain. We took her to the dentist, and he numbed her up, telling her that it shouldn't hurt to take out the root, which was necessary again due to the infection. Well, it hurt anyway, and she was squirming and crying so much it was painful as a parent to watch. I just held her hand and prayed for her. I couldn't even watch. The dentist said that it shouldn't hurt, that her fear was multiplying the pain, but to me, her pain was very real. After he was done, he said that while it might hurt a bit when the anesthesia wore off, it should be fine after that. Well, it wasn't. She was up most of the night crying and in pain. As a parent, to see her in all that pain and not being able to take it away hurts me, too, maybe as much as her toothache was hurting her. Thanks be to God, when she woke up this morning she was pain-free.

I vow with all that is within me that that is the last root canal any of my kids will ever experience. I never want to have to see them in pain like I saw Mia yesterday. Maybe I won't be able to prevent it, I don't know, but I do know that I am going to try. Ten root canals in one family is more than enough.

*I failed. Abby is now in the process of getting root canal #3.

#5 Rice—A National Obsession

I am writing this during the Super Bowl. The Super Bowl always makes me think about how crazy Americans are about football in general and the Super Bowl in particular. Many people who don't even like football get together anyway for Super Bowl parties. Maybe it is an excuse to just eat and drink a lot.

Anyway, thinking about national obsessions made me think about rice. Today I was thinking a lot about rice. The Japanese are absolutely crazy about rice and think that it is the staple food of a healthy diet. Many students I know eat rice three times a day, sometimes a couple of bowls at each meal. The Japanese government even puts out promotional ads about rice, encouraging people to begin their day with a nice bowl of hot rice. Schools here even encourage the kids to eat rice and not bread for breakfast. There is a strong sentiment here that if you eat bread, you will get hungry not long after; however, if you eat rice, you will stay full for longer. Interestingly enough, I find the opposite to be true. I am always hungry not long after eating rice.

Part of the reason I have been thinking so much about rice lately is that I have been eating it a lot since trying to reduce gluten from my diet. It is not that I didn't like it before, but I just much preferred bread. And since the media has been harping on the evils of too many carbs for years, I figured that since I couldn't eat both, I would choose bread. I never ate rice as a kid. I grew up in the mountains of Southwest Virginia, and we ate typical American cuisine: hamburgers, hot dogs, lasagna, roast beef and lots of casseroles. And Doritos. Can't forget them! In fact, I don't even think I ever ate real Asian rice until I was in college. That instant Uncle Ben stuff that you have to eat with a fork doesn't count. (To a Japanese, rice that cannot be eaten with chopsticks doesn't really count as rice!) I remember I had a date with this dreamy guy, and he took me to a Chinese restaurant for dinner. It was my first experience with rice. I don't really have much recollection about my opinion of it, but that probably means that I thought it was pretty bland like most Americans do. To remedy that of course, for subsequent rice-eating experiences, I drowned my rice with soy sauce, which is about one of the worst cultural taboos ever. I liken it to a Japanese coming to America and eating pizza with green tea.

I tried rice off and on throughout college and grad school, and got a rice cooker as a graduation gift. The first time I made rice, I forgot to put water in the rice cooker. Uh yeah. That was a problem. I even tried it with my favorite food of all time–peanut butter. Gross, you may say, but..yeah, you're right. It was gross. Anyway, when I moved to Japan, I started eating rice more and actually developed quite a taste for it. It really goes well with Japanese food, and the flavor of the food made up for the fact that I still thought rice was pretty tasteless. I was, however, still committing the taboo of putting soy sauce on my rice at that point.

Recently, I have developed a love for *haiga mai*, a healthier alternative to white rice, somewhere in between white rice and brown rice on the fiber scale. I wish I knew the English equivalent, but when I looked it up, it didn't make any sense, so I will stick with the Japanese here. My kids and Riz aren't crazy about it, but I make them eat it anyway since it is healthy. My kids, along with most of the Japanese population, think that white rice tastes so much better than *haiga mai* or brown rice. I just don't get it. White rice, to me, is so bland, and the more healthy varieties are so flavorful. In the U.S. white rice, along with white bread and most other white foods, is criticized as being void of nutrition, carb-heavy and a pretty much useless, empty-calorie food. You don't really hear that here, though. Most Japanese families still eat white rice everyday. I did hear recently, though, that a lot of Japanese kids today don't really like rice, preferring to eat bread for breakfast instead. This is unbelievable to me, the culinary equivalent of American kids turning their backs on pizza for sushi. To be sure, it is much easier for working parents to stick a piece of bread in the toaster than prepare a traditional, healthy Japanese breakfast.

As a side note about *haiga mai*, I found out a week or so into my quest to reduce gluten that it is one of the only kinds of rice to contain gluten. Oh well, so much for that experiment. It only has trace amounts, though, so I am still feeling better than when I loaded up on multi-grain bread. My kids still don't like it, but they do like brown rice. Brown rice is so chewy and flavorful there is not even a need to drench it in soy sauce. Since the family hates *haiga mai,* and we all love brown rice, I have abandoned *haiga mai* recently. Instead, I make mostly white rice, with an occasional brown rice day thrown in.

I have found that many Japanese tend to be a little ignorant, though, about the caloric content of rice. Many of my friends think that rice is the ultimate health food, and because it is, they can eat as much as they want to. In fact, rice is very high calorie, and high in carbs as well. Some people wonder why they cannot lose weight, and don't even think to blame the two bowls of rice they are downing everyday at dinner right before bed. To me, it is kind of like the misconception Americans have about bagels or granola. Many people think they are both health foods, but in reality a bagel with cream cheese has almost the same amount of calories as a Big Mac, and some granolas have more sugar than a donut. That being said, you cannot really argue with the Japanese conviction that rice is the key to a healthy body. I mean, for years they had the longest life expectancy in the world, only falling back a little recently thanks in part to their new national obsession--Western food.

So, I guess the moral of the story is this: eat anything in moderation and you probably will be okay, unless you have some kind of allergy or food intolerance, of course. I agree that rice is high carb and high calorie, but it is so much a part of this culture and goes so well with traditional Japanese dishes. I mean, the Japanese are much skinnier than bread-loving Americans, so rice cannot be all that bad. As for me, I will keep eating my brown rice (minus the soy sauce. That is gross), and my family will be like the 125 million Japanese people who eat evil white rice every day and they will still live to be 90 years old. There are too many other GMO products and chemical-filled food impostors in today's world to worry about rice killing my family, don't you think?

#6 What's a *Freeta*?

I was talking to someone the other day about work, namely, making sure that you find something you really enjoy doing. I was telling her not to settle for a job that she might possibly hate, and be miserable doing it for at least a year. It seems that in Japan, most college graduates who find a job are committed to sticking with it for at least a year, no matter how unhappy or miserable he or she may be. I am not sure if they hang in there this long because they want to make sure they really hate it, or if they feel like it is unfair to the company who hired them to quit earlier than this. But if you think about it, a year is a really long time to be unhappy in a job, waking up every morning and going to a place you don't like, doing something you don't want to do. I still remember how miserable Riz was when he started working a new job in the U.S. after our time in Kobe. He would hide under the covers in the morning dreading going to work. He eventually came to like his job, but it was hard for me to see him so unhappy. I advised my friend that since she has a place to live, and no real money concerns, why not work part-time somewhere until she finds something she really likes?

She told me she has thought about this, but is worried about what everybody around her thinks about her and is saying about her. That is so big here in Japan – the opinion of those around you. If she were to forgo a low-paying full-time job for an equally low-paying part-time job, she would join the ranks or the *freeta*. The term *freeta*, an excellent example of Japanese English, is used to refer to young people who choose to prioritize their freedom and happiness over stability and salary by choosing to work part-time instead of finding a career. The number of young people bucking the trend and not interested in lifetime employment is increasing these days. Unlike most Japanese, I don't really have a negative opinion of the *freeta*; after all, they are being responsible and working, most of them at least five days a week. While they are not full-time employees, many of them often work schedules comparable to them. I sometimes wonder if a *freeta* can make more money than a full-time worker in dismally low-paying positions such as preschool teachers. But of course, society thinks more highly of someone in a stable full-time job. To me, most *freetas* work hard, make money and take care of themselves. That is nothing to be ashamed of.

The NEET on the other hand, is a different story. This term comes from the abbreviation of the English words, Not in

Education, Employment or Training. The NEET is pretty much a lazy bum mooching off his or her parents, doing nothing. Traditionally, Japanese parents tend to be kind of soft on their kids. The number of NEET, unmotivated and uninspired Japanese young people, is also increasing in recent days. Of course, I don't think being a NEET is acceptable adult behavior in Japan or anywhere else for that matter. My mom would kick me out on my tush if I tried pulling that off...

The main issue that leads to all this rebellious behavior towards work is the growing independence of Japanese young people. They are no longer content to stay with the same company doing the same things their whole lives, especially if they are not happy and not finding satisfaction in their work. In addition, the long Japanese economic recession doesn't even guarantee lifetime employment anymore anyway. Changing jobs several times is not uncommon, and many young people will leave a company if they are not happy. Some young people will use a working holiday visa or go backpacking around the world for six months to a year after quitting their jobs as a time of respite, to think about and reflect upon what they want in life, and what will make them happy. And being happy, being personally satisfied is much more important now than it used to be. It seems young people are becoming more and more unwilling to sacrifice personal happiness for the sake of their company or the sake of society.

Regarding work, I am one of the lucky ones. I have found

a job that I absolutely love, and I feel blessed to be able to get paid to do something I enjoy. Of course, it is not perfect, but nothing really is. I love my students. They make me happy and they make me laugh. I enjoy my relationships with my co-workers, and am learning so much from my research. I think deep down, more than anything, most people just want to be happy and satisfied in life. And in Japan, a huge part of that happiness is found in a having a meaningful job. I mean, you are at work for eight to ten hours a day, five or six days a week. That is a huge chunk of time to be either happy or unhappy. I, for one, am really thankful that I have found happiness in a meaningful job, and then get to go home everyday to the happiness and love of my family. I am a lucky woman indeed. I hope that Japanese young people can find what they are looking for, too.

#7 Mind Your Manners

Japanese people are pretty serious about having good manners. It seems that everywhere you go, you will see signs around neighborhoods, in parks, in supermarkets and on the train reminding everyone to mind their manners. "If your dog poops, make sure you scoop it up and take it home with you." "Turn off your phone or put it on vibrate so you don't bother those around you." "Don't make too much noise when you are outside." "Don't sit on the floor of the train." "Give your seat up for the elderly, handicapped or mothers with small children." The word "manners" has even become Japanese, and everywhere Japanese people go, they are reminded how important good manners are for an orderly society.

The thing is, I think the Japanese idea of manners and my idea is a little different. To me, manners=respect. You should show respect to the people and places around you, and treat them according to the value they have. Because humans are created in the image of God, they are infinitely more valuable and worthy of respect than anything else. Treating others with respect, even if you don't feel like it, is the most important manner to cultivate. Maybe that is why I get so annoyed with the lack of respect I see towards family members in Japan. Parents yell at their kids in public, sometimes smacking them on the head. Children order their mothers around like they are servants and rarely get scolded. "Hey, Mom, buy me that!" "Give me that!" "I'm thirsty!" "Where's my drink?" I cannot stand to hear the way kids talk to their moms here. It is even harder on the ears since I know Japanese so well, and am aware of the very informal language used by them, and it always lacks any form of "please."

My husband and I don't stand for any talk like this. The kids know that we are in charge, we are above them, and they are required to treat us with respect. When they say, "I'm thirsty," I say, "So, what do you want me to do about it?" At that point they realize they are supposed to say, "Can I have a drink please, mommy?" More often than not, I will also make them get it themselves, if they are able to. I am their mother and I love them and want to serve them with all my heart, but I am not a slave or a servant.

Recently, I have been so bothered by how kids talk to their moms that I correct them. I rebuke them right there in front of their mothers and tell them to say "please." Their moms don't mind my intervention a bit, and are even thankful for it. I think Japanese moms don't like how their kids talk to them, but maybe they think it is too late, it's the way society is, and that the kids are too old to do anything about it. My kids may lapse a little at times, but they are generally very polite and respectful towards their parents. They know we are in charge, and if they want anything, they have to be nice about it. We also don't tolerate endless sibling bickering, fighting and disrespect. While we recognize that sisters as close in age as ours are will fight, we refuse to have a there-is-nothing-I-can-do-about-it attitude. We are teaching our kids that they must respect all people, and that it must start at home.

Japanese people are so polite and nice to strangers, friends, customers, and business associates. In fact, Japanese manners and respect are famous all over the world. However, the Japanese, like people all over the world, are oftentimes ruder and more disrespetful to people they love than people they don't know. I know that Japanese kids love their mommies, but sometimes I feel moms are really taken for granted here. Everyone, from kids to husbands to grandparents to friends seem to think that it is the duty of a mother to sacrifice who she is, her very identity, for her children. Because everyone expects this and this is normal, there is a tendency to take mothers for granted and not appreciate them as they should be appreciated. All mothers want to give of themselves for their children, but we still want to feel appreciated, to feel like our children and husbands are aware of what we are doing and are thankful for it. We don't need much, just a "Thanks, Mom! I appreciate it" and an occasional "That dinner was awesome!" will suffice. And please, don't forget our birthdays! One of my friends told me once her kids and husband totally forgot her birthday, and she looked so sad.

Even Mother's Day is not that big of a deal here. Some kids will give their moms a flower or take her out to dinner, but that is about it. Many kids forget altogether. My mommy friends about my age are so concerned about doing something for their own mommy that they forget that they are mommies, too, and should be appreciated. My church even had the yearly church cleaning on Mother's Day until me and some other moms complained about it.

My kids don't take me for granted, but that is because Riz doesn't let them. This year, they made me breakfast and drew me pictures; Riz cleaned the bathtub and made me a video. But more than what they do on that day is the love and appreciation they show me everyday of the year. All the kids, especially Mia, say thank you after almost every meal, even when it is not all that yummy (which I think is pretty often). On days we get take out, Mia prays, "Thank you God for this food Mommy bought." She is always thinking of me and always thankful. When I feel appreciated, it makes my day. That is all I need. My husband Riz appreciates me, and he is instilling that appreciation in our kids. I certainly don't take my own parents for granted and I am so thankful for all they have done for me in my life. It makes me sad when kids, whether young or old, do not appreciate all the sacrifices their parents make for them. Of course, there are scores of kids all over the world who take their parents for granted, and I am not meaning to single out Japan. It's just that Japan and the U.S. are the only cultures I know much about.

I want my kids to show respect for everyone, whether it is their parents, their siblings, their teacher, their friend's mommy, or the cleaning lady at their school. These are the type of manners that I am most strict about, and we do not let them get away with bad behavior in this area.

Although I am super strict with myself and others about manners regarding respecting other people, I am often much more lax regarding rules or manners that I think are not all that important. For example, I don't think there is anything wrong with wearing a hat in class (sometimes I even do it). I don't mind it if students have a drink, either. I do wish they would keep their shoes on, though. That one is a little too stinky for me. I know that at Costco or a bakery the standard manners when getting a food sample is one per customer, but I have been known to take more than that if it is something I really like. My friend and I were at a bakery once, and her daughter said, "Mommy only let me get one bread sample, but she took two! She is so sneaky!" That one cracked me up, and I must admit that I do the same thing sometimes. Although I think there is absolutely no harm in taking two pieces of a bread sample, particulary when I spend hundreds of dollars at the bakery, it is probably not a good idea to tell my kids they can only have one, then proceed to take two (at least do it when the kids aren't looking!)

I am not justifying my sometimes poor manners, and I know that some people probably see me as a way too casual laidback American. I guess what I am trying to say is, manners are important, but respecting another person trumps not wearing a hat in class any day of the week. I want to instill good manners in my kids, to value the environment and their surroundings, but I don't want kids who may not chew gum in class, but who treat their parents like servants. I want to focus more on the big things, and be a little more lax on the little ones. While eating three servings of a food sample may make others think my kids are greedy or not being properly fed at home, it will not cause the scars that are possible when disrespecting others. So, the next time you see three American kids chowing on all the free *bulgogi* and salmon at Costco in Kitakyushu, they are probably mine.

#8 No Debt, Please

Japanese people hate being in debt for anything. When given a gift, they will almost always give a return gift called an *okaeshi,* a gift which is often of equal or more value as the gift received. This system of returning gifts stems from an underlying desire of not wanting to owe anybody anything. If you give me something, and I don't return the favor, I owe you. The Japanese try to avoid owing a debt when at all possible.

This feeling naturally overflows into the finances of the Japanese people, especially in regards to credit cards. When I was in America, my mailbox was flooded everyday by credit card companies offering me "Instant Credit! No questions asked!" I got offers like this all the time, even when I was a college student with absolutely no income, and no way to ever pay off the debt I was bound to ensue if I applied for one of those evil things. I mean, you hear it all the time in the States: Person A gets a credit card with a $1000 limit. She cannot pay it, so she gets another credit card and maxes that out, while of course paying the minimum payment on credit card #1 with credit card #2. This cycle continues until finally, Person A has a pile of credit cards, all maxed out, and she is unable to even pay the minimum monthly payment on any of them. So, in other words, she cannot even pay the interest. How many stories have you heard of people who end up calling credit card debt managers to rescue them from the debt by negotiating with the companies? It is either that or personal bankruptcy. Interestingly enough, credit card debt used to be the number one cause of personal bankruptcy, but now it is sickness and being unable to pay medical bills. Go USA.

Anyway, the first time I applied for a credit card in Japan, I received it relatively easily, but my monthly spending was capped at $1000 a month. And, at the end of the following month, the entire amount would be withdrawn from my bank account. It sounds to me a lot like a U.S debit card, only the funds are taken out the following month. What a novel idea! A credit card debt that people actually have to pay off every month! Brilliant! Now, of course, there is also the 'revolving' option, where you can choose to pay off a certain purchase over the period of several months. But it most cases, the 'revolving' option is also capped pretty low, in my case at about $1000.

I really love the idea of not having credit card debt in Japan. I can have a credit card to pay for something if by chance I don't have the money at that time, but I have to be sure that there is money in my account the following month to pay it off. Sometimes I get annoyed when I go over that limit for the month (darn you, Costco!), but later I am thankful that I will never see the credit card debt in Japan that I saw while I lived in the U.S. Yes, I too, had a mountain of credit card debt that I finally got out from under.

As far as I know, Japanese credit card companies do not market to students, trying to reel them in and get them into debt so early in their young lives like you will see in the U.S. In fact, the approval process for getting one is pretty tough. I got rejected just a couple of years ago, even though I have a more than decent salary, a good job, and a respectable workplace. In fact, I already had been approved for one credit card at the same company that rejected me. The only possible reason for rejection I could think of was that I am a foreigner with no permanent residency. So, of course I whined discrimination. They wouldn't tell me why I got rejected, of course, but that was all I could figure out. But I rarely get discriminated against in this wonderful country, so I will let that one slide.

Of course, there are seedy loan companies just like in the U.S. where heavies will come after you if you don't pay your exorbitant monthly interest fees, but you will see that kind of place anywhere you go. Unfortunately, many Japanese fall into debt with companies like these, and maybe some credit card debt too, but I rarely hear of it. In fact, I have never heard of anybody having credit card debt here. Of course, in this shame-conscious culture credit card debt is not exactly something that you go and shout about from the rooftops...

#9 Swimming in a Sea of Gluten

I am now on day seven of an elimination diet, trying to figure out if years of digestive ailments can be attributed to some kind of food intolerance. Being a novice, I am trying the best I can to eliminate the most reactive foods, but I fear that I am probably unknowingly eating something I shouldn't. It seems there are so many kinds of elimination diets out there and they are all done in different ways for different lengths of time that I have been a little confused at times. But I am trying to mainly eliminate soy, gluten, dairy, caffeine, sugar, and eggs. I figure that is a pretty good start. It has been incredibly mentally, physically and emotionally challenging, and honestly, I am trying to just take it one day at a time. I did find an organic store that had gluten-free pasta. Although I am not a pasta fan, I was so tired of eating the same old stuff that I think it was one of the best pasta dishes I have ever eaten.

Japan is the land of gluten. Maybe you are surprised by this, as most people assume that since the Japanese eat mostly rice, veggies and fish, all of which is gluten-free, that this would probably be a pretty good place to live. These foods are the staples of the Japanese diet, but the sauces used to season everything here contains gluten. The big three – soy sauce, *dashi*, and *miso*, all contain gluten. My personal favorite *ponzu* sauce, since it is made with soy sauce also contains gluten. I couldn't even find gluten-free soy sauce at the organic store. It is virtually impossible to eat Japanese food unless you can find gluten-free sauces. Italian and olive oil is the only way to go. I did find gluten-free everything on Amazon.com, even my beloved *ponzu* sauce, but unfortunately they don't ship over here for a reasonable price. Call me crazy, but I am not willing to pay 30 bucks shipping for a four dollar bottle of gluten-free soy sauce. I am sure there are some Japanese companies that offer such items if I dig into it a little bit. But for now, pass the olive oil, salt and pepper, please.

There is very little incidence of gluten intolerance in Japan, probably because the eating of bread and heavily gluten-filled foods is a relatively new thing here. There are a few cases of gluten intolerance, like the around 1100 people who suddenly became intolerant when they used a soap infused with massive amounts of gluten, but still, compared to the U.S., there are very few people who are gluten intolerant. In fact, when I speak to my friends, they don't even know what gluten is. They know of a wheat or flour allergy, but not gluten. I think the terms are mistakenly used interchangeably, when they are not the same at all. The causes, treatment, and symptoms are different. In fact, testing for celiac disease is not even covered by the National Health Insurance system here because it is so uncommon. My doctor told me that it costs hundreds of dollars and the samples must be sent off to the U.S. for analysis. Because my regular blood tests showed no sign of gluten problems at all, my doctors doubt I have Celiac, but I could very well be gluten sensitive like 7-12% of the U.S. population.

My favorite bakery has no gluten-free bread (where are you, Trader Joe's?), so in the mornings, instead of drinking coffee and eating my favorite bread, I have only water and good conversation with my friends there. I don't know why I torture myself and go anyway. But, it's okay, because you know what? I am feeling a little better already. My tummy doesn't hurt quite as much and my body feels lighter. And, I found a bakery only an hour away (only?) that makes gluten-free bread. Toasted, it is excellent and crunchy; eaten as is, dry as sawdust, crumbling at the slightest touch. Note to self: there is a reason gluten is used in bread other than taste.

Anyway, for now, I am subsisting on my rice, veggies, nuts, fruits and chicken, and for now, I am okay with that. I don't know how long I will make it. I hope to make it 21 days, but I am just taking one day at a time. I am proud of myself for making it this far. In fact, I don't even think about coffee all the time anymore, although the smell of fresh bread still gets to me…

I ended up going ten days with no bread or other gluten products. I eat bread now, but in moderation, and try to avoid noodles and processed foods as much as possible. I feel better, but not perfect. For me, figuring out what foods are best for my body is a lifelong process, but I am pretty sure that too much gluten is not a good thing for my sensitive colon.

#10 Where's the Soap?

Sometimes I write thought provoking, deep comments about Japanese culture and society. That is a good thing because I am a deep-thinking religion major that wants people everywhere to really think and not just blindly accept all that they have been told or thought they knew. But not today. Today, I just want to talk about soap. Or rather the lack of it in public toilets in Japan.

Being mildly obsessive-compulsive about cleanliness, the absence of soap in toilets in Japan irritated me for years. Actually, I'm not all that OCD about cleanliness, but about having clean hands. I don't mind being sweaty, stinky or covered in mud. But my hands have to be clean. Early in my time in Japan, it seemed it was hard to find soap in any public toilet. It has been slowly appearing on the scene more and more in recent years, but something that happened when my daughter Emmy was a baby has really put me on a crusade to get soap in public toilets all over Japan, or at least in Kitakyushu.

I went to a children's and baby clothing store near my home called Birthday. This store had just opened, and it was popular because of the hip children's clothes it carried, and for the cheap prices. Emmy had a diaper explosion, so I took her to the store bathroom, and since this was a baby store, after all, I assumed would be 100% diaper-changing friendly. After changing her diaper I went to wash my hands and…that's right!

No hand soap. Just water and paper towels. Now, I have been especially obsessive about washing my hands thoroughly after diaper changing since I caught meningitis when Mia was a baby. My doctor thought it was highly possible I caught it from her, who, although she didn't have meningitis did have diarrhea, and could have been a carrier of the virus. My doctor thought that maybe I didn't wash my hands well enough after changing her diaper and as a result, contracted the disease. I am no expert, but I am pretty sure that warm water and paper towels won't kill most viruses that lurk on the hands after changing the diaper of a sick baby.

So, being the loud-mouthed American that I am, I went to the counter, dirty hands and all, and asked a cashier why on earth they would not have hand soap in a bathroom where parents regularly change diapers. I was told they must follow the policy handed down by the head office. I am all for obedience and all, but I don't think the manager would get fired for putting a little container of hand soap in the bathroom at a customer's request. I haven't been there recently, but I think I will go and check to see if there is any soap in there now...

Many public restrooms have soap now in Japan, and I am happy that strides are being made on that front. But, still, for reasons unknown to me, most multi-purpose toilets, and sinks specifically designed for children, still don't have soap. Mysterious, isn't it? The multi-purpose toilets are big rooms that can be used by disabled persons or by families with babies and young children. There is usually a place to change diapers in these toilets, but often, no soap. So, I usually have to go to the regular women's toilet to wash my hands after changing a diaper. Many regular toilets often have low sinks for small children to wash their hands, and they don't have soap, either. Maybe it is a design problem or something, an issue of not knowing where to put the soap, but I always have to get soap for my kids and put it on their hands before they use these low sinks.

Most Japanese have little awareness of the lack-of-soap problem. Once, I noticed that the multi-purpose toilets at my school didn't have soap, so I went to the main office to request that they put soap in there. The next day, an email circulated around campus informing everyone that all multi-purpose toilets at school now had hand soap. I don't think there is a resistance to the idea, I just think that most people are unaware.

I have relaxed my rigorous hand washing requirements in recent years. I was militant about it with my kids during the Swine Flu outbreak, carrying around hand sanitizer and squirting their little hands every chance I got. But they all still caught the flu. Now, I still try to get them to wash their hands as much as possible, and I am thankful that many shops and restaurants provide hand sanitizer, a vestige from the Swine Flu outbreak. I must admit that sometimes I am lazy about hand washing. The kids are tired and cold, the toilet is far away, and I don't have the energy to take them. But since this year the flu and *noro* virus seem to be particularly nasty, I think I need to step it up a notch.

I often wonder if anyone else ever says anything about the lack of soap, if anyone else ever thinks about it as much as I do. Maybe I am just way too perceptive about stuff, but if my being loud and outspoken can make even a small difference, keeping a person or two from getting sick with flu germs, then I guess I will keep being loud and outspoken.

#11 Skinny Girls

A couple of years ago, I headed to a local massage parlor for some much needed relaxation. I only go a couple times a year, but I totally LOVE getting massages. Outside the parlor there was an advertisement for some kind of massage-based weight loss therapy, something weird like rubbing the earlobe to speed metabolism or something like that. There was a before/after picture of a woman standing on a scale. The before picture showed this woman with a bulging tummy, thunder thighs, and a look of despair and shock on her face as she glanced down and saw that she weighed a tremendous 54 kg (121 pounds). The picture on the right showed her all slimmed down, flat tummy, slender thighs and a look of satisfaction on her face as she had gotten down to 48 kg (106 pounds). I was incredulous as I looked at this, as at that time I was exactly 54 kg, and had been told by many people that I was too skinny. I certainly didn't think it was fair advertising to call a 54 kg woman fat.

This is just one of many advertisements that have made me think Japanese women are obsessed with being thin. Of course, women all over the world want to be thin, a desire fanned by the super-skinny models and actresses all over TV and magazines. But Japanese women, in particular, want to be thin. Not just have no fat, but to be thin. What I mean is, they don't really want to be toned or muscular like American women. Most girls I talk to have no interest in that kind of body. They care most about being thin and that number on the scale being less than 50 kg, if possible.

Now, going back to that fat 54 kg woman advertisement at the massage parlor. I know very few women in the U.S. who weigh less than 54 kg, and many who would give their right arm to get even close to that number. I know that the Asian body type is quite different from the American one, and that they are naturally smaller and more petite than we are. I mean, no matter how little I eat or much I work out, I will never be as thin as a lot of women around me. And to be sure, if you are less than 5 feet tall, 54 kg may make you look fat. But for the majority of people 54 kg is a weight to be satisfied with. It disturbs me that this kind of ad may make perfectly normal-weight women feel like they are fat. Maybe, they are fine with their weight until they look at that ad declaring them to be grossly overweight.

Once, in a culture class, I did a lecture about women and body image. I put up a slide, and on the left I inserted a picture of the famous South Korean figure skater Yu-Na Kim, who is incredibly slim and svelte, a perfect example of an Asian beauty. On the right, I put a picture of Dara Torres. She is an American Olympic swimmer who made the news for making the Olympic team at age 41 and after just having given birth a year or so earlier. She had to me what was the perfect female athlete's body. Not an ounce of fat anywhere, but muscles everywhere. She is buff. I mean, buff. Not bulky, but buff. As someone who loves to work out, I would love to have a body like that. But when I asked my female students whose body they would rather have, almost all of them said Yu-Na Kim's. We don't want muscles, they said. We want to be thin. The guys also said they would prefer the thin woman to the buff woman. Maybe a guy would feel intimidated by a woman with more muscles than him…

Once Riz showed me an ad for a diet magazine with more before/after shots. We were shocked at how the women in the before shots looked beautiful and healthy, and in the after shots they looked like emaciated sticks. He was convinced that the pictures had to be Photoshopped, but I wasn't so sure. I mean, a 5 foot 4 woman weighing less than 90 pounds probably really looks like that. We showed the pictures to our friends, and without exception all of them were highly disturbed, and in some cases grossed out. When did looking like that become beautiful in our culture? Remember the days of Marilyn Monroe when curvy was beautiful? The media has definitely changed the way we view beautiful. As someone who has had eating issues for years, these ads targeting young Japanese girls make me really mad. I think if I ever see an ad like that at my massage parlor again, I might just open my big American mouth and say something. Why not? Someone has to.

#12 Girly Guys

One day I was talking to a friend and she told me most Japanese guys pluck their eyebrows. No way, I said, but I thought I would observe the guys in my classes to see if this were true. Sure enough, as I looked around, there in front of my eyes were perfectly manicured, rounded eyebrows on my male students! Growing up in the U.S., I had never seen a guy pluck or shave his eyebrows, unless of course, they were growing together into the now-famous Unibrow. I mean, I am a girl and I have never even plucked my eyebrows! Of course, I grew up in the days before the advent of the modern, cool chic guy, the Metrosexual.

For those of you who don't know this term, the metrosexual guy is traditionally defined as an upper-middle class man who spends excess income on beauty treatments, trendy colorful clothes, expensive haircuts, and gym memberships. The metrosexual guy works out a lot and has lean muscle, not the bulky body that is found on the traditional macho man like Vin Diesel, Bruce Willis or Arnold Schwarzenegger. In the West, classic metrosexuals are David Beckham, Zac Efron, George Clooney, and even Bill Clinton. Some modern women seem to prefer the metrosexual type, so the more feminine, sensitive male is on the rise even in the West. However, not nearly to the degree that can be found in Japan.

Almost all male pop stars here are girly guys. I mean, they are actually beautiful. Perfect, smooth skin, skinny bodies, frilly wild clothes. It has to take those guys more time to get ready in the morning than in takes me, especially the hair. Of course, that is not saying much. The hair is perfectly done and spiked up with all kinds of gels and hairsprays. All the groups from the famous Johnny's Jimusho, groups like SMAP, ARASHI and w-inds, are metrosexuals. Many movie stars and TV stars are, too. In fact, I rarely see a non-girly guy on TV. This influence of TV and pop stars has exerted a big influence on the everyday male in Japanese society. Even some of my male students in the boonies here pluck their eyebrows and spend lots of time on their hair. One guy even told me once that he put on sunscreen in the mornings so he wouldn't get a tan on the twenty-minute walk from his house to school. The worst thing ever in Japan is to get a tan, especially for women. However, even some guys hate it. White is beautiful. But this hatred of the sun deserves its own separate discussion so I will leave that for another day...

So, the girly guy is all the rage now in Japan and even to some extent in the West. I taught a culture class once, and I asked my female students if they prefer girly guys like Zac Efron and Johnny Depp, or macho guys like Bruce Willis, and all but maybe one preferred the girly guy. I personally greatly prefer the more manly guy. Riz has never plucked his eyebrows and I like that. He wears jeans, t-shirts and sweatshirts. I don't really like being all that girly myself, but for some reason I just think guys were made to look and act different from girls. I had a boyfriend once who got mad every time I touched his hair because he was afraid I would mess it up. It drove me crazy. Maybe that is why I have such an aversion to girly guys now. Call me old-fashioned if you want, but I just don't think it should take a guy longer to get ready in the morning than a girl…I am definitely a non-girly guy type of gal.

#13 Here Comes the Bride, There Goes My Money

The first wedding we ever attended in Japan cost us $1200. No kidding. First of all, we had to travel by overnight bus to Tottori Prefecture, which cost about 500 bucks. Then, we had to present a cash wedding gift of $500, the going rate for a couple like us. It is apparently $300 for a single person, as for some reason $200 is too cheap, and $400 is bad luck, as the pronunciation of number four in Japanese can also mean death. Of course, as much as it hurt financially, the bride was a dear friend and we didn't even think of not attending. She did pay for our hotel room, which was nice. This past October, we paid $1700 dollars on travel costs to Okinawa to attend another friend's wedding. Luckily, we were exempt from paying the $500 gift due to the crazy costs we were incurring to travel to the wedding.

Now, for someone who comes from a country where really good friends maybe, just maybe, will spend $50 on a wedding gift, the Japanese way seemed crazy to me. I mean, what is all this money for anyway? Well, it turns out that most of the money goes to paying for the wedding, including the luxurious 10-course meal given to all the guests. None of the *el cheapo* finger foods that were found at my wedding. No way, baby. We are talking endless French food (sometimes Chinese), the majority of which I had never seen before and had no idea even what it was. Japanese weddings are really pricey, costing on average 30,000 to 50,000 dollars for everything–very often cheesy Western-style chapel ceremony with a cheesy tall white foreigner with a horrible accent presiding; wedding dress, kimono, and cocktail dress rental, since many brides will change two or three times during the reception; full-course meals for all the guests; way overpriced photography package, which is not nearly as good as my amazingly talented photographer husband; reception hall rental; professional MC, wedding cake that nobody eats and is often fake. You get the picture. It is a scene to behold. The happy couple uses most of the cash to pay for the whole shebang. So, more or less, guests are paying for their own meals. Of course, because the bride and groom are indebted that the guests took time out of their busy schedules to attend the reception, they present each guest with a big bag of bling, sometimes some really nice bling…

The ceremony is really not a big deal in Japan. It is all about the reception. Most Japanese get married anyway before the ceremony. Huh? That's right. Almost everyone I know goes to the City Office and signs the marriage certificate, officially entering the woman into the man's family register months before the ceremony. Since most Japanese are not Christian, the chapel ceremony is not really the focal point of the day. Many of the guests don't even attend that part–choosing to attend only the reception. Some couples even make it a point to say during the ceremony that they are not making a pledge before a god, but before family and friends to be loving and faithful to each other.

As for the reception, it is usually full of numerous wardrobe changes, way too much food and alcohol, cheesy and sometimes vulgar musical or dramatic performances from the groom's friends; a couple of speeches full of formal Japanese, the bride reading a letter of thanks to her mom (inevitably producing tears all around!), more eating, more speeches, and a slideshow or two. Receptions last two or three hours, and just like in the U.S., the bride and groom are too busy to eat anything. For most couples, the next day is back to life as normal, as many husbands cannot get time off to go on a honeymoon. They often postpone it until the husband can take some extended time off.

I have attended five weddings or so. I gave a speech at one and sang at two. Once, I sang a really moving mushy Japanese love song that I practiced a million times, and I nailed it. Afterwards, this old guy came up and said, "That was so beautiful! I didn't understand it at all, but it was beautiful." Oh well, at least the bride appreciated it.

Very often, after the wedding, there is an after-party, or *ni-ji-kai*, which is much more informal and usually reserved for close friends of the bride and groom. If one attends the after-party, he can say goodbye to another 50 bucks or so to cover food and drink expenses. I feel guilty sometimes for hoping that I don't get invited to the wedding (cost to me=$500) but only to the after-party (cost to me=$50). I am sure that I am not the only person who has these hopes. It is really hard to turn down a wedding invitation once invited. There is even a term for young people who fall temporarily on hard times because all their friends seem to get married at the same time, meaning of course, it costs them $300 a pop. I enjoy going to Japanese weddings and rejoicing with my friends on their happy day, I just wish it didn't cost me so darn much. Maybe I am just a cheapskate, but I much prefer the American way of registering for gifts. Of course, brides and grooms who do it the traditional way, with the bride's family paying for the ceremony, and the groom's paying for the honeymoon, make a huge killing. Parents pay for everything and they get to keep the loot! Three cheers for the American way!

#14 Death and Chopsticks

I distinctly remember the first time I learned about the Japanese way of doing funerals. I was in Kobe in 1999 or so, and I was teaching a private English lesson to a Japanese housewife. Somehow or another we ended up talking about death and funerals. My student told me that upon death, Japanese people must be cremated by law, probably due to a lack of land for burial. Unlike Western cremations, though, in Japan, most of the bones remain after the tissues and organs are cremated. Then, close relatives and friends will hold ceremonial chopsticks and pick up bone pieces, passing them person-to-person and placing them in an urn. This ceremony is the reason that it is considered bad manners and bad luck to pass food from chopsticks-to-chopsticks at mealtime. For men, in particular, the bone that makes up the Adam's apple is very important, as it is seen to be in the shape of the Buddha. The bones in the urn are then placed in a family grave; leftover bones are ashes are discarded.

Now, I am very different from many Americans in my thinking about burial. I think it is pretty barbaric, and I have no desire to be buried for the bugs to eat me, and time to erode my body so that I eventually look like one of the walking dead from Michael Jackson's "Thriller." I also have been freaked out by the numerous TV shows and movies that have depicted people who have been buried alive, thought to be dead only to wake up hours later entombed. So, for many years I have thought that cremation is the way to go. I have to admit, however, that my Westernized self is a little disturbed by Japanese funeral practices. I know that it is cultural and for the Japanese, it is heavily influenced by religion and it is just the way they have always done it. I know all this. I really do. Maybe this cremation ceremony brings closure for the Japanese like burial does for Americans. But it is so different from anything I have known, it is still hard for me to understand. I cannot imagine my 7-year-old daughter picking up Granddad's bone and putting in into an urn; or as a parent, picking up the bone of my child. There is no way in a million years I could do that. But Japanese parents who lose their children can and do. They have an incredible amount of fortitude to be able to do that.

I have never been to a Japanese funeral. It is hard to believe, considering I have been here 13 years. As my friends and I are getting older though, I am sure that I will end up attending one in the near future. My husband Riz attended the funeral of a colleague about eight years ago. This 27-year old American guy was found dead in his apartment, apparently from complications with asthma and the flu. His family thought that since he was here and loved Japan, he should just have a Japanese-style funeral. So, they asked his company to make plans, and they would come get the ashes when it was over. Riz said it was weird since the guy wasn't Japanese or Buddhist. It was also incredibly sad. Riz attended the service, but as a Christian did not attend the cremation ceremony afterwards.

Most families have Buddhist altars to remember the dead in their homes, and they regularly pray and offer incense at the altar in front of a picture of the loved one. They also prepare food, often a bowl of rice with chopsticks stuck in the middle. It is terribly taboo in Japan to stick your chopsticks in your rice when taking a break from eating a meal because it is the symbol of death. Many foreigners in Japan, or those eating at Japanese restaurants overseas don't know this, and are often corrected for their cultural *faux pas.*

Personally, I don't really care what happens to my body after I die because it is not me anymore. I will be in Heaven partying with Jesus. I guess I have never really understood all the rituals associated with death and funerals. Elaborate coffins, expensive headstones, visiting graves to put flowers on them. Maybe it is more for those left behind, those who are grieving than for the person who has died. I guess that treating a loved one with respect and honoring their memory brings a kind of closure. For me, when I leave this earth I want two things really badly at my funeral. First of all, I want to be 100% cremated—no bones, please. Maybe my ashes can be scattered over somewhere special to me like my favorite bakery or something! That is probably impossible and illegal, but it would be fitting.

The other thing is that I want people to not mourn, but to remember the good things and remember how crazy I was. Of course, being sad is normal when someone you love passes away. I understand that. But I want people to celebrate my life, not mourn my death. The Bible says, "to be absent from the body is to be present with the Lord," so I believe as soon as I die, I will be with Jesus. So, I am not afraid of death. Now, I don't want to die, of course. I love my life, my kids, my husband. But I am not afraid of death. I cannot really imagine what it will be like to be in heaven, but I figure since it is pure joy and happiness, there has to be coffee and bread there…

#15 Japanese Religion 101

During the first few days of a new year, you will always find faithful Japanese flocking to shrines, to pray for good fortune in the coming year. For many Japanese, it will be their only visit of the year to the shrine. Does that mean they are not a very religious people, that they don't really think much of the supernatural? That is a very complicated question…

I once heard that when a survey was taken of people in countries all over the world as to what their religious affiliation was, Japan was the only country in the world with a total of more than 100%. For example, Country A would be 75% Christian; 10% Muslim; 2% Jewish; 10% Non-religious; 3%

Other. For Japan, it was something like 75% Buddhist; 80% Shinto; 1% Christian. Sounds ridiculous when you think about it, but actually, nothing could be more telling about how the Japanese view religion in their daily life.

The average Japanese will probably tell you that he is not religious and doesn't believe in God; however, many of the practices and rituals of daily life are permeated with religious influence. The two main religions here are Buddhism, which was first brought over from China, and Shintoism, a traditional Japanese religion of nature and ancestor worship. Many Japanese are Buddhist at birth, the first ritual being a visit to the local temple to pray for blessing at one month old, and another ceremony at 100 days praying for health. They are many times Shinto on their wedding day, with many couples choosing to have a traditional Shinto wedding ceremony, mostly often conducted at a shrine. Once, Riz and I attended one for which he was the photographer. I didn't understand any of the Japanese used in the chants, prayers or blessings, but my Japanese friends said that they didn't understand either. However, recently, many Japanese are choosing Christian wedding ceremonies in a "chapel." Japanese friends tell me that Christian ceremonies are much more cheery than Shinto ones, and many brides long to wear a white, Western wedding dress. Many English teachers and missionaries work part-time performing weddings. The funny thing is that most wedding halls don't require that you are even a Christian, as long as you are foreign-looking, and preferably white (Riz got turned away from one because he isn't white). My friend, a long-time missionary here, does work for one that requires real Christians, and he even makes it mandatory for the bride and groom to undergo premarital counseling. Finally, many Japanese are Buddhist at death, with Buddhist funerals being by far the most common type of funerals in this country.

What about daily life? I must admit that as a devout Christian, my husband and I are always torn as to whether to allow our kids to participate in traditional Japanese events and holidays, because it seems that just about everything has some tie to Buddhism or Shintoism. For example, *Tanabata*, the Star Festival. Most Japanese see it as a traditional kids' day where children write their wishes on strips of paper and hang them on bamboo. But even this holiday has religious ties. How about other seemingly harmless events? Do we let our kids throw beans at the *oni* (devil) like the other kids (yes)? Do we let them do the traditional Bon dance, in August, which beckons back the spirits of departed loved ones (definitely not)? Do we let them ring the bells at the shrines (no, no, no)? It is tough navigating daily life as Christians in a country that is at first glance very non-religious, but in reality, very spiritual. In fact, most Japanese don't even see much spiritual significance in many traditional events.

Ask a Japanese person what they think will happen after death, and you will often hear that good people go to heaven and bad people go to hell, which is actually what many people in

Western countries think, too. Others admit that they have never really thought about it that deeply. I often wonder how they reconcile going to heaven, reincarnation, and the return of their ancestors every August during the O-bon holiday. It seems to me that if someone goes to heaven or is reincarnated, how can they come back every summer to encourage their families? Maybe many people don't really think about it all that much. I think Japanese religion is so tied to Japanese culture, that it is just who they are and what they believe. I don't think it really even matters if they really believe it, but participating in these rituals is very important to what it means to be Japanese. In my opinion, religion and spirituality are in many ways much more a part of daily life here, and influences how people think and act more than in many overtly religious countries. This is the most non-religious religious country I have ever seen!

This past summer, my kids joined in the traditional Bon dance at a summer festival when I wasn't looking. We need to have a talk with them next year...

#16 Show Me the Love!

Yesterday I walked past a dry cleaning shop, and I noticed a sign saying something like, "You need to trust your beloved clothes to us." The Chinese character used for this was *ai*, which means "love." This character is often used in front of nouns, for things that mean a lot to a person. For example, *aisha* (beloved car), *aiken* (beloved dog) and even *aijin* (mistress). But interestingly enough, Japanese people rarely use it to refer to people that are the closest to them, like a wife, husband or child. There is a word for beloved wife (*aisai*), but my friend tells me it is rarely used, and when it is used, it is used by others to refer to someone else's wife, not their own. In fact, it is more common for a husband to refer to his wife as *gusai*, or foolish wife. Of course, he probably doesn't really think his wife is foolish, but it is just an exercise in Japanese humility. Pride is bad, humility is good here. For example, when a person moves into a new neighborhood, he will take a gift to neighbors saying "*Tsumaranai mono desu ga...*" (It's nothing special, but here you go!)

You see the word *ai* used a lot in music. It can be found in most songs at karaoke, but rarely will couples use this word with each other. My friends tell me that it is really a strong word, and that the English "I love you" is much lighter and easier to say than the Japanese *aishiteru*. Sometimes, younger couples will use the less strong *daisuki,* which means "I like you very much," but most older couples won't express their affection in words; maybe they just assume that their partner knows how they feel. Of course, most hopeless romantics like me want to hear it, even though we may know it is true. Most of the time I hear my friends say *aishiteru*, they are goofing off, not really being serious at all.

So why is it that Japanese people can easily talk of loving their dog or their car, but not their family? Who knows? Maybe they are embarrassed to verbalize their feelings. To be sure, any PDA (public display of affection) is a no-no here. I rarely see Japanese couples holding hands and never see them kissing in public, not even young people on my college campus. In fact, some students are so rarely together on campus that sometimes I don't even know they are dating. Of course, off campus they are freer to hold hands, and once I saw some students holding hands in town and they quickly let go of each other's hands as soon as they saw me.

The Chinese international students are very easy to find, though. They are the ones always holding hands. Shows of physical affection even among parents and children are rare in Japan. While moms and dads hug their kids until they enter elementary school, something changes around that time, and most physical affection stops. I remember when I first came to Japan, how badly I was in need of a hug. Even my closest friends didn't really hug me. Things are changing now, and I think my love of hugging has rubbed off on my friends. Most of my friends who study abroad come back to Japan as hugging maniacs, much to the shock of their family and friends. I guess people everywhere need some hugging, but don't really realize it until they are exposed to it. I am crazy about hugging, and I hug my parents and brothers like crazy every time I go back to the States.

So, Japanese people love their families just like everyone else, maybe they are just a little shy about showing it. This is just one of the many of the cultural differences I have trouble getting used to. I think I am going to go hug my kids now…

#17 Smoking Gun

I just returned home after a peaceful time by myself at Joyfull, a local family restaurant. Yes, I know that "Joyful" only has one "l" but this is the land of Japanese English, after all. I actually kind of like that spelling. It makes it seem to be a little more full of joy. Anyway, my regular morning coffee shop and bakery is closed for the New Year Holidays, so Joyfull was my only option. I can hardly stand the smell of myself, as I reek of smoke after two hours in the place. I detest the smell of smoke, and have since I was a child. Why didn't you sit in the non-smoking section, you might ask? Oh, I did. The thing is, in many restaurants in Japan, the system of separating smoking from non-smoking sections is ridiculous. At Joyfull, where I went today, both sections are in one big room, the back half being smoking, the front half being non-smoking, with nary a wall or any kind of separator in the middle. As soon as I entered the restaurant the smell of smoke overwhelmed me. If there is even one smoker there, the entire restaurant will smell of smoke. So, that is why I smell terrible even though I was in the non-smoking section of the restaurant.

To be fair to Japan, things have gotten much better in recent years. In the past, there was not even a non-smoking section in many restaurants. Now they can be found at almost all of them, even if they are pitiful sometimes. The hospital near my home has made the entire hospital grounds non-smoking, so at any given time scores of hospitalized patients can be found huddled just beyond the hospital grounds in their pajamas, gripping their IV stand, lighting up. Something disturbing about a guy with an IV smoking but that is another topic for another day. My university went non-smoking a couple of years ago, too, except in designated areas. Prior to that, teachers could even smoke in their offices. So, Japan is making strides to provide a more comfortable environment for non-smokers, but they still have a ways to go. I don't plan on taking my kids to Joyfull anytime soon, because I don't want them exposed to the dangerous secondhand smoke. I was planning on staying in my sweats all day, but I think I need to go change. I can't stand the smell of myself.

#18 The Happy Bag and Weird Food

My family always enjoys the slow life of the week-long New Years holiday in Japan, but after a few days, we start getting a little stir-crazy and want to leave the house. There is not much open the first three days of the year, but the huge shopping malls always are. Not so many years ago in Japan, everything was closed during this period; even ATMs were closed, so if you didn't have any cash you were out of luck. But like Thanksgiving Day and Christmas Day in the U.S., retailers are realizing there are a lot of bored people like me and that since nothing else is open, staying open during the holidays might be a cash cow for them. So while most places, including many restaurants, hospitals, clinics and schools are closed, shopping malls are open, hoping to cash in on the mass of bored Japanese on New Years.

One of the major money-making endeavors is the *fukubukuro*, or happy bag. I just love that word. *Fukubukuro. Fukubukuro.* I never get tired of saying it. Come on. Everybody say it with me. *Fukubukuro.* But while it is called "happy bag," which is a direct translation, the closest thing in the U.S. would be the grab bag. Retailers fill up paper bags with a variety of goodies, and have one set price, or perhaps two or three different prices, depending on the size of your happy bag. Due to many skeptical, frugal Japanese, many retailers recently have begun informing shoppers exactly what is inside the happy bag. For example, a 10,000 yen bag may have a jacket, two shirts, a pair of pants, three pairs of socks, etc. Of course, the surprise factor is gone, but I guess shoppers are much more willing to shell out the yen if they know what they are getting. There is still a little surprise, because, while the shoppers know what is in the bags, they don't know (most of the time) what color or style they are getting.

These happy bags are usually filled with leftover merchandise from the previous season, and there definitely are some deals to be had. I am a sucker for the happy bag, and while I don't get one every year, I do enjoy buying one every now and then. Due to spending way too much money this holiday season, I don't think there is a *fukubukuro* being bought by the Crescini family this year.

Japanese people, just like Americans, are gradually moving away from some holiday traditions that used to define the culture. For example, more and more people are forsaking the traditional New Year's food, called *o-sechi ryori,* for more modern dishes like *nabe* hot pot, or even eating out. Many of my students tell me they don't even like *o-sechi ryori.* It seems that Japanese housewives slave for hours and hours to produce three days worth of this traditional food, but something in me wonders if husbands and children would rather not just eat *nabe*. But then again, maybe even if *o-sechi ryori* is not all that delicious, that is not the point of making it; maybe, families make it to preserve tradition, and keep the same New Year's spirit alive. If so, I think that is a good thing. Too often, families lose tradition due to modernization of society. I mean, how many families still play board games or put puzzles together? Maybe some still do, but not as many as before the invention of the computer, Nintendo Wii, Play Station or social networking.

I am not a big fan of *o-sechi ryori*; I don't think it tastes good, and I don't even know what it is. Most of it seems to be some mysterious something made out of fish paste. But this year, we bought some prepared New Year's Food at the supermarket to try it out again. I didn't recognize most of it, so I asked the lady working there what is was. "Well, you know, it's *fu*," she said. "Okay," I said, "What's *fu*?" "You know," she responded, "the stuff that is often in miso soup." "Okay," I said, "but exactly what is it?" She didn't know, so another customer waiting beside me told me it is kinda like *mochi*, a gluttonous rice cake. I thought it humorous that even the people who make the stuff don't always know what it is! That being said, there was something special joining millions of Japanese people eating *o-sechi ryori* and watching New Year's Programs on TV, although I think we ate it a day too early!!

Many Japanese also go to shrines and temples to pray for a prosperous, happy year. While the Japanese are, in general, not a very religious people, most of them go to the shrines during the New Years holiday. Maybe it is kinda like the C and E Christians in the U.S. You know, the Christmas and Easter Christians who attend church only on those two days of the year. Because we are Christians we don't participate in this tradition, but once we did go to see what it was like and to take pictures. Mia wanted to know why she couldn't ring the bell and put the purifying water on her hands like everyone else. We explained it to her, but I doubt she understood at four years old. We will try again later…

Anyway, New Years in Japan is a special time, and while I get bored sometimes, the kids trash the house, and I don't really like the food, I like it. I like seeing the always-busy Japanese relax and do nothing, staying home and spending time with the family (or going shopping for Happy Bags!) This is probably the only time all year that most people can have such an extended time of relaxation. Many just sleep, eat *mochi* and watch TV. I always wondered how Japanese gain so much weight over New Years when *o-sechi ryori* is so healthy. I was told because they sleep, eat *mochi* and watch TV. Apparently, *mochi* is so dense that one little *mochi* cake has the same calories as an entire bowl of rice. In other words, they don't move much for a week, and they eat a lot of sugar and carbs. Every now and then, I think this is just fine. They have the other 51 weeks of the year to be busy, but this one week is a time to relax, spend time with family, and get ready for the coming year. I think New Years is one of my favorite Japanese holidays.

#19 The Red and White Song Battle

Every New Year's Eve, the Japanese media powerhouse NHK puts on a music monstrosity called *Kouhaku Utagassen*– literally the Red and White Song Battle. The guys are white, the girls are red, and the most popular and successful singers of all genres in Japanese music of that calendar year battle it out on stage for four hours. There are pop singers, rock singers, rappers and Japanese *enka* folk song singers. 80% of it is pure cheese. I mean, it is over-the-top crazy outfits, weird choreography, bizarre arrangements, and just general outlandishness. That being said, it is very entertaining and we enjoy watching it every year for the most part. Every now and then, there is some severe cheese that we cannot stomach. A couple years ago, there was this song about the god of the toilet, which we couldn't take seriously, but many Japanese were moved to tears by it; must have been something cultural that we just couldn't understand.

We are not big *enka* folk song fans–it is not my cup of tea when it comes to musical genres. But one thing that my husband and I agree on is that they are definitely the most talented singers on the stage. Some of the pop singers are so bad that I cannot believe they are famous or popular. They must have some kind of popular appeal that I just don't get. Of course, it is the same in the States. There are plenty of famous singers, who are more famous for their looks or personality than for their singing skills. I guess there is a lot more to being a famous singer than singing no matter what country you are in.

I can't tell you just how huge this event is in Japan. To be invited to participate is the crowning achievement of an artist's career. To be invited back again and again is even more of an honor. In fact, as each artist or group is performing, the number of years they have appeared on the show is shown at the bottom of the screen. Some of the *enka* folk singers have been going strong for 40 or 50 years. It is amazing. It is truly an entertainment extravaganza. I do not even want to know how many billions of yen are spent on the production every year. The costumes, make-up, sets, technicians. You could probably feed a small country for a year on the money that is spent preparing for that one evening. This one lady was wearing a dress and standing on a platform like twenty feet high, and the dress reached all the way to the ground. I think she was going for a peacock theme or something.

•

So, anyway, I gotta get back to seeing how much cheesier the Red and White Song Battle gets. No matter how bad it gets, I am sure I will keep watching. No matter how much Japanese people complain about how boring and outlandish it has gotten in recent years, you can be sure they are watching it too. As cheesy as it is, it is a highly entertaining and cherished New Year's Eve tradition in Japan. So, like most of the rest of the country, I will spend the next two hours glued to the TV seeing if the girls can finally beat the guys. Pass the cheese, please!

*In 2013, I plan on initiating my new-to-Japan American friends to the Red and White Song Battle tradition. You cannot really understand the Japanese spirit until you watch it.

#20 The Weather Bugs Me

I tell you, I must really love Kitakyushu because it, by far, has the worst weather of any place I have ever lived. It seems to rain all the time, not just during the miserable rainy season in June and July. The wind in my area of the city in particular is so strong; in fact, my umbrella this morning was broken by strong winds as I was walking to the bakery in the middle of a rainstorm. The winters are cold, not as cold as other areas of Japan, but with terrible insulation in buildings, the cold seeps in everywhere. There is no central heating, and it can get below 50 degrees Fahrenheit inside the house. My hometown of Wytheville, Virginia was much colder when I was growing up, but at least I could get relatively warm inside buildings.

And you know what? If it is going to be cold, the least it could do is snow and bring some joy to my kids. We get flurries every now and then, but accumulation only once every few years. It is hilarious to watch people here freak out over a few flurries. Growing up where two feet of snowfall was not unheard of, the panic of Kitakyushu citizens over a few flurries is fun to watch. Maybe Riz and I get a little too arrogant over our snow expertise at times. This past March, we went up north to the Sendai area to volunteer with tsunami relief. It snows like crazy up there, even in March, and we were unprepared to say the least. Snow tires? What are those? We had a couple of close calls, the scariest one being almost sliding into a frozen lake at 10 pm. Maybe we should stop being so cocky...

Summers are hot and miserably humid in Kitakyushu, but I actually love that. Give me hot weather over the cold any day. It cannot get too hot for me. But, my kids and Riz are miserable, and the mosquitos torment us all summer long, even early in the morning. The cicadas chirp so loudly at 5 am at sunrise (no Daylight Savings Time here), that it is hard to have a conversation outside. This past summer, in an effort to save energy and avoid possible rolling blackouts due to power shortages caused by the disasters in Northern Japan, many public institutions implemented strict energy conservation policies. At my university, the outside elevators were shut down, lights in the halls turned off, and hand dryers in the bathrooms covered with trash bags so we couldn't use them. But the worst measure was setting the temperature in the classrooms at 28 degrees Celsius (about 83 degrees F). Wow. It was so hot in those rooms I thought I was going to pass out, and the students didn't look much better. Once I had to stick my head out the window to keep from keeling over. I don't know how my students managed to concentrate in that environment, but they did. Finally, near the end of the semester the temperature setting was changed to 26 degrees C. What a difference two degrees can make! As hard as that summer was, the entire city worked together and rolling blackouts were avoided.

Despite the horrible weather, I totally love this city and don't want to go anywhere else. I visited Okinawa earlier this year, and wow, the weather there suits me just fine. The food is awesome, too. But there is something that keeps me in Kitakyushu. It has got to be the people. I guess warm-hearted people trump cold weather any day of the week.

Summer 2013 in Kitakyushu was one of the most brutally hot summers on record. We endured weeks of no rain, constant humidity, and scorching heat. It rarely got below 82 degrees Fahrenheit in July and August, even at night. Everyone in the entire city was miserable except me. I was in heaven. Except for the mosquitoes.

#21 Traumatized Kids

Yesterday was Christmas Day. Unlike in my home country of the United States, Christmas is not a public holiday in Japan. And, since I work at a public university, I had to come to work and had classes 1st, 2nd, and 3rd periods. Up until a few years ago, classes for the year always ended before the Emperor's birthday on December 23rd, but recently classes have been getting later and later, this year going all the way up to December 27th. I could complain and whine about it, I guess, but it is my choice to live and work in this country, so I have to abide by Japanese national holidays and work schedules. It stinks to work on Christmas Day, but it is not an awful event for me. I do, however, feel very sorry for my kids.

When I was growing up, there was nothing like the excitement of Christmas morning. I remember some years waking up before the sun came up, and knowing that my parents would not like it if I got them up before six or so, I laid awake in bed waiting for six to come. My brothers and I would run downstairs and start opening presents, and my Mom would make coffee for herself and hot chocolate for us to drink while opening presents. After we were done, Mom would make a big breakfast, usually including what we call Heart Attack Casserole. It is a sausage, egg and milk casserole, and it is not the healthiest thing in the world. We didn't call it Heart Attack Casserole until 2006, the year my Dad had a heart attack after eating it (I am sure it was a coincidence?) My Dad recovered, but it took years for Mom to make that casserole again.

So, we would stay in our pajamas all day, play with our new presents, watch TV, and eat. Sometimes it was relaxing, sometimes it was boring; this was still a time when everything was closed, there was no Wal-Mart yet in town, and it was considered taboo to bother your friends on this special family day. Fun or boring, I have great memories of Christmas Day, some of the greatest memories of my childhood. So the fact that I couldn't give this experience to my own kids was pretty depressing for me this year.

The day before, we talked as a family about celebrating Christmas on the 26th since we had much more time to relax on that day, and it was still Christmas Day in the U.S. Mia freaked out and said, "But Mommy, tomorrow is the 25th! Tomorrow is Christmas! Why can't we open presents on Christmas?" It broke my heart and I felt bad, but classes for both Riz and I started at 8:50 in the morning, and since we had to first take Abby and Emmy to preschool, and Mia to a friend's house, we had to leave the house by 8:15. The kids were up late on Christmas Eve, and getting them up too early would make them grouchy. So, we decided to only open the presents from Santa in the morning, and open the rest after work finished for us. However, there wasn't time to both open presents and eat breakfast, so the kids wound up eating in the car on the way to school.

One of the hardest things for me about living in Japan is not being able to give my kids some of the great holiday experiences I had as a kid, particularly Thanksgiving and Christmas. I will talk about Christmas in a later chapter, but Thanksgiving is hard to celebrate primarily because the main guest of honor, the turkey, is really hard to cook in small Japanese ovens. Plus, being culinarily challenged, I probably couldn't properly prepare one anyway. The biggest part of Thanksgiving that I cannot give them is celebrating with extended family. Sometimes, we celebrate with our American friends the best we can and it is a blessing, but it is not the same as gathering at Grandmother's house and lounging on the sofa after eating a way too much and being barely able to breathe.

Of course, they are having experiences here in Japan that most American kids could never even dream of. I realize every day that living in a foreign country requires sacrifice, but that there is also so much to gain. My kids are learning to be global citizens, and I guess that going to school in the morning on Christmas Day is not too high of a cost to pay for that.

#22 Cake, The Colonel and Love

When I first came to Japan, I remember being mystified by the Japanese take on Christmas. Christmas cake? Who eats Christmas cake? Well, it turns out many Europeans do, and that is where this tradition came from. I am not really sure where the tie between Christmas and Kentucky Fried Chicken came from, but it probably is the brainchild of some marketing whiz in Tokyo who figured that chicken is close enough to turkey, the Christmas food of choice in the U.S. Once, I tried to get some KFC on Christmas Eve, but there was not a wing or breast to be found. Costco, which is about an hour drive from my house, has both huge Christmas cakes and rotisserie chicken, so you can imagine the crowd there on December 23, two days before Christmas and a national holiday. We waited in line 40 minutes

JUST TO GET IN THE DOOR. Yep, that's right. Just to get in the door. There were no carts, we were told, so line up. I said, "I don't need a cart. Can I just go in?" Well, of course not! That would totally go against the Japanese concept of fairness and equality. Everybody has to *gaman* (endure, persevere, suffer) together.

Somewhere along the line, Christmas Eve became a lover's holiday here. Couples go out to expensive dinners, sometimes paying up to $100 a person, and singles bemoan the fact that they are alone on Christmas. I thought that America had commercialized the holiday, but they have nothing on Japan. Sometimes I feel like I am surrounded by Christmas lights, decorations, trees, and music, but it feels absolutely nothing like Christmas. Even the Christmas trees look like impostors to me. They look so skinny and underfed, with weird cotton-looking stuff hanging off of them.

Not only Christmas, but Japan takes whatever she likes from the West and makes it her own. Take pizza. Every topping known to man and some yet unknown ones have found their way onto the Japanese pizza: corn, mayonnaise, tuna, gluttonous rice cakes, seaweed, tofu. Some of it actually tastes pretty good, but it just doesn't seem right to me…I know that America takes Asian food, like sushi, and does weird things with it (California Roll, tempura rolls), but seaweed on pizza just seems wrong, man. Wrong.

Three years ago, my family went back to the U.S. at Christmas. It had been seven years since I had experienced an American Christmas. And let me tell you, it was a really stereotypical, perfect American Christmas. Christmas dinner at my sister-in-law's parents' farm. Snow on the ground. Horses in the background. A huge dining room table covered with every kind of food you can imagine: turkey, ham, stuffing, yams, and a zillion different desserts. It took us hours to open all the presents on Christmas morning with my parents, my brother, and his enormous family. We stayed in our PJs all morning, eating homemade cinnamon rolls for breakfast.

It is amazing how the Christmas lights in Japan look the same, the songs playing in the stores are the same, and even some of the foods are the same, but the atmosphere feels totally different. Christmas caroling, baking cookies and making fudge, playing in the snow. That was Christmas as I remembered it, and I treasure the Christmas that my family got to spend in the U.S. three years ago. I love Japan, and the Japanese Christmas is for sure better than no Christmas at all. But it is just not magical here like it is to me when I go home. This year, on Christmas morning, instead of opening presents in my pajamas with my kids and making pancakes, I rushed my kids off to school as the ate bread covered with Nutella in the car on the way to school. Riz and I taught on Christmas Day, and tried to salvage the rest of this special day after we got home. Maybe not the magic of Christmas in the States, but we somehow managed to make our own magic and enjoy the time as a family anyway. Because when it comes down to it, the presents, the food, and the music don't make the holiday special anyway--it's the people you spend it with.

#23 Land of Masks

When cold and flu season rolls around in Japan, out come the masks. I remember the first time I saw someone wearing a mask in Japan. I was at the train station in Osaka, and this guy with a two hundred dollar haircut and expensive Italian suit was wearing this totally unattractive white mask on his face. What the heck, I thought. Was there some deadly outbreak of a mystery disease or something? I found out later, the mask is just a part of common winter attire in Japan. Most Americans I know who care a lick about fashion wouldn't even think about this hideous accessory, but in Japan, a country where fashion and appearance are so important, oddly enough the mask is not seen as taking away from your looks at all.

Reasons for wearing masks vary. Some people wear them to protect others from germs when they are coughing or sneezing. Others wear them when they are not even sick, to protect themselves from catching anything. One of my students told me he wears a mask most of the winter because he just feels more comfortable that way. Some people even wear a mask to cover stuff up. Some wear them to cover cold sores on their mouths. I even met this lady in a shop yesterday who told me she was wearing a mask because she hadn't had time to put on makeup in the morning! She was so embarrassed by her appearance without makeup that she felt like she had to cover it up. That made me sad. I think she is pretty without it.

I, for one, know that while there are times I should probably wear a mask, I just cannot do it. I find that I cannot breathe, that I feel like I am suffocating when I wear a mask. Sometimes when I go the hospital I will wear one because I know there are germs floating around everywhere. But I find myself tearing it off as soon as I leave. When I wear glasses, I find my breathing under the mask fogs up my glasses as well. I can't understand how Japanese people can wear them all day long and it not bother them at all. My students will even get up in front of class and do a presentation wearing their masks. Unbelievable to me.

I did find myself wearing a mask during the swine flu scare, as well as sanitizing my hands and those of my children fifteen times a day. I heard, though, that masks offer virtually zero protection from airborne virus. What they do protect against, though, is germs transmitted by touch. People touch their eyes and mouth with their germ-infested hands hundreds of times a day, and wearing a mask prevents you from at least touching your mouth.

The wearing of masks in Japan shows just another way

that the Japanese are always thinking about others. Many people I know don't go out if they are sick, or take out sick kids, because they do not want to infect others. This is another of the major reasons they wear masks. I like how they sacrifice fashion for consideration. While I can't wear a mask without hyperventilating, I respect and admire those who can, and do so to protect others. Maybe someone can teach me someday how to wear one without my glasses from fogging up...

#24 End of the Year Party!

In Japan, the end of the year party is one of the most important work events of the year. Drinking parties are huge in Japan, and are some of the only times co-workers will let their guard down and talk freely about anything and everything. There is a set price for everyone, usually between $30 and $70, and there is lots of drinking and lots of eating going on. I am not a very big fan of these parties because I don't eat much at them and don't drink at all. I always feel like there should be a special Anne price, but that is not the Japanese way. Sometimes, the non-drinkers will pay a little less than everyone else, but I still feel like I am paying a fortune to hang out with my co-workers and hear them talk about stuff they would never talk about at work.

The end of the year party is the mother of all drinking

parties. The Japanese word is "*bonenkai*," which literally means, "forget what happened this year party." That is exactly what many people try to do. Although I am not a big fan of drinking parties, I try not to miss the *bonenkai*. It is a good chance to hang out with co-workers and get to know them better. My department is really cool, and everyone gets along pretty well. Usually, work and family are kept so separate in Japan that families are never invited to company parties or events. I remember my shock at being invited by a co-worker to her wedding, my first in Japan. I found out later that only I was invited, not my husband. It made me sad to go alone, because in America it is assumed that you can bring your husband or mother or whoever to the wedding with you and enjoy the day together.

My department is pretty laid back, and families are invited to this year's party. This is really, really rare in Japan; in fact, I have never heard about something like this anywhere else. It is going to be a blast having my kids interact with the children of my colleagues. There are a lot of young teachers in my department with young kids, so bringing them to parties is not only acceptable but encouraged. I really like that because I often dislike the strict separation of family and work in Japan. You will never go into an office in Japan and find the walls or desk decorated with family pictures like you do in the States. Well, that is except in my office. There are pictures of my kids and husband everywhere.

Tonight's end of the year party is at a Japanese hot pot *nabe* place, one of my favorite places to eat. Everyone eats boiled veggies, fish, meat and tofu from a steaming pot. Probably not the most sanitary thing in the world if you think about it, but I love it so much that I try not to think about it. *Nabe* is a great way to get in a lot of veggies at one sitting, and still feel full when you are done. During winter my family eats *nabe* at least twice a week. It can get a little pricey if you have a carnivorous family like I do. They always seem to complain there is not enough meat. But for this party, I don't need to worry about money, because whether they eat a little or a lot, I will pay the same price. So, my little carnivorous ones, eat till your little hearts are content, but save the tofu and veggies for me.

#25 Health Checkup Lottery, Part I

Tomorrow, I am going in for an extensive physical. It includes pretty much everything–blood and urine work, chest x-ray, bone density test, EKG, echocardiogram, mammogram, abdominal ultrasound, vision and hearing tests and Upper GI. The last one, Upper GI is pretty common here, but I don't know anyone who has ever done it in the States. It is done by swallowing a camera on the end of a scope that snakes its way down into your tummy to have a good look. I have done it twice before (What can I say? I am a test junkie). They can put the camera through your nose or your mouth, but both are uncomfortable since it has to pass through your throat either way. Not good for people with a strong gag reflex. The reason Japanese do this test so often is because of the high incidence of stomach cancer here. In the West, colon cancer is much more common than stomach cancer. Japan used to have very few cases of colon cancer, but with the introduction of the Western diet, colon cancer is increasing right alongside stomach cancer.

Anyway, I won the health check up lottery this year. My insurance group offers these tests every year, but not everyone can get them done. I have applied three times and won all three times, so I am wondering if most people who apply get it. The insurance pays about $400, and I pay about $70. Pretty good deal for all these tests, don't you think? People who do not win the lottery for the extensive check up participate in the yearly regular health checks required by their employer. These are far simpler, but still include blood and urine tests, EKG, chest x-ray, and vision and hearing tests. Sometimes I wonder if people who don't win the lottery might be unlucky enough to die of some undiagnosed disease.

It is weird that the Japanese are so proactive about some kinds of testing, but so lax about others. I know many women in their 40s who rarely have pap smears, and others even older who have never had a mammogram. The Japanese government is sending out free tickets for pap smears to try to encourage women to get them, but only every five years. I am pretty sure that a cancer can get pretty bad in that five-year interval. I think that these coupons, while meant to encourage women to get tested might actually be detrimental, causing women to have the tests done only in the years they get the free coupons. Maybe they don't know that It only costs about ten bucks without a coupon; or maybe it is that many people either don't want to pay even ten dollars, or are too embarrassed to have the pap smear every year. Not me. I guess all my health issues especially my colitis struggles have made me oblivious to medical embarrassment.

When I get a pap smear, my doctor and I just chat away through the lace curtain that hides the patient's upper body during pelvic exams to protect women from embarrassment in Japan. "Hey, doc! Still running everyday? Doing another marathon soon?" I figure, cancer is worse than the test, and I am willing to go through a little discomfort to better my chances to be around for my kids and grandkids. But, just like the colonoscopy, the invasive, embarrassing aspect of the pap smear keeps people from being tested. It's a shame that embarrassment can inadvertently lead to cancer and even death. The government is ratcheting up efforts for preventative testing, but they still have a long way to go to increase the national consciousness of the importance of these tests.

But they don't have to worry about me. I am on the other end of the scale, maybe even a mild hypochondriac. So tomorrow, bright and early I will be off to the hospital with my winning lottery ticket in my hand and 70 bucks in my pocket, having another round of tests, all of which I have done before, all the while thankful that I live in socialized Japan. I love this country.

#26 Health Checkup Lottery, Part II

Well, I am back from my extensive health checkup. I had to get to the hospital by 7:30 in the morning, of course after not eating anything since they were going to do an Upper GI stomach camera. I got there, paid my $70, and was told where to change into the test-appropriate clothes. I was assigned my locker, and inside were a set of pajamas, a warm bathrobe, and some slippers. After changing, I was led from one test to another at an astonishing speed. I mean, like, no waiting time at all. First was vision and hearing check, followed by blood work, and a consultation with the nurse. Then after about a two-minute wait, I was led to the first floor for an abdominal ultrasound, lung function test, eye pressure tests, EKG, mammogram, chest X-ray, and bone density test. Unlike many people I know, I don't really think the mammogram hurts all that bad. Contorting my body into all the crazy positions to be able to smash my breast appropriately is much more painful.

After these tests were done, I was led back upstairs for the Upper GI. In order to numb my throat, I had to gargle this gel-like concoction for forty seconds. Then, I was led into the testing room, where the nurse gave me a shot to make me loopy. At first I thought it didn't work very well since I could feel them putting the probe down my throat and it was making me gag. But from that point on, I remember nothing. I woke up an hour later still feeling woozy, but so glad I decided on using the drugs. One of my friends opted not to use the anesthesia, and she was gagging uncontrollably the whole test, totally miserable.

The last test, the pap smear, was done in another building which was an incredibly far 50 yards away. But, since the hospital couldn't have their patient getting cold, I was driven over there in a minivan. 18 seconds later, we arrived. After the test was finished, the car was late in coming, so we walked back. I think the nurse felt bad for making me walk 50 yards in the cold…

So, all the tests were done, and all that was left was to wait to talk to the doctor and get the results. While waiting, the nurse brought me coffee and a cake on a cute little tray. It took a while to see the doctor, so I got a free refill on the coffee. Finally, after waiting 20 minutes or so, I saw the doctor. Thanks be to God, the results that came back today were normal. I still have to wait on the results of the mammogram, but I seem to be fine.

After leaving the doctor's office, I was given a ticket for a free lunch in the hospital cafeteria. Since I was in kind of a hurry, I got a steak, vegetable and rice lunch to go and gave it to Riz when I got home. Free food makes us both happy--me because it is free, and Riz because it is food.

The last thing I want to say in this post is this: the Japanese find a way to bring in excellent customer service to everything, even health checkups. I felt more like a valued customer than a patient. I was treated with respect and professionalism. In addition to the thorough medical care, I got a lot of extra perks too. I mean, I paid $70 bucks for tests that would have cost me thousands in the States, and I got coffee, cake and a free lunch to boot. Yes, I love this country. And, Riz really enjoyed my lunch.

#27 Embarrassment and Culture

I was thinking yesterday about how the things that embarrass people varies from culture to culture. For example, here in Japan, the toilet-making powerhouse company TOTO has come up with an invention called the *otohime*, or "sound princess." This is a little device installed on the walls of many public toilets. When women go to the bathroom, they can push a button that produces a static sound, covering up any sounds they make while doing No.1 or No.2. I asked Riz if they can also be found in the men's toilets, but he laughed and said of course not. I find this toilet contraption ridiculous since all people make the same noises. What's the big deal? In fact, the one at my workplace is triggered by a sensor, so it goes off even if I don't want it to. And I don't want it to. It is really annoying and loud, almost like scratching your fingernails on a chalkboard.

Just today, I went to the drugstore to buy some feminine stuff for that monthly visitor, and the cashier placed my purchase in a black plastic bag so no one could see through it. They do the same thing with pregnancy tests. Again, I don't see what the big deal is since all women need this kind of stuff. I wonder if any Japanese husbands are sent on feminine product runs by their wives like husbands in the U.S. are sometimes. I really, really doubt it.

On the other hand, they are not really all that embarrassed to bathe with strangers in the hot springs or public baths, an act which horrifies many first time visitors to Japan. They are also not all that embarrassed by farting in public. When my husband was in the hospital, the other three guys in his ward had no qualms about letting it rip. And while blowing your nose in public is considered bad manners, clearing your throat of phlegm and then hacking it onto the sidewalk is not all that bad. Go figure.

Lastly, for some reason, laughing is embarrassing here, and many women and sometimes men cover their mouths when laughing. In fact, sometimes they do it when just talking. I wonder why? Bad breath? Bad teeth? Modesty? I talked to an older lady once, and she covered her mouth with her hand for the entire 20-minute conversation. That was pretty annoying because I prefer to see someone's mouth when having a conversation. I had actually never thought about how important it is to see someone's mouth during a conversation before, but yes, having a conversation with a hand is a little distracting.

Oh yeah, don't ask Japanese women their age. That is really embarrassing. I am 39, by the way. I'm 39 and happy to still be alive. My dad always says, "If you are not getting older, you are dead." I like that.

#28 Bonus Day

Today is one of my favorite days. Bonus day. It is one of two days a year that I, and most of the full-time working population in Japan, get this huge chunk of money deposited in our accounts. It is not really a bonus if you think about it logically. My workplace just takes money out of my monthly salary and puts it aside, paying me a big chunk twice a year. It usually amounts to about two months salary, and the winter bonus is slightly more than the summer bonus. On bonus day, I feel rich for about two hours, then it starts to disappear into a web of bill payments, savings plans, tithing, and daily expenses. It sure is nice to feel rich for two hours, though.

Many people with mortgages have to set aside around half of their bonuses to put towards their loans. There is nothing fun about that! I mean, the bonus is something that I really look forward to, and if I had to cough up half before even getting a single yen, that would be pretty depressing. While many of my friends think that paying 100,000 yen (1000 dollars) a month for rent is wasteful, I don't really see it that way. Buying a house is a huge commitment--one we are not willing to make. Besides, we don't even know if we are going to be here forever or not.

I enjoy not having any loans. No car loans. No housing loan. No credit card loans. We enjoy our simple life and enjoy my twice yearly bonuses. The only time that I have ever really splurged, though, was a few years ago when I went out and bought a massage chair. I had always wanted one, but they usually cost $2000-$3000 and there is no way I am going to shell out that kind of money for a chair. I am my mother's daughter. But when I found one for $700, I figured we may just be able to afford it. I had just had a baby, and I felt like pampering myself. Man, was it worth it. We use that chair all the time, and my friends immediately sit it in when they come over. Sometimes I wonder if they are visiting me or my chair.

That is the biggest splurge you will ever get out of me. Most bonuses go towards paying for airfare to get the whole Crescini brood to the U.S. to visit family every two years, which by the way, is way more important to us than buying stuff. You cannot put a value on time with the Grandparents. I am sure that it is a much better feeling for the kids to sit on Grandmother's lap than in that $700 chair...

#29 Costco is Coming! Costco is Coming!

There are a few words in the English language that bring instant joy to my heart: family, Jesus, peanut butter, cookies, and coffee are a few. Another one of those words is Costco, a word that can bring joy into the darkest gloom of any homesick American living in Japan. I'll never forget the first time my host family drove me to the nearest Costco soon after I moved to Kitakyushu. The sight of those giant American carts, the big, carb-loaded yummy bagels, the 80 yen sodas and footlong hotdogs. And the smell. It smelled like America. I wasn't homesick yet, and was very happy to be in Japan, but the knowledge that Costco was there for me if I needed her was so comforting. Even though it was over an hour away and I didn't even have a car, to me Costco was going to save my American self in more ways than one. It would save me from having to have my mom send me peanut butter like she did when I lived in Kobe; it would save me from having to go for years without a slice a pizza that didn't have corn or mayo on it; and it would save me from having to actually bake a birthday cake. I didn't care that it was so far away because it was so much closer than America. Even before Riz and I got our first car, we paid our 4200 yen to become Costco members. We would figure out later how we would actually get there.

Eating was hard during my first stint in Kobe, Japan from 1997-2000. Even though Kobe was a big city, there was not much foreign food that I could find, although I learned later during my time there of services like the Foreign Buyers Club (FBC) and Price Club, places that had American food at exorbitant prices. I still use FBC at times, swallowing my pride and paying five bucks for a box of cake mix. I hated Japanese food at first, and was always asking my Mom to send over my favorites. I remember once trying to bake chocolate chip cookies in my toaster over. Didn't go so well. I got entirely giddy if I was able to find my all-time favorite snack food ever–Nacho Cheese Doritos. Never mind they cost three times what they do in the States.

My first time to Costco, I bought way too much stuff. Come to think of it, I still buy way too much stuff. It seems that no matter what I go there to buy, I always spend 20,000 yen (200 dollars). It is a mystery to me. No matter what I get, a lot or a little, it always comes to 20,000 yen. I go to buy peanut butter and bagels, and come back with new pajamas for the kids and a cooler that I didn't really need. Anyway, I figure, Costco is so far away, and they may not have what I want the next time I go, so I better buy it now. Which brings me to the single most important thing any foreigner in Japan needs to remember about Costco: get it while you can! If you want something really bad, never, ever say, "I'll think about it and maybe get it next time." There will be no next time. It is 99% guaranteed to be gone by next time. And don't even thinking about asking when they will get it again. That is more secretive than Roswell. Eight years ago, Nacho Cheese Doritos disappeared from the shelves of Costco, never to be seen again. And please, don't tell me those salsa-flavored Japanese knock-off Doritos are good enough. They are good, but they are not Doritos. Other favorites disappear for a couple of years and then mysteriously appear again. Still others are one-shot wonders, appearing briefly and then disappearing forever. Like turkey lunch meat. There was one window of a month I was regularly enjoying turkey sandwiches. Then, like my Doritos, it was gone in an instant.

Of course, the Japanese love Costco, too, so there are tons of bulk Japanese products as well. The Japanese are so crazy about Costco that honestly, it is a headache to go anymore. The lines can be torturous on weekends and holidays. Like I said, two days before Christmas, I waited 40 minutes just to get inside because there were no carts to be found. Darn you 700 yen rotisserie chickens and cheap Christmas cakes!! And don't even get me started about the ability or lack thereof, of the average Japanese to maneuver skillfully the giant Costco carts. I have never seen carts so big anywhere else in Japan, and from the way they push them around, they haven't either. Most supermarkets have these little baskets you place on a small cart that holds maybe three loafs of bread, two cartons of milk, and a few veggies. Being unaccustomed to the oversized carts, people will park them anywhere, causing a huge traffic jam. The worst place is near the meat with all the free food samples. People will line up, carts and all, and make the entire meat area inaccessible. Sometimes people even stand in line 20 minutes just to get a sample! It's a sample, people! The ends of the aisles are also traffic jam hazards, as they are another favorite location for free samples. To be honest, I am probably guilty of causing a traffic jam or two myself, but of course, it only annoys me when others do it.

Well, about the title of this post...I found out last fall that Costco was building a new store in my city of Kitakyushu. Now, Kitakyushu has a population of almost a million people, and a huge land area, so depending on where it was to be built, there was a good chance that it wouldn't be much closer than the one an hour away in Fukuoka. Imagine my glee when I found out it would be built a mere five-minute drive from my house! The euphoria! I was having a long day when I found that out, but I tell you, I walked around with a smile on my face the rest of the day. I have no doubt that it will become just as crowded as the one in Fukuoka, but the difference is, I can go there during the week or late at night when it is not so crowded. No longer will going to Costco be a half-day trip. And hopefully, no longer will I spend two hundred dollars a visit. Maybe I can talk the management into giving free classes on cart etiquette?

Costco Kitakyushu Warehouse opened on March 21st, 2013 to great fanfare and the presence of lots of white, non-Japanese speaking employees flown over for the occasion. My husband is proud of the fact he was the first foreigner to set foot in the new Costco, the only one crazy enough to line up at 4 am in the freezing cold. I am happy to report that while it is unbearably crowded on weekends, it is a very pleasant place to visit on weekdays. I think this is how Costcos around the world are supposed to be.

I am proud to say that I no longer waste money on garden lights or portable coolers; I go there for what I need and that is all. I have yet to spend 20,000 yen there. Unfortunately, there are a lot of people like me who shun the carts and just pick up a couple things, and there have been rumors that tightwads like us have put Kitakyushu Costco is danger of going out of business. I am not worried, though. I have never heard of Costco going out of business anywhere.

#30 Japanese English, Part I

Most people know that I am a teacher, but because I am a university teacher, I have another equally important role—researcher. To be honest, education is my passion, so at first I was very lukewarm about the whole research thing. Sure, I would write textbooks and short papers, but I just couldn't find a topic that got me fired up enough to spend hours researching, writing and doing surveys. But since university in Japan is like university everywhere else, it is publish or perish baby! If I wanted to keep my dream job, teaching, I had to get promoted. To get promoted, I had to do research. It was that simple. So, I started trying to find something that was both interesting and useful. I had no desire to write papers that no one would read, and that would not help anyone anywhere. Finally, two years ago, I hit the jackpot. I became enthralled by Japanese English. Japanese English is a distinctly made-in-Japan creation—creative use and manipulation of English in such a way that the majority of native speakers will not understand it. Some classic examples are 'mansion' (small apartment); 'magic tape' (Velcro); 'salaryman' (businessman) and 'virgin road' (wedding aisle). I could write pages and pages about this colorful topic, but I want to focus on one area of usage: words that are real English words but have a vastly different meaning in Japanese English.

A couple weeks ago, my oldest came home and announced she was running in a marathon at school. Well, this got my attention, and if I hadn't heard about this event earlier from other mothers, I may have run to the school crying child abuse. How dare they make my 7-year old run 42.1 kilometers? Actually, they weren't. In Japanese, the word 'marathon' just means any kind of foot race, regardless of the length. Mia is only running a one kilometer or so.

Last week, at the beginning of the church council meeting, I was handed the 'resume' of the meeting. Much unlike the English meaning of the word, in Japanese 'resume' means meeting agenda. Likewise, when my students tell me they are going to bring over 'juice' I know better than to expect only fruit juice. While they might bring some, 'juice' in Japanese means soft drinks and sports drinks, too. The words are endless: a 'jumper' is a light jacket; 'cunning' is cheating; and lastly, my favorite, 'my car.' Alas, 'my car' in Japanese doesn't just mean my car like you might think. It may also mean your car, his car, their car, Kenta's car, my mom's car, Kenta's grandmother's friend's sister's car. You get the picture. It means one's own car. So when you say, "Hey, are we going in my car?" you cannot really know who's car the speaker is talking about out of context.

This inventive usage of the English pronoun is being affixed to just about everything these days: my bag (a personal shopping bag); my pace (one's own pace); even my *hashi* (one's own chopsticks). As weird as it may seem, I actually like some of these words. Sometimes I even make up my own. My favorite linguistic creation is 'my peanut butter.' Yes, I admit it. I have been known to carry around a small jar of peanut butter in my bag. But more on that later.

And that brings me to the title of this book. Do you know what a 'body bag' is in Japanese English? Well, it is definitely not a black vinyl bag into which medical examiners place victims of violent crimes like on Law and Order SVU. In Japan, a 'body bag' is a sling-type bag worn around the chest. I love it. I got my daughter a Phineas and Ferb body bag for her birthday, and every time she wears it she says, "Mommy, thanks so much for my body bag!"

I am happy to report that in April, 2013, I was promoted to Associate Professor after the longest serving tenure as a lecturer in the history of Japanese universities. Thank you, Japanese English. Thank you, body bags.

#31 Funny Japanese Mistakes

Anyone who has ever learned a foreign language is bound to have stories of humiliating languages gaffes. It is bad enough when you can't communicate any better than a two-year old, but when you go one step further and say something embarrassing, it is a hundred times worse. Even though my husband and I have been here 13 years and speak fluent Japanese, it amazes me how we still at times find ourselves the providers of entertainment with our flawed use of the language. Just a few months ago, I made one of my funniest gaffes ever. Recently, that famous Master Card commercial about stuff being "priceless" has become popular over here too. You know them, "Tickets to Fenway Park: $120; refreshments at the game: $40; memories of the ballpark with Dad: priceless." That kind of emotional cheesiness that everybody loves is a hit, even in stoic Japan. So, I was talking to a friend and I wanted to tell her that she is priceless to me. Although the word "priceless" can be pronounced in Japanese thanks to the commercials, it is probably not all that well-known, so I wanted to say it in Japanese. So, I told Junko, *"Anata wa kachi ga nai"* which means, "You have absolutely no value, you piece of dung." Oops. I realized my mistake and fixed it quickly, but Junko and several other friends were already on the floor laughing.

RIz is always good for a few laughs, too. My favorite one is when we had a party at our house. Japanese people always begin a party with a speech and a toast, so Riz decided to ask me in Japanese in front of everyone to say a few words. But instead of asking me to say a few words, he told me to start talking to myself. I got so tickled I had a hard time eventually saying a few words. The two phrases for say a few words (*hito koto*) and talk to yourself (*hitori goto*) sound understandably similar to each other.

I guess the moral of the story is that no matter how good your language skills are, you are bound to butcher it from time to time. I mean, we even butcher our native language at times, so it is guaranteed to be much worse in another tongue. For us, the key is to be able to laugh at ourselves and our mistakes instead of being horrified by them. I feel like cracking up even as I think about all my goofs. The Japanese have a proverb, "Failure is the root of success." Maybe that is why I can speak Japanese so well.

*Last weekend, my family visited a castle in Oita Prefecture. When I went to pay for admission, I said, "Two adults, one elementary school student, and two preemies, please." Darn word preemie sounds too much like preschooler in Japanese!

#32 I am a Foreigner

When I first came to Japan in 1997, I knew very little Japanese. I mean, very little. My vocabulary consisted of a few greetings and apologies, and the incredibly useful phrases of "What's that?" and "How do you say that in Japanese?" Still, I decided that when possible, I was going to be as Japanese as possible to try to fit into the culture as best as a tall, white American who couldn't speak the language at all could. I lived for three months with a very kind host family, and am very grateful to them for helping me acquire many new vocabulary words as a result of my expert usage of "What's that?" and "How do you say that in Japanese?" However, my host family's house was over an hour away from Riz's place, and I was getting weary of traveling that far almost everyday to see him. And, yes, I absolutely had to see him everyday—we were young and in love (still are, in love that is) after all.

I found a really small place only about a 50-second walk from Riz's place. What luck! After paying a highway robbery fee of ten months rent for key money (the scandalous Japanese hybrid of a security deposit and thank you gift to my landlord for the incredible kind act of letting a wretched soul like me rent his beloved apartment. More on that later), I moved in and began getting settled into my new life. But before getting settled in, I was obligated to take a gift to my new neighbors, introducing myself and letting them know I was there. I went to the store to buy the standard self-introduction-after-moving-to-a-new-place gift—dishwashing soap. I figured one wasn't enough, so I got two or three. I can't remember. You may be laughing at the idea of such a gift, but the Japanese are very practical, and practical gifts like these are highly appreciated by the receiver. I remember at my kids' preschool recital, there was some time to kill while the teachers were setting up the props, so the school principal started a trivia game with the audience. The prizes were…you guessed it! Incredibly practical garbage bags!!

So, armed with dishwashing soap and my determination to be a good Japanese neighbor, I knocked on the door of the lady living next door. From inside, I heard her ask in Japanese, "*Dare desu ka*?" (Who is it?). I found myself in the conundrum I often found myself in at that point in my life; I understood the question, but had no idea how to answer it. Although I now know to say, "*Tonari ni hikkoshite kita mono nan desu kedo…*" (I am the one who just moved next door), at that point, I had no idea how to say "move" or "neighbor" or anything remotely acceptable as a response. I wracked my brain, but to no avail. Finally, in a moment of panic, I blurted out, "*Gaijin desu.*" I am a foreigner. What an idiot. Not only did I say something stupid, but I even used the sometimes derogatory Japanese word for foreigner, *gaijin* (literally "outside person), instead of the more socially acceptable *gaikokujin* (outside country person). Right after it came out of my mouth, I was horrified. I heard the lady chuckle and say she was coming out. I handed her the soap, and mumbled, "*tsumaranai mono desu ga…*" (literally, "Sorry for giving you such a lousy gift." The Japanese always degrade themselves, family members and presents because they think it shows humility).

I left with my tail between my knees. As I was walking to Riz's house, I started laughing out loud as I thought about what an idiotic thing I had said, and how I really need to learn the word "neighbor" in Japanese. Note to self: Next time I embark on an encounter for which I have inadequate language skills, do a little preparation beforehand! However, I thought at the time what a great story this language gaffe would be, and sure enough, I have been making fun of myself and entertaining Japanese friends and students for years with the retelling of this story. I can tell you one thing, though. I will never forget the Japanese word for "neighbor."

#33 Funny Japanese Mistakes, Part II

Since in a previous post I shared embarrassing Japanese mistakes Riz and I have made since coming to Japan, I thought in this one I would recount the best stories I have heard of the language mistakes of others. After all, making fun of others is much more fun than making fun of yourself!

My friend Marla, who now speaks fluent Japanese, couldn't speak Japanese at all when she first arrived in Japan more than fifteen years ago. She was invited to the house of a very prominent area pastor, and was treated to an excellent meal. Being stuffed to the gills, she sat back, patted her tummy and intended to say, "I'm full" in Japanese (*onaka ippai*). Instead, this wet-behind-the-ears newcomer patted her tummy and committed a classic Spoonerism, switching the letters around and said, "*inaka oppai,* (country breasts). She was embarrassed, but everybody in the room had a good laugh.

    I think my favorite one is of a guy who wanted to learn polite Japanese so he asked for some advice from a friend. He was told that you needed to put (o-) in front of nouns to make your speech very polite. Some examples are *o-cha* (honorable tea), *o-bento* (honorable lunch box), *o-miyage* (honorable souvenir), etc. That sounds easy enough, he thought. So one day, he had to walk in front of his boss, an action considered rude here if you don't say anything. The best thing to say is *mae shitsurei shimasu,* which means, "Sorry for being so rude as to pass in front of you." But this guy decided he was going to practice his new polite vocabulary, so when he passed in front of his boss he said, "*o-mae shitsurei.*" A great idea, except that in Japanese the word *o-mae* is a low, vulgar way to say "you," and when joined with *shitsurei* it literally means, "you are so rude, you moron." Not the best thing to say to your boss…

    Lastly, there is a story I heard of a woman riding the train home, exhausted from a long day at work. People were staring at the curious foreigner again as usual, and she found that she just couldn't take it anymore. She stood up and yelled in Japanese, "Why are you guys staring at me? I am a person!"

She then pointed to those seated around her and said, "Look! He is a person. She is a person. That guy is a person! We are all people." She found that people were staring at her as if she were crazy, and she had a feeling that it wasn't because she was a crazed foreigner going on a tirade on a train at rush hour. She realized that she had mistaken the Japanese word for person (*ningen*) for the word carrot (*ninjin*). So, the Japanese aboard the train that day got treated to a stressed out foreign woman yelling, "I am a carrot! You are a carrot! We are all carrots!"

There are numerous other funny gaffes I've heard. For example, foreigners often confuse the words *kawaii* (cute), *kowai* (scary), and *kiroi* (yellow). An American guy told me once that he once told a Japanese mommy that her baby sure was yellow. Oops. Then there was the guy who was told to bring over some *shuu cream* (cream puffs), and instead brought over some shoe cream, thinking the speaker meant shoe polish. I could talk about this topic forever. And the good thing is, as long as we are non-native speakers (forever), my friends and I are sure to be providing future party material for years to come...

#34 *Shaken* to the Core

I remember once I was looking through the ads in a magazine for foreigners. I liked looking at the want ads, and at all the stuff foreigners living in Japan were trying to get rid of before moving back to their home countries. I kept coming upon ads by people trying to sell their cars, and they kept saying that the car was shaken. I thought, "What on earth is a shaken car?" It baffled me for a while, but I finally figured out it referred not to the English word "shaken," but to the Japanese word *shaken*, which is an abbreviation meaning car inspection fee.

Now that I was armed with the knowledge of what *shaken* was, I had to figure out why it was such a big deal that it needed to be mentioned in the ad. In the United States, where I am from, you must get your car inspected every year, for the crazy expense of $15 or so. Now, if your car has a major problem, the car will not pass inspection until you get that problem fixed. I found out that this extensive Japanese inspection must be carried out every three years for new cars, and every two years for older cars. It costs anywhere between $700 and $1500 dollars a time depending on what kind of car you have, how old it is, and where you get it inspected. What?? $1500 for a car inspection? I thought, well at least if you have to pay that much, if there is a big problem, such as the need for a new alternator, timing belt, starter, etc., that would surely be included in the cost, right? Wrong. Those things are additional. The *shaken* fee is only for the inspection.

So the reason that people always have to mention the *shaken* in an ad is this: if they are selling a car for $500, but the new owner will have to pay the $1000 *shaken* fee in a month, it would be unethical not to mention it. Conversely, if the *shaken* has recently been taken care of, that is also a positive selling point, as the new owner will not have to worry about paying it for at least another two years.

Before my third daughter, Emmy, was born, we decided that we needed a new minivan because our old one could not hold three car seats. We asked around, and a friend of a friend offered to give us a 13-year old Honda Odyssey with only 70,000 miles on it for $500 dollars, the *shaken* fee of about $1000, the yearly taxes of $500, and some minor repairs that added up to about $500. So, thanks to God's grace, we got a very reliable minivan, which was perfect for our growing family for only $2500. We paid for it in cash, and have had it for almost four years. Because the previous owner worked at a Honda dealership, the maintenance was perfect, and it has given us no major problems to date.

We paid the *shaken* two years ago for the first time, and three months from now, we will have to pay it again. The thing is, it also needs new tires that will cost us about $800. We are trying to decide if we want to put $1800 into a 17-year old car with 110,000 miles on it. On the other hand, it is a good car, and has had no problems so far. There is no way we will find another good used car for that price, and we definitely don't want to take out a loan to pay for a new car. But what if the car falls apart right after we pay *shaken*? (I doubt it—it is a Honda). It is a risk, to be sure, and we are not quite sure what we will do. I think I will ask a mechanic friend to check it out and tell us what he thinks. One thing I do know: the cost of *shaken* is definitely more than the monetary value of the car. But to us, the emotional value and the practical value of that car is priceless. We will probably try to drive it to 300,000 miles...

We ended up keeping the car and paying the shaken and for new tires. It now runs like a dream. Go Honda.

#35 Key Money

My husband and I have rented six different places during our 13 years in Japan. For five of those, we have had to pay key money. Key money is the best English translation that anyone can come up with for the bizarre Japanese system of paying thousands of dollars to your landlord for God only knows what reason. Is it a security deposit? Well, kind of, but you will not get it all back, even if you leave the place in pristine condition. You will be lucky to get any of it back. Is it a gift? Hmm. Maybe we are getting closer. After all, the landlord is being kind enough to let us borrow his place. In my Kobe apartment, I had to pay the equivalent of ten months rent up front as key money before I was allowed to move in. Ten months! My rent was cheap, about

$300 a month, but still, that was $3000 and I didn't have it. Maybe I really needed to say thank you because the landlord was nice enough to let me move in even though I was a foreigner. What a nice guy! The realtor had to call and check just to be sure, because some landlords have been known to turn away foreigners. Anyway, I could move in, but I had to ask Mommy for help. I didn't have that kind of cash. I cannot remember how much of it I got back after I moved out a year or so later, but it was not more than half.

Apparently, each area in Japan has different rules regarding key money. The Kansai area (Kobe, Osaka, Kyoto) has very high key money, sometimes up to ten months like in my case. In Kyushu, where we live now, the norm is three to five months. However, you are more likely to get money back in Kansai than in Kyushu.

In 2006, when Mia was a baby, we moved to our first house. The rent was about $1000 a month, so we had to pay four months of key money--$4000. We did not know much at that time about our rights as renters, but we signed what is known as a regular contract, and we hoped to live there indefinitely, as it was a nice house in a convenient location. However, in the spring of 2010, not even three years into our contract, we were informed that the owner would like us to move out by the fall. We were shocked and very worried. We had been under the impression that we could live there as long as we wanted, and we wanted to stay longer. After speaking to the real estate agent, we found out that the owner was buying a new house and needed cash quickly, so he wanted to sell the house. We also found out that he would like us to buy it. Now, we liked the house, but we didn't love it. Besides, we didn't have permanent residency yet, and without that, it is next to impossible to get a housing loan. So, we politely declined and tried to figure out what to do next.

The real estate company felt bad, and I got the impression they were as surprised as we were. They helped us to find a new place, and it was an even better house and in a better location than our old house. We then set about trying to figure out the finances of it all. We thought because he asked us to leave so suddenly after such a short time, that he should return most of our key money. Seemed only fair. Moving is so expensive, and we hadn't budgeted for it at all. We were going home to the U.S. for two months that summer, so even though we could stay in our old house until the fall, we had to get out and moved into our new place before we left for the States in early August. The owner, through the real estate agent, refused to return any more than one month of key money. Well, this did not sit well with us, and we decided to do some investigating.

We discovered there are two types of housing contracts in Japan—regular (*futsuu*) and term-limit (*teiki*) contracts. The term-limit contracts state specifically how long you can stay, and then when that term is up, you can negotiate with the owner about staying longer. He may allow you to stay longer, or he may ask you to leave. We had signed a regular contract, which meant that legally, we could stay indefinitely, as long as the owner was not returned to Kitakyushu for work. Wanting to sell the house was not a valid reason for asking us to leave. Of course, although we didn't have to leave, we didn't want to be nasty about it and stay somewhere that we were not wanted; at the same time, we knew our rights and just wanted to be treated fairly. So, I called the real estate agent again, and told him that one month of key money was not acceptable, and that I was aware of our rights as renters under a regular contract. I requested fair treatment, and a return of more key money. I was proud of myself, because I was finally good enough at Japanese to be able to argue and stick up for myself.

A little while later, the real estate agent returned our call, and informed us that not only was the owner going to pay ALL the key money for our new house, but he was also going to pay for most of our moving expenses. Wow. We weren't expecting that. Thank you, Jesus! I figure the owner got scared that we knew the law and was worried we would give him trouble. So, it turns out, that we were able to move safely in early May all in one day, thanks to our generous friends, and we ended up only losing about $400 on the whole deal. That is so much better than the $6000 that I was worried about when this whole ordeal started. The best thing is, we are much happier in our new place. God really took care of our needs.

The contract we signed for our new place is a four-year

contract. It is up in a year a half, so we do not know what will happen. We hope to stay longer, but we have a great realtor, and we know if we do have to leave, she will do her best to help us find a new place. We were told up front that we will not be getting our key money back. That stinks, but at least we knew about it at the beginning. We love our neighborhood, and we would love to stay there as long as we can, but who knows? The thing I learned from all this is how important it is to stand your ground and fight for your rights. I wanted to stand up for myself and for my family with dignity, and I think I did that. I wonder how many people just accept bad situations and figure there is nothing they can do to change them. Well, there was something I could do, and I did it, and could not have been happier with the results. But at the end of the day, I still think the key money system is whacked out.

We just found out that we have to move again next year. I refuse to pay key money again, so we will probably end up living in university housing. It is small, but cheap, close to campus, and best of all, requires no key money.

#36 Driving School of Highway Robbery

The next time you are complaining about the long waits at your local DMV, maybe you should consider that it costs an average Japanese $3000 and takes two or three months for him to get a driver's license. Not kidding. Most Japanese go to driving school in their late teens or early twenties. It is paid for either by months of working part-time, or if they are lucky, by generous parents. Now, attending driving school is not technically required, but there are few people who can pass the difficult driving test without it. Just ask my Chinese friend who failed the test nine times before finally passing it. It seems to the wary foreign eye that the driving schools and DMV may have some kind of under the table agreement, as it is pretty rare for a driving school student to fail the driving test. Or maybe, they just practice the difficult turns so often that they can perform them in their sleep.

While many students attend driving school when they can during the school year, others go to intensive driving school camps during summer and spring vacations. These camps, usually about three weeks long, house and feed students who attend lectures and driving classes all day long. My students tell me that these intensive camps are much cheaper than regular driving school, but they still cost around $2000 to attend.

Foreigners are not required to attend driving school. The requirements for getting a Japanese driver's license vary from country to country. I hear that people from countries who drive on the same side of the road as the Japanese (England, Australia), the left, are only required to take a written test. I mean, this test is a laugh. "If the light is red, you should stop. True or false?" Hmm. That's a hard one...Of course, before that stage, all foreigners must go to JAF, the Japanese equivalent of AAA, and get their home countries' license officially translated into Japanese. This was a hassle for me, because I had just renewed my license, so it seemed like I had only a few months driving experience, not the years and years that I actually had and that was required by the city government to get a Japanese license. So, adding to the paperwork, I had to contact the Virginia DMV for proof that I had been indeed driving for years and had a stellar record.

People unfortunate enough to come from countries that drive on the right side of the road (U.S., China) must not only take the written test, but also the road test. Now, the road test is conducted on a real driving course, and is very difficult. In fact, those foreigners who actually pass on the first time are legends here. My husband, Riz, passed on his second try, earning him much respect from me and the rest of our foreign friends here. The problem is, how can you pass the road test, when you don't have a license so you cannot legally drive, and therefore, practice? It is a huge catch-22. If you don't practice, you cannot pass; but you can't practice because you don't have a license. Many of us practice in parking lots and hope we won't get caught, but practicing in parking lots is not nearly good enough practice to prepare you for the horrors of the actual course.

After I had all my documents translated by JAF, I went to the Japanese Licensing Center for my first try. All test takers must arrive by 1:30, pay the fees (about $40), fill out forms and then, wait. Driving school students are prioritized over foreigners, so the usual pattern is pay, fill out forms, and wait for hours in nervous dread and fear. Finally, about 3:00 or 3:30, my time came. I was taken to the course, looked carefully around the car, and got inside. The examiner had his clipboard, and I spoke to him politely in my best Japanese. I wonder if it is a better idea to fake not being able to speak Japanese. Maybe he will feel sorry for me and pass me sooner. But alas, this is dishonest, and therefore, I cannot do it. Darn you morality!

My first try ended quickly. I ran over the curb in the crank, the most dreaded part of the course, and the area likely responsible for 99.9% of all failure. It is a ninety degree turn, and running over the curb is an instant fail. Everything else was all right, so the instructor told me to try again soon. A week or so later, I was back. I arrived at 1:30, paid forty bucks, filled out forms, and waited hours. This time, I ran over the curb on the S turn, another instant fail. My third try, I ran over the curb on the crank again, at the very last obstacle before success. I was so upset I was brought to tears. Finally, on my fourth time, I passed. I was so happy, that after I got out of the car, I skipped to Riz with a big smile on my face. I was one of the lucky ones—only three fails. I have heard of others failing more than ten times...

So, while I think the whole driving school and test taking system for foreigners is a racket, it does produce relatively safe drivers, unlike in the U.S. I mean, I loved getting my license at 16, but do 16-year olds really belong behind the wheel? And just how much do we really learn in Drivers' Ed? I do hear that in some places in the U.S., high school Drivers' Ed is being replaced by non-public school related driving school. I seriously doubt, though, that it costs $3000 to attend.

My license expired while I was in Japan, and because at that time it couldn't be renewed online, I was required to retake the test upon a visit home to the States when I was 27 years old. I went to the DMV and passed the computer test with flying colors. I was then told that I could only receive a learner's permit at that time, and had to wait a few weeks to get a real license. I went home furious and humiliated that I couldn't even drive myself to work. I was 27 years old, had over ten years driving experience, and here I was being given a learner's permit. I did what any self-respecting adult would do—I cried to my mommy. "Mommy, the mean lady told me I had to get a learner's permit!! Do something, Mommy!" And anyone who knows my Mom, the Iron Lady, must know that she indeed did something. She immediately got on the phone with the State DMV in Richmond complaining of the gall of the local staff giving her adult daughter a learner's permit. The lady at the head office apologized, said it was a mistake, and told me to go the next day and take the road test. Go, Mom! Even after all these years, my Mom still has my back, and I don't know what I would do without her. Thinking about it, I don't really blame the lady in the local office; I mean, how often do they get an application from someone whose license had expired while overseas in Japan? Not your everyday training exercise in the country town of Wytheville, Virginia.

Anyway, before that long tangent, I was going to say how simple the driving test was. The instructor had me get into the car and go straight about two miles, then turn left, turn right, and then start heading back to the DMV. Finally, I was told to park in an empty parking lot anywhere I wanted to. That was it. I passed. The whole time the instructor, a friend of my Mom's, was asking me how she was and engaging me in small talk. Needless to say, that softball exam didn't come anywhere near to preparing me for the brutal Japanese driving test.

I got my license three years ago, and have no desire to ever give it up. Not after all I went through to get it. No way. Never. Even if I go back to the States someday, I will probably come back to Japan every few years just to renew my license.

#37 The *Gambaru* Spirit

No one in Japan will ever forget the horrible events of March 11, 2011, when a terrible earthquake, tsunami, and nuclear accident devastated the Tohoku region of Northern Japan. Although there are no final tallies of the number of lives lost due to this triple disaster, the number is estimated by most to be between 20,000 and 25,000. In the days and weeks that followed the tragedy, the world got a glimpse of the remarkable Japanese spirit, one that can be characterized by the word *gambaru*.

Japanese students and friends often ask me how to translate this term into English. That is a tough one, because there are so many different meanings and nuances associated with this word. For example, if one is taking a big test, and a friend says, "*gambatte ne**." the best English translation would be "good luck." However, during a game or race, if the fans are screaming "*gambare!*" the best English equivalent for this would be "go!" or "fight!" or "you can do it!" When a friend is down, depressed or having a hard time and someone says, "*gambatte*," it means, "hang in there." So, you can see this is a word with various nuances, meanings, and inferences. I think this must be one of the most used words in the Japanese language because of the variety of situations in which I hear it used. Shortly after the March 2011 tragedy, I began to see signs popping up all over the place: "*Gambarou* Nippon!" "*Gambare* Tohoku!*"* The meaning was clear, mixing together a little of many of the varied meanings of the word. It more or less meant, "Let's stick together, Japan, and fight together, work together, and overcome this terrible tragedy."

While this is a word that really strikes a chord with the public consciousness in Japan, I personally felt that it was not the appropriate one on this occasion. I mean, the wounds were fresh, the pain real, and the sadness and grief overwhelming. I am sure there were many Japanese feeling, "I don't really want to *gambaru* right now; I just want to cry." To me, this phrase, which is often used at sporting events, school activities and events I would consider trivial in light of the tragedy, was not the appropriate one to use at a time like this. I realize that marketers were looking for a catch phrase to unite the country, begin the healing process, and encourage people's hearts, but I wonder if they did more harm than good. I wonder if any Japanese felt as disturbed by the constant use of this phrase as I did. Thinking about it, though, there are not many other words in the language to express what they wanted to express. This word, *gambaru*, seems to be the fall back term, the all-encompassing word with which you can say whatever you want to say, no matter the occasion. As hard as I myself try not to use this word, I am always finding it slipping from my lips anyway. When my student is looking for a job or having a hard time, there it is: *"Gambare"* I say, annoyed with myself as soon as it leaves my lips.

I think this is a great word than can express so many different feelings and emotions. I just think because it can be used on so many different occasions, maybe, just maybe, at a time of national tragedy, it was not the word that should have been chosen for recovery slogans. The country was depressed, and I am sure that I am not the only one who didn't feel much like *gambaru*-ing. That being said, this nation did tap into the communal *gambaru* spirit and pull itself out of tragedy, moving people all over the world with its strength of spirit and unity. Japan has indeed *gambaru*-ed together and is on the way to recovery and healing. But I cannot help but feel that there are still thousands of people in the Tohoku region who still have no desire, and maybe even, no strength to *gambaru*. I think maybe we should just be quiet and give them a hug.

There are many grammatical variations of the term gambaru; for example gambatte, gambare and gambarou.

#38 I Cannot Eat Fish With Eyes

When I first came to Japan in the fall of 1997, I couldn't eat anything. I hated Japanese food with a passion. I remember very clearly my first meal. Riz had asked some friends to drive him to the airport to pick me up, and on the way home, we stopped off for dinner—my first-ever Japanese meal. It was an *okonomiyaki* place. *Okonomiyaki* is like a Japanese pizza or pancake. The base ingredient is cabbage, and then you just add whatever else you like--noodles, seafood, meat, veggies, cheese—and then fry it on a hot plate. When you are done, you top it off with a sweet or spicy sauce, seaweed flakes, mayonnaise, or whatever other toppings you may like. Now, there are ways to make this dish very foreigner-friendly. All you have to do is stay away from the seafood, instead choosing pork, cabbage, corn, cheese, and top it off only with the sauce, and so avoiding all the fishy stuff that so many Americans like myself are averse to. I couldn't speak a lick of Japanese at that time, but Riz and I did our best to communicate that under no circumstances did I want seafood in my *okonomiyaki*.

Well, out comes mine full of squid, shrimp and octopus. Interestingly enough, Riz's was very safe, although he likes seafood very much. But my appetite was ruined, as was my first dining experience in Japan. I went home that night and ate a bowl of chocolate rice crispies, something I would never eat in the U.S., but which was comfort food for me in my new home. I would be doing a lot of the comfort food thing my first few months. I had such a hard time adjusting to the food, that I ended up eating an unhealthy amount of junk food, which led to a ten-pound weight gain.

My basic eating rule was this: nothing that came out of the sea would pass these lips. Now, there are a lot of Japanese foods these days that don't contain seafood, but at the time it seemed that the only food choices around me were seafood. Even the staple of the Japanese diet, the rice ball, was wrapped in seaweed. So while I may have liked what was inside, Korean beef or chicken teriyaki, I never made it past the seaweed. Imagine my glee on the occasions I found seaweed-less rice balls, instead wrapped in egg with chicken and ketchup inside, almost like an omelet. Yes! I could eat something besides chips and chocolate!

Changing was hard. I was a country girl brought up in the mountains of southwest Virginia. Our staple foods were bread, potatoes, roast beef, casseroles, pizza and lasagna. I never once ate Asian sticky rice during childhood, and in my eyes, seafood was Long John Silver's buttered deep-fried fish fillets and the school cafeteria's fish sticks.

But over time, I realized that life like this would be hard, especially if I was going to live here for a while. I don't really remember exactly when I started changing, but the first item from the sea that I started to enjoy was seaweed. I really wanted to enjoy rice balls, and to do that I needed to like seaweed. Along with the rice balls, I started to love *miso* soup, which also contained seaweed. Many of my friends say it tastes fishy due to the *miso* paste used to make it, but I have never thought so. After that, I began to enjoy certain grilled fish dishes. My friend's husband went fishing once, and the fish fry we had afterwards was one of the most delicious meals I have ever had. I am still not a big fan of raw fish like sushi and sashimi, but I can eat it if I have to. I would just never choose to order it on my own.

I have come a really long way in the past 13 years. I love most Japanese foods, especially boiled vegetables dishes which the Japanese call *nimono*. I love traditional Japanese vegetables and beef and chicken dishes, but I am not that big a fan of the modern, Westernized fried Japanese foods that are so popular with young people. I now love Japanese pickles, and sometimes eat Korean seaweed with my brown rice for breakfast. I would much rather eat a boiled radish than a piece of pizza. Yes, I have come a long way, and my husband is very proud of me.

Now, there are just a few rules I have regarding food. The first is, I cannot eat fish with eyes. That just creeps me out. This applies to cooked fish, raw fish, and especially the little snack fish. Now that is gross. Who wants to eat crunchy little fish (with eyes) as their afternoon snack? Believe or not, all my kids do. Not only do most fish with eyes smell gross, they seem to always be looking at me.

The other outlawed food in my diet is *natto*, the fermented soybean paste. I must be truly forthcoming on this matter and say that I have never tried it, but that is because I cannot get past the horrendous smell and slimy texture to get it to my mouth. I know I am a total hypocrite for making my kids try everything, yet refusing to try *natto*. So be it. I will wear a sign screaming 'hyprocite' all through town before I will try that nasty stuff. It is so stinky and stringy, and makes an incredible mess, especially when eaten by toddlers. Yes, my kids, love *natto*. My husband does, too, making me the only member of the family who doesn't like it. As much as I dislike it, it is so cheap and so healthy that I feel obligated as a mommy who loves her family to buy it. I hate cleaning my kids mouths after they have eaten it, and I have to scrub the dishes and table endlessly to get them clean from *natto* residue. The stuff is so sticky that some people wash natto dishes first to hold in the soap bubbles, thus not having to use as much soap and as a result, saving money. I have such a *natto* sensitivity that I can smell that stuff coming a mile away. When we go to a sushi restaurant, you know, the kind that carries sushi around on a conveyor belt, I can smell the *natto* rolls coming. Sure enough, a few minutes later, there they are. Once Riz decided to play a joke on me; he fed the kids *natto* and then told them to go kiss mommy. My joy of being loved faded under the overwhelming stench of *natto*…

Yes, I have come a long way, but I am still the most selective member of the family when it comes to eating Japanese food. Maybe one day I will come to like *natto* and fish with eyes in the same way I have come to like seaweed. Nah. That will never happen. Never.

#39 When Japanese People Can't Use Japanese

Anyone who has ever studied Japanese knows about the incredibly complex web of polite language. There is nothing even close to it in English. I mean, in English something becomes polite if you stick "please" on the end, or change "Can I?" to "May I?" This is not that tough for learners of English as a Second Language, and certainly a piece of cake for native speakers. Japanese, however, is a whole different animal. I can think of five words right off the top of my head for the English word "give." Which one you choose depends on whom you are giving it to, who you are, and what you are giving. While understandably a nightmare for Japanese learners like me (it is the area of Japanese proficiency in which I have the least confidence), I have found that even native speakers make a mess of it, often using the polite language (called *keigo*) because they think it sounds good. In reality, they are using it when not necessary or in the wrong way, and sometimes, even me with my flawed Japanese can catch the mistakes.

I have a favorite mistake that I always hear Japanese native speakers using. My #1 favorite is *"...ni narimasu."* For example, *"pan in narimasu."* I often hear this when receiving a free food sample at Costco, or upon getting my food from a waitress at a family restaurant. The speaker intends to use the polite form of Japanese meaning, "Here is your honorable bread," but translated literally it means, "This is becoming bread." I remember the first time at Costco someone gave me a food sample and said, "*pan ni narimasu*" my smart-aleck self wanted to retort, "Oh yeah? And what was it before it became bread? Flour and eggs?" Of course, I am a polite foreigner who wants to respect my host country, so I would never actually say that, but I have thought it and joked with my friends about it many times. I asked a Japanese teacher once, and she told me that this usage is incorrect, that a simple "*pan desu*" (This is bread) would suffice. I am certain that the users of this incorrect phrase have no idea that it is wrong; in fact, I am sure that they are trying very hard to be polite and have good customer service. Not many people would continue to use bad grammar if they knew it was bad. Well, except for me sometimes when I am trying to annoy my grammarian mother…

I have been amazed at how much Japanese grammar that young people actually don't know. When I was studying for the Japanese proficiency exam, there was one question which my students regularly got wrong, some of them saying they had never even heard of the grammar being used. Of course, middle-aged Japanese people all got it right. Granted, it was a pretty obscure grammar structure, but still, students should have known it.

Once, my student was remarking that English was so hard. Poor me, she whined. I responded, "Yeah, but Japanese is hard, too. I mean, just to count stuff you have to know a million different words." Well, maybe not a million, but there are lots and lots of different suffix counters in Japanese, which are used depending on what you are counting. For example, long cylindrical objects are –*hon,* like *enpitsu 2-hon* (2 pencils); flat objects are –*mai*, like *kami 2-mai* (2 sheets of paper); cars and machines are –*dai,* like *kuruma 2-dai* (2 cars); and animals are –*hiki,* like *neko 2-hiki* (2 cats). The list goes on and on and it is a real headache to learn it all.

I learned that even chopsticks have their own special counter, which is –*zen. For example, o-hashi 2-zen* (2 pairs of honorable chopsticks). I was giving my own language-learning sob story to my first-year students when one of them said to me, "I have never heard of chopsticks being counted that way! For real?" She then turned to a classmate and asked her, "Have you ever heard of chopsticks being counted like that?" Nope. That friend had never heard of it either. Of course, being a non-native speaker, I started to panic that maybe I was mistaken, but later I confirmed the way to count honorable chopsticks with my friends, and was assured I was correct. That friend was horrified that the students had no idea how to properly count chopsticks. I make sure when I am asked at a convenience store how many pairs of chopsticks that I want to respond with my chopsticks counter that is so advanced that not even some native speakers know it. Maybe it is bad and a little prideful, but there is some kind of pleasure in knowing something about Japanese that some native speakers don't even know. On the other hand, I am sure there is some obscure English grammar that my students know that I don't.

Have you ever noticed that most native speakers have no idea why something is said a certain way in their own language? Most people just speak it—they have never thought about why. That is one reason I think it is laughable that a person thinks they can be a great language teacher just because they are a native speaker of it. I am always asking my Japanese friends for language help, or asking why something is this way or that, but few of them can help me. The truth is, you just don't think about stuff until you are forced to. I was this kind of English teacher before I got training in graduate school, and I am the first to admit that there is a ton of stuff that I still don't know. When I don't know the answer to something, I will say, "I will look it up." "Don't know. Just memorize it," or "That is just the way it is." Some grammatical complexities really do have reasons, but I find that more often than not, it is just the way it is, and just needs to be memorized. I mean, why do we say "hotter" but not "funner?" That doesn't make any sense at all.

In the meantime, I will continue to try to use polite Japanese the best I can, and trying to keep myself from giving a smart aleck response when someone says, "*pan ni narimasu.*" Sometimes I wonder if I should correct someone using this phrase incorrectly, but how can I do that without coming off as an arrogant jerk, and embarrassing the already easily embarrassed Japanese? I think I will just keep my mouth shut and enjoy the bread.

#40 Japanese Food...Kind of

People all over the world regard traditional Japanese food to be one of the healthiest ethnic cuisines in the world. The main elements of a Japanese meal are fish, boiled vegetables, rice, pickles and *miso* soup. With the exception of the extraordinarily high sodium content thanks to the use of *miso* and soy sauce, I agree that Japanese food is one of the healthiest cuisines I have ever eaten. There are few spicy or fried foods, and the cholesterol content is relatively low.

Of course, the emphasis must be placed on the world *traditional*. While these traditional dishes have been largely praised for contributing to the world's longest life expectancy, recent assaults on the Japanese palate are beginning to wreak havoc on the health and waistlines of the Japanese people. Many people blame the newfound popularity of Western food for the decline in the health of the Japanese people. To be sure, hamburgers, pizza, steaks, and pasta have become favorites of Japanese people of all ages. In addition, Western snacks like potato chips, ice cream and chocolate have also become popular in recent days. I, however, think more of the blame needs to be placed on the modern "Japanese foods," foods which Japan has adapted from other countries and made her own. I think these foods may even be more evil than the hamburger—a food which, by the way, Americans do not consume everyday contrary to popular opinion.

Let me tell you what foods I am talking about. First and foremost, there is ramen—the versatile noodle dish borrowed from China. Japanese people, especially men, are passionate about ramen, and everyone is boorishly opinionated about which region of Japan has the best-flavored ramen. It is not uncommon for guys to go out for a bowl of ramen after a drinking party, sometimes in the wee hours of the morning. Ramen is carb-loaded and the broth is oily, high-calorie, salty, and generally just bad for you. Of course, ramen lovers don't care about any of that, just as lovers of the Chicago deep-dish pizza don't care if one slice has over 1000 calories. Ramen lovers are passionate about their ramen, and when Momofuku Ando invented instant ramen in the 1960s, he made it possible to eat ramen anytime, anywhere, for a relatively cheap price. Ramen became to Japanese college students what macaroni and cheese is to American college students—cheap, delicious carb-loading heaven.

Then there is *omuraisu*, a hybrid of an omelette and rice. Simply speaking, rice mixed with chicken and ketchup is fried up, placed on top of a fried egg, and wrapped up so the egg covers the rice. Then it is covered in your favorite sauce and served with your choice of meat. Some restaurants are entirely devoted to this dish, with over 30 different menu items. While not the worst offender, it does have a lot of oil, butter and mayonnaise. I must confess to liking this one much more than I like ramen. The only ramen I can stomach is *tantanmen*, a spicy ramen with veggies and pork, and even then, there is no way I would eat it in the middle of the night.

The next offender is *karaage*, the Japanese take on boneless fried chicken. It is a staple convenience store food, and popular with people of all ages, especially kids and young people. My kids absolutely love *karaage*. Most foreigners I know will tell you that they are not exactly sure what it is, but Japanese *karaage* is way better than the fried chicken they grew up with. They will also tell you unequivocally that they don't care if it is high calorie—they will eat it anyway.

There are other fried and greasy foods that the Japanese love, too. Tempura, deep-fried battered shrimp and veggies are oily, but oh so good. This is my favorite bad-for-you Japanese food. Riz and I had an argument once because he thinks it is not all that bad. Granted, it is not as bad as other deep-fried foods, and you can get deep-fried veggies, but it is still deep-fried. Deep-fried is deep-fried, right? Riz is a diehard tempura lover, though, and he says it is much better than our next offender…

Tonkatsu. Deep-fried breaded pork cutlet. This is a bad boy. Very greasy, very high calorie, and very yummy. Plus, it doesn't really taste good unless you eat it with a lot of high-carb rice. There is this nearby *tonkatsu* restaurant that we love that gives you all-you-can-eat rice, Japanese pickles, salad and *miso* soup with your *tonkatsu* order. That is a dangerous thing, because you need a lot of rice to eat with all that *tonkatsu*.

Personally, I prefer the pickles and salad so I just eat a lot of them as my kids chow down on my *tonkatsu*, but when I eat a lot of *tonkatsu* and rice I always leave feeling gross and disgusted with myself.

And lastly, give it up for *okonomiyaki*, the Japanese equivalent of a pancake that was my first meal in Japan. It is a flour-based batter filled with cabbage and your favorite veggies, noodles, meat or seafood. Sounds pretty harmless, and if eaten responsibly it can be harmless and even healthy. A nice, normal-sized portion with veggies and pork, topped with a sweet sauce is not all that bad. But the really yummy version is huge, filled with pork, cheese, noodles, sometimes hot dogs or gluttonous rice cakes, and topped with sauce and mayonnaise. The word *okonomiyaki* actually means, "Cook it as you like." And if you like, it can be good for you. If you like, that is.

And so, I have taken you on a culinary journey through the maze of modern Japanese cuisine. To be fair, of course, people don't eat like this all the time, and there are plenty of times they eat traditional meals of fish, veggies and *miso* soup. But these new foods are becoming more and more popular, especially among young people. The rates of diseases like diabetes are increasingly like crazy here, and part of me wonders if instead of blaming Western food, perhaps the Japanese should look internally and question the foods they have borrowed and made their own instead. But alas, it is much easier and more fun to blame the fat Americans for bringing over McDonalds and their irresistible hamburgers.

#41 Japanese Bakeries Kick Butt

Let me start off by saying that I am a huge bread lover. But recently I have begun to fear that I may have what bread lovers around the world fear more than anything else. That is right—I am wondering if I may have gluten sensitivity. Although I have eaten bread, pasta, and pizza all my life, I can't help but wonder if it is the bread that I have eaten since moving to Japan that may be the cause of all my newfound intestinal woes. I want to say here without bias, without reserve, and with complete confidence that the bread made in Japanese bakeries is way more delicious than anything I ever had growing up in the U.S. Way more. Not even close.

Before you fall over in shock that I would make such an outrageous statement, let me explain. Yes, the staple food of the Japanese diet is rice and not bread. Yes, American homemade bread made in bread makers is probably still much better. And yes, we kick butt with our spreads—peanut butter, jelly, Nutella (I know it's European but we stole it!), almond butter, cream cheese, butter and my all-time favorite, Trader Joe's Cookie Butter. Have you ever had that stuff? Oh my. Cookie Butter aside, the Japanese creativity with bread is maybe just a notch below their creativity in the electronics realm. They can come up with the most unusual, the most, there-is-no-way-that-will-taste-good-but-it-does creations.

I think it is because bread is not the staple food of the Japanese diet that it is so yummy. You see, bread is seen as a treat here, something to be really enjoyed, because Japanese people don't eat it everyday. Most Japanese don't really care if it is healthy or not, because they think of it like they think of dessert. It is a splurge, so why not go all the way and eat it regardless of the calorie content? Most delicious bakeries are French-style bakeries with a Japanese twist. There are four main categories of bread. Here goes.

The first group is what I call the healthy breads. These are the harder breads like baguettes, rye loaves, and wheat, nut and berry breads. These are the ones that are usually popular with older folks (and me, but I am not old), and these are the ones I blame for my gluten sensitivity. But I will talk about that later…

The second group is the sandwiches. Now, when I say the word "sandwich" you may conjure up images of Subway or huge honking slabs of meat between two big pieces of bread. Japanese sandwiches are much more petite, especially the bread. In most cases, the bread is thinly sliced with the crust cut off. Popular fillings are egg salad, ham, lettuce, tuna salad, and tomatoes. Many sandwiches at my local bakery have a Japanese or ethnic twist. For example, Indian tandoori chicken wrap, pork cutlet sandwich, pork marinated in soy sauce and ginger sandwich, minced beef sandwich, avocado and shrimp sandwich, and raw ham and cream cheese bagel sandwich. There are also several variations of the hamburger and chicken sandwich, and my favorite, the tofu burger. Most of the sandwiches are light and healthy, with the exception of the excessive use of mayonnaise, but I'll talk about that later.

The third kind of bread is the bread the Japanese call "*chori pan*." I guess the best translation would be "bread that can be eaten as a meal." Now, these are different from your average sandwich, and this is the group that sets Japanese bakeries apart from their American counterparts in my opinion. These breads are made with various different kids of crusts, fillings, and toppings, but most commonly use meats and veggies with a Japanese twist. For example, the most popular bread at my favorite bakery is the deep-fried curry bread. Curry sauce and meat are put inside the dough and then deep-fried. Another popular bread is the focaccia with various toppings such shrimp and avocado, salsa and veggies, corn and mayonnaise or egg and ham.

Other popular breads include a tuna sandwich made to look like a rice ball, boiled octopus baked inside a round baguette and then sprinkled with sauce and fish flakes, various croissants, several kinds of hot dogs baked inside baguettes, and soft kid-friendly breads shaped like koalas or other animals. In my area, *mentai* fish roe is very popular, so of course, there is also a French bread lathered in spicy *mentai* paste mixed with you guessed it, mayonnaise. It is one of the most popular breads at the bakery, and is on its way to becoming legendary. There are various other fish-based breads, one of which contains a fish hotdog that I think looks like it was run over by a car, and by far is the most disgusting thing there, but is very popular with the Japanese customers. Most of these *chori pan* are doused in mayonnaise, which is on the same level as soy sauce as a national obsession in my opinion. They put mayonnaise on everything here, including pizza and hotdogs, both of which by the way, you can find at a Japanese bakery.

The last type of bread is the sweet bread. This can be found in the form of a donut, Danish, or gluttonous *mochi* rice cake. Popular Western sweets can be easily found—sugar donuts, donuts with sprinkles, chocolate breads, cinnamon churros, etc,, but there are also Japanese sweets mixed in with the rest. Creations like donuts with sweet bean paste in the middle, green tea scones, and my all-time favorite (I am being sarcastic) cherry blossom donuts. They are hugely popular in the spring, but every time I try one, I feel like I am eating a flower. If I want to eat a flower, I can go to the park. I don't want to pay for it. That being said, the cherry blossom scones are growing on me...

The bread at Japanese bakeries can be horrifying for a diet. I was once told that my favorite bread, a huge piece of Texas toast slathered with maple syrup and butter, has over

1000 calories. I don't think I have eaten that since I found that out three years ago. Another favorite, the Milk Ball bread, contains what should be an illegal amount of condensed milk. But like I said, for the Japanese, bread is a splurge, so they don't really care.

What I think makes Japanese bakeries so special is the incredible variety and creativity. I heard there are more than a hundred and forty kinds of bread available at my local bakery. The owner is always trying to come up with new creations, trying to make something tastier than all the other bakeries around. He does it, too. He never ceases to amaze me with the crazy but yummy concoctions he dreams up. Most bakeries that I have been to in the U.S. just have lots of variations on loaf bread, but not the tremendous varieties of different kinds of bread like I have found in Japanese bakeries. So, no matter what your tastes, you will be able to find something you love at a Japanese bakery.

Which brings me back to why I blame rice-loving Japan for my gluten sensitivity. I love sweets, and I love bread, but I don't really like sweet bread. Call me crazy, but to me, bread should not be sweet, but instead should be toasted and spreads like peanut butter should be applied generously. I started getting addicted to the healthy breads at my local bakery. My favorite one is the Cereal and Nut Campagne Bread. While I am slowly breaking my addiction, at my worst I would eat it every morning for breakfast. Because it is so full of different kinds of grains, I am convinced the higher gluten content did me in. Years of eating this bad boy could not have been good for me. I guess because it is so much healthier than all the other breads there, I figured I could eat it as much as I wanted to. I guess there can much too much of a good thing...

If a friend were to visit me from the U.S. and asked me what she should do in Japan, of course I would recommend the standard sightseeing spots and Japanese cuisine. But I don't think any trip to Japan would be complete without a visit to a Japanese bakery. People will never look at bread the same again...

#42 Booze

I am sure the title of this one got your attention! I decided today to write about something I know absolutely nothing about —alcohol. But I figure that because I know nothing about that gives me a unique perspective on drinking, and what it looks like from the outside.

I never touched alcohol until I came to Japan, not even a drop. Well, unless you count the sip of beer Dad gave me as a kid. My Grandpa loved beer, but it destroyed his liver and he died way too young. I remember going to visit him in the hospital and his tummy being bloated like a balloon because his liver wasn't able to function properly and remove all the waste. I still remember that long needle they stuck in there to remove the fluid. To me, every experience I had ever had with alcohol was bad, and it had taken away my Papa, so I had no interest at all in doing the same thing to myself. Even in college, when I went through a slight rebellious period, I still never drank a drop of alcohol.

I came to Kitakyushu at age 27, still never having tried alcohol. I remember being shocked at how openly people drank here, even underage ones. While many college students also drink and party in the U.S., I.D. checks to prevent underage drinking are strict, and drinking in public for all people is illegal unlike in Asian countries. I remember once when I was a TA in graduate school having to warn a Korean exchange student for popping open a can of beer at the beach, perfectly normal behavior in Korea but a crime in the U.S. It is not uncommon at all to see people drinking deer or sake on the trains or at the beach, and I have never in all my years here seen anyone asked for their ID when ordering alcohol.

All Japanese people, young and old, love the *nomikai,* or drinking party. These events are some of the only times that the normally reserved Japanese will let down their guard and share their true feelings about everything. If you ever want to know what a Japanese person really thinks, just take him drinking. For some reason, ridiculous behavior that would be otherwise frowned upon is accepted if someone is drunk here. The *nomikai* is a huge part of the culture, and many businessmen are expected to go to *nomikais* late into the night many days of the week. Some people say that real business happens not during working hours, but during these frequent drinking parties.

I don't drink by choice, and everybody around me knows it. People are always saying to me, "Oh, so you can't drink?" The Japanese word is *nomenai*. I always respond, "I can but I don't want to." I use the word *nomanai* or *nomitakunai*, which mean "I don't drink" and "I don't want to drink" respectively. They always look puzzled when I respond like this. Why on earth would you not want to drink? I remember early on in my time in Kobe I went to dinner at a friend's house and the friend asked if I wanted beer or wine. I asked for juice and he looked at me like I was crazy. I don't ever remember going to dinner at a friend's house in the U.S. and being asked if I wanted alcohol with my meal.

I am not at all ashamed of my non-drinking ways, but sometimes I think many Japanese people are. So many times I hear people say "*nomenai*." They say they cannot drink, that they get sick, pass out, get red-faced, whatever as soon as they start drinking. I am not buying it. There is no way that such a high percentage of the Japanese population is unable to drink. I think that it is much more likely that they don't want to drink, but saying it that way is not socially acceptable. On the other hand, if someone can't drink because of a physical reaction, well, there is nothing you can do about that so people don't give you a hard time.

I am capable of drinking. Once I went to a restaurant with some friends and decided to try something for the first time in my life. I like sweets, so I ordered a Kahlua with milk cocktail. Oh my. Hello, Ms. Kahlua. Where have you been all my life? I only had two, but for the first time in my life I understood how it was possible to become an alcoholic. Still almost ten years after that first drink, Kahlua with milk is the only alcohol I ever consume, and even then, only a couple times a year. I have never been drunk in my life, although I think I may have had one too many at a wedding once and felt a little buzzed. As a Christian, I feel drunkenness is inappropriate and a bad example of Christ to those around me, so that is the main reason I don't want to drink. Another is that being a very health-conscious person, I just have no desire to take in so many calories through beverages. I would rather get my calories from food.

Despite the fact that the Japanese are quite heavy drinkers, the laws about drunk driving in Japan are very harsh, which they should be. Japan has a zero tolerance policy towards drunk driving, meaning that even a little alcohol in your bloodstream makes you legally drunk. Most people who attend *nomikais* will take the bus or train home, or if it is close, walk. When I attended the mandatory three-hour lecture to renew my driver's license, much of it was taken up by preaching against drunk driving. This is awesome, I think, but I wish they would devote even a little of that time to car seat safety, which is a topic sadly never discussed by anyone around me…

Luckily for the peace of my family and our family budget, Riz is not a drinker, either. Like me, he may have a drink or two at a party, but we never keep alcohol in the home. It is just not something that tempts either of us. I wish we could say the same thing for chocolate chip cookies (me) and Doritos (Riz).

Americans probably consume just as much alcohol as the Japanese, but it just seems to me that drinking is a much more important part of the culture here than it is there. It seems to be the key that opens the door of honesty and communication, and if you don't drink, it is almost like you are disappointing those around you. But as for me, I will have to find another way through that door, because except for an occasional Kahlua and milk indulgence, I have absolutely no interest in alcohol. Maybe I am not as Japanese as I thought I was…

Oh, I almost forgot. Are you wondering about the title of this chapter? I went to a restaurant once, and the heading for beverages was written in English as "Booze." It would have been funny enough if they were referring to only alcohol, but alas, that is not the case. Coke and Ginger Ale were apparently booze, too. Gotta love the Japanese and their liberal use of the English language.

#43 My Kids English Not at All Cannot Speak, Part II

I wrote in a previous chapter about the challenges of raising bilingual kids here in Japan. Despite the fact that my kids have language issues, and I am proud of them and their ability to change between the two languages at will (most of the time), and while I may lament about their strange word choices and language mixing at times, I am confident that they are all three good English speakers. There are times, though, that cause me to doubt this…

Like yesterday. My oldest daughter Mia and I were invited to an interview to appear on a cooking show for the Japanese broadcaster NHK. Apparently, a famous Japanese cooking show host wants to come to Kitakyushu and teach a foreign mother and child how to cook easy, delicious Japanese dishes. Well, since Mia and I are honest to goodness full-blooded foreigners, we were invited to interview for the show. At first, we were told it was an audition, which made me laugh, because I was trying to figure out how we would audition for a cooking show. Turns out, it wasn't really an audition but an interview. We were asked to fill out an information form about ourselves, and told to come to the interview at an Italian restaurant yesterday afternoon. I am not really sure why we were interviewed in a smoky, noisy restaurant, but we were.

Two young guys met us at the restaurant to conduct the interview. I am not really sure of their positions, but I think they were on the production team. The questions were just basic stuff about our lives in Japan, experiences, interest in cooking, hobbies, etc. Riz and I prepped Mia before the interview about how to answer questions assertively and that, no matter what, she was not to be shy. Mia has the tendency to be shy when she meets people for the first time, so we told her she couldn't be shy if she wants to be on TV.

She did great, answering our mock questions with energy and enthusiasm. We also told her to please not say that she loved my instant ramen. That was a big no-no. Well, after we arrived, the NHK guys bought us some drinks, and started asking questions. It went really well as I am not at all shy, and was prepped and ready to wow them with my friendly personality and rocking Japanese ability, which I did, I hope. When they got to Mia, though, she seemed to forget everything she liked, and worse, she started doing the infamous Japanese head tilt. Anyone who has lived here knows what I am talking about. You ask a Japanese person a question, and she gets this look of perplexity on her face that says either I don't know or I don't care, and then she slowly tilts her head to the right, all the while not answering the question. I hate it when my kids do this and they know it. But there is was: the head tilt.

She was able to get out answers to a lot of the questions, but the restaurant was so loud that they couldn't hear her. I found myself having to repeat her answers all the time, making me look like a lawyer leading a witness, or worse yet, a controlling Hollywood Mom trying to live her dreams of stardom through her helpless child. Mia said that she likes to read, but then when they asked her about her favorite book—well, total blank. She was struggling in Japanese but not because of the language ability, but because of the introverted head-tilter that she morphs into when she is meeting people for the first time.

About halfway through, we were asked to look into a video camera and introduce ourselves in English. Since this is a program for NHK World, the intended viewers are foreigners living overseas. The program was to be entirely in English, so if the white American mother and her child couldn't speak English, well, that would be a problem. I breezed through mine with an air of confidence, speaking English almost as well as Japanese. Mia followed my lead. She was out of the starting gate strong. "My name is Mia Crescini. I am seven years old and I go to Mitsusada Elementary School." Yeah, that is my girl!! Next, "My *shumi* is *o-ekaki* and *ehon*. Thank you." Huh? What was that? Apparently, she didn't know the word for hobby (*shumi*), and so after saying it naturally in Japanese, she just kept on going by saying that she liked drawing and reading, probably not even realizing that she was saying that in Japanese, too.

I was horrified for a bit, then I wanted to start laughing, especially after what happened next. She was asked, "When your mommy cooks Japanese food, what is your favorite dish?" Yep, you guessed it. Instant ramen, the one thing we told her not to say. She just said ramen, but the guys were so shocked that I could make ramen that I felt compelled to fess up that she was referring to my highly honed and intensely practiced skill of pouring hot water over prepackaged noodles. With a nervous laugh, hee hee, I explained that she really loved ramen, and was a little confused that it wasn't really considered home cooking.

Mia did okay on the final few questions, and was asked by the interviewers if she would be able to speak only in English on the program. She assured them that she would (I am not so sure), and I finished up the interview with machine-gun like answers to questions trying to sway in our favor their wavering opinions of the Crescini pair. We were told that they were interviewing several other mother-daughter combos, and would only be choosing one, so there was no guarantee we would be on the show. They told us we would be contacted in a week or so, and then we said our goodbyes.

After they left, I told Mia I couldn't believe she was so shy after all we had practiced, and she apologized, sad that she had let Mommy down. But you know what? She didn't let me down. I don't really care about that show. Sure, it would be nice if we are chosen, and who knows, maybe we still will be. But she is my daughter and I love her no matter what. It is not her fault that she couldn't do some of the tasks well. She has never in her life been asked to introduce herself in English, or been interviewed like that by people that she doesn't know. It is not her fault that she is so crazy about ramen that she blurts out the word the moment she is asked about food. Sure, maybe her English is a little sketchy, but her Japanese is perfect, and her heart is beautiful. I realized yesterday two things: first, even though her English is good, Riz and I still need to do a lot of work with her on our own to teach her not only how to speak, but how to conduct herself in both English and Japanese. We particularly hate that Japanese head tilt and accompanying silence. We want her to be able to respond self-assuredly to any question whether in Japanese or English, to be a woman of confidence. That is something we must teach her.

The other thing I realized anew was how much I love her. She was so worried about disappointing me, and she felt like she had let me down. I remember when I was a kid how much I wanted my parents' approval. I know that there is nothing worse than feeling like you have let your parents down. I wanted her to know that that did not happen. I am her mother, and I am proud of her no matter what. She is much more important to me than being on a cooking show.

Come to think of it, I also learned that I need to hone my Japanese cooking skills a little to avoid future embarrassment...

Sadly, the Crescini mother/daughter team was not chosen to be on the NHK cooking show. Our TV debut will have to wait for another day...

#44 What's in a Name?

The answer to that question is, a lot, in Japan. Japanese names are made up of Chinese characters called *kanji*, and there are a million factors in play when naming a Japanese baby. First, the number of strokes in the name is important. It is bad luck to have a certain number of strokes, or an imbalance with the family name. Of course, the meaning of the characters is also very important. Parents try to give their kids names that convey their dreams or hopes. That is, if the parents even name the baby. Sometimes, grandparents are given charge of the naming process and the parents just humbly accept it. This is changing these days as more and more parents are deciding on baby names together, but I still have some friends who either leave the naming to the grandparents or to the father-to-be. From what I can see, sound is not as important as meaning and the number of strokes. In English names, the sound of the name, and how it sounds in combination with the family name seems to be the most important thing. Meaning is not that big of a deal. Heck, I didn't even know what my name meant until college. In fact, I cannot even recall it off the top of my head. Time to Google it…

Speaking of my name, I love it for a lot of reasons. First, I have always loved the 'e' on Anne. It is the less common way to spell it, and I am not your run-of-the-mill Anne. Despite my annoyances throughout childhood when people constantly left off my 'e', I have always loved my name. Little did I know that leaving the 'e' off was the least offensive way to butcher my name. When I came to Japan, not only was the 'e' left off, but one of my 'n's was as well. At times I found my name written as An. An in Japan.

Which is just a transliteration of how my name is written in the *katakana* script, a special Japanese alphabet for foreign words and names. Can't blame people, I guess, for that one. This brings me to another reason I love my name: it is so easy to pronounce in Japanese. The pronunciation changes a bit, kinda like the first syllable of the word '*encore*,' but it is still way easier for Japanese people to pronounce than many other foreign names. I always feel sorry for people with 'r' or 'l' in their names, notoriously hard sounds for the Japanese to pronounce. Before we came to Japan, the faculty at Riz's school thought that he was a girl. Why? Because his name has the same *katakana* as the name "Liz," and the only Liz the Japanese know is Elizabeth Taylor.

I feel doubly sorry for anyone with both 'r' and 'l' in their names. A name like "Laura" is a nightmare for Japanese speakers. Also high on my list of sympathies would be anyone named Gary or Ben, as those words in Japanese mean diarrhea and poop, respectively.

So, the potential minefields for names in Japan are significant. When I came here and found out how easy it was for Japanese speakers to pronounce my name, my long-held secret suspicion that my parents are geniuses was confirmed. Because my name is so easy to pronounce and my family name, Crescini, isn't, everybody here just calls me Anne. My friends call me Anne-chan, and my students and the office staff call me Anne Sensei. I like my name, so that is okay with me. There was one time, though, that I returned to the States and introduced myself to someone. She couldn't understand me to my amazement. That was when Riz pointed out that I was pronouncing it in Japanese.

When my kids were born, Riz and I really thought long and hard before naming them. We wanted names that would be easy to pronounce for both Japanese and English speakers. If I had given my kids Japanese names like Ryosuke or Ruriko, both impossible for Americans to pronounce, my mom would have killed me. Likewise, Laura and Larry were out unless I wanted my kids to be bullied for all eternity. We settled on short simple names, Mia, Abby and Emmy. All three are simple to pronounce in both languages, and all three sound cool with Crescini. In Japanese, all five of our names—Riz, Anne, Mia, Abby and Emmy—are two katakana letters. This sounds trivial, but I like the idea of having symmetry when we write our New Year's cards.

So, we are getting by in a land that is totally not used to foreign names and doesn't even have a uniform system for writing them. No matter where you go, the post office, bank, city office, etc. you will always be told to write your name in a different alphabet in a different order. Maybe one day Japan will get on the ball and make it easier for themselves, maybe one day, people will look at my family name written in katakana and not panic, suddenly being unable to read their native tongue. That day is not here yet, so until it is, I will fight the urge to write Tanaka or Yamada on the waiting list at restaurants, be proud my Crescini name, and sit back and watch with humor as the waitress tries to read my name written in this complex alphabet that she learned when she was seven...I love this country!

#45 Naked

In my first book I wrote a whole chapter about *onsens*, but recently I have been thinking about them more and more. For those of you who don't know, *onsens* are Japanese hot springs. There are many rules and manners associated with *onsen* usage, but the main ones are you have to shower before you enter the *onsen*, and no clothes are allowed. Bathers are expected to scrub themselves meticulously clean, and then relax in any one of a number of different kinds of baths. Other common courtesies include tying your hair up to keep loose strands out of the water, not talking too loudly (the little old ladies ignore that one), and not bothering any of the other bathers. To illustrate a typical trip to an *onsen,* I will talk about the one nearby us, *Otogi no Mori.*

Maybe it should technically be classified as a bathhouse. I am not quite sure the difference, but hot springs seem to me a little moe luxurious, with numerous baths and a hotel often connected to the bathing facitiies. Semantics aside, it is a great place. It costs about eight dollars for general admission to *Otogi no Mori,* and for that fee you may use all the bathing facilities. There is a main bath that is set at about 40 degrees Celsius, and a number of other smaller baths set at between 37 and 40 degrees. One of the freakiest ones is the electric current bath, which feels like getting shocked by an electric eel. It is supposedly good for curing a variety of ailments, and I cannot decide if I love it or hate it. Totally freaks my kids out.

There are all kinds of power stream pools that shoot out water at such a speed that it is like getting a water massage. This kind is my favorite. There is also a cold pool situated outside the sauna area where a lot of bathers go for a dip after relaxing in the ridiculously hot sauna.

Then there is the *rotenburo,* the outside bath. That is a treat. The air is freezing cold but the milky white bath is nice and toasty. There is something so soothing about relaxing in the middle of nature.

Recently, my tummy has really been bothering me, so I decided to take some time off from work to pamper myself. The last two days I went to *Otogi no Mori* by myself, which I almost never do. I am always with my kids, who love *onsens*, but see it as a water park adventure. Needless to say, going with the kids is not very relaxing at all. They don't share my desire to sit and relax; instead they want to splash around from one pool to the next, spending an average of 1 minute 28 seconds in each pool. Plus, since kids cannot enter the sauna, I am unable to enjoy one of my favorite parts of the *onsen* when I am with them. I love going with them, and I love the joy they have when they are there, but it is not relaxing.

The first day I stayed in the *onsen* for over an hour. I could feel the stress just draining away. The funniest thing is listening to the conversation of all the old ladies in their harsh Kyushu local dialect. Being a weekday, 90% of the people there were old ladies, whose bodies are so wrinkled and saggy I got a glimpse of what is waiting for me in the future. Some are so saggy that I think their boobs are about to meet their tummies. They are so animated, obviously enjoying life, friendships, and the freedom to just hang around a bathhouse all day. There were the obvious stares at the curious foreigner (me) and the occasional friendly greeting.

After my bath, I felt clean and relaxed, and headed off for my massage downstairs. Many *onsens* and bathhouses have massage parlors and barber shops attached to them. I had a very painful 20-minute massage, and left feeling totally and utterly relaxed. I repeated the same routine the next day, and coupled with healthy eating, I am feeling much better.

As much as I love the relaxation that *onsens* give me, I must admit that I am still not comfortable being naked with strangers. I can't help thinking that everybody is staring at me, comparing my body with theirs. The old ladies there seem to be totally content with their fluffy, flabby bodies and don't seem to be uncomfortable at all. They do, however, try to show a little modesty by covering up their private parts with a little while towel. Not that it covers up much, but they are trying. I think old people whose prime has past are much more comfortable with their bodies than younger women, who are much more self-conscious. Maybe the older ladies have realized that it is a part of life for things to start sagging like that, and they just shrug it off.

Most of my friends love *onsens*, but I do have a few who tell me they are self-conscious and have no interest in bathing with strangers. Luckily for them, there are private family baths that can be reserved at major *onsen* resorts, as well as many rooms in resort areas with private *onsens* as well. One of my close friends in her 60s told me that she has never once entered the public *onsen*, and the very thought of it creeps her out. I won't go that far, and I must admit that the relaxation and rejuvenation the *onsen* gives me helps me overcome the dread of being naked with strangers. I do wish, though, that bathing suits were allowed. That would make my experience much more enjoyable. But they are not, only birthday suits. I think that not only my mother but the majority of the American population would freak out at the prospect of being naked with strangers.

#46 Home Parties: Could You Spare an Hour or Seven?

Yesterday, my family and I attended a Cheese Fondue party at the home of one of our very best friends. There were about 15 or so other people there, all very close friends. We usually get together like this at her house 4 or 5 times a year—BBQ in the summer, hot pot party in the winter, cheese fondue all year round!! Woo Hoo!! This time was actually to celebrate together the time-honored spring tradition of cherry blossom viewing in Japan. Every year at the end of March or early April, depending on when the cherry blossoms feel like blooming, Japanese people get together to look at them. We got together at our friend's house to look at one very pretty tree, transplanted from our church's garden when we had to bulldoze our garden to make a parking lot a couple years ago. I found it humorous that 15 people were getting together for an afternoon to stare at one tree. It sure was a darn pretty tree, though.

So, the party started about 1:00, but Riz was off in Fukuoka doing a photo shoot because, of course, Japanese love birds also want to take romantic pictures under the cherry blossom trees. The cherry blossoms, or *sakura*, are such a huge part of Japanese culture that they deserve their own post. So, more about that later.

Anyway, Riz was off to a photo shoot early in the morning, and hoped to get back to the party by three in the afternoon. Maybe you are thinking, "3:00? If the party starts at

1:00, then all the food will be gone and everyone getting ready to go home by 3:00." No, no no, my friend, you do not understand Japanese parties. Japanese parties are all day, hanging out, grazing extravaganzas. We arrived at 1:00, Riz arrived finally at 4:00, and we went home at 8:30. Yep, that's right. It was a seven-and-a-half hour party. This is quite normal for a party in Japan. This is how they work.

So, everyone arrives whenever they can. Most of us got there between 12:30 and 1:00, but Riz came at 4:00, and others arrived at different intervals during the day, with the last guest getting there about 6:30. At about 3:00, we were all wondering where she was and the host said, "Oh, she is just getting on the bullet train in Kyoto; so, she should be here in three hours or so." Imagine a party in the States where someone says, "Well, Linda is just boarding her flight in Chicago, so she should arrive here in D.C. in a couple of hours and get here in time for dessert." Sounds crazy, but here, there's nothing weird about waiting around for a good friend who is five hours late. We were all just so happy that she was going to make it at all.

So, by the time we got there at 1:00, the cheese fondue was ready, all the veggies cut up and boiled, the bread sliced, the chicken cooked. It was a feast. I am trying to cut down on carbs these days, so I stuffed myself with veggies and chicken, pretty much not able to eat another bite by 1:30. The kids were outside running around under the lone cherry blossom tree, so I figured they would be eating on their own schedule. After eating, we just hung around the table and chatted for a while, drinking strawberry tea and looking at the cherry blossom tree. I must have had seven or eight cups of tea.

A little while later, out come the snacks. This is the part about home parties I find to be funny. In the U.S., the snacks like chips and crackers usually come out before the meal, holding people over until the main dishes are ready. In Japan, it is the opposite. Because parties here are so long, the chips and other snacks come out an hour or two after the main meal. People are all still hanging around the table, and after a while, they get the munchies. Of course, the kids have junk food radars, and as soon as they heard the rustling of the potato chips bag, they were all gathered around the table attacking those chips like those zombies on *The Walking Dead* go at an animal carcass. The chips and cookies were gone in minutes, and at about that time someone comes in with oranges, which are soon cut up and devoured. An hour or so later, a new guest arrives with fruit mousse, so that is passed around and gone in no time. Around 4:00, Riz comes rolling in, so the cheese fondue is heated up again, and of course, the others felt compelled to eat with him since it is right in front of them after all. There is something about these parties that make me not want to move an inch. I just want to sit at the table or lounge on the sofa all day long—all seven hours. I don't want to move. And of course, if there is food in front on you, the average person will eat it regardless of whether he or she is hungry or not.

Riz ate his fill and went out to play with the kids. I was amazed at his energy after having walked around all morning taking romantic photos of newlyweds. I, on the other hand, had been lounging all day, and yet had no desire to move away from the table. I did pretty good, though, not eating all the junk the food that came in after the main meal. But since I drank eight cups of tea instead, I did find myself making frequent visits to the bathroom, forcing myself away from my comfortable spot at the table.

At about 5:00, in comes a new person with ice cream, so that is passed around, too, and gone in no time. Of course, for all junk food, the kids seem to get dibs, and the ice cream was no different. And of course, she is hungry so the cheese fondue is fired up again. She eats her fill, the others nibble here and there, and then we all start drinking coffee. Finally, about 6:30, the last guest comes in with piping hot beef buns. Well, heck, it is dinnertime, so those are scarfed down in less than five minutes. And, of course, she is hungry, so the cheese fondue is fired up for the fifth and final time. Everyone seated around the pot gives in to the creamy temptation, polishing off the last of the veggies and bread, along with another bag of chips. In the end, we ended up going through an innumerable amount of veggies and chicken, and eight loaves of French bread. Eight loaves. Unbelievable.

So, after over seven hours of great food and greater conversation, we said our goodbyes. My exhausted, napless kids went right to sleep after getting home, and I followed soon after. It is amazing how eating and staying in one place all day can wear you out. I always marvel how I have absolutely no idea how many calories I consume at these parties. Is it a lot? Or a little? I have no clue. Yesterday, although my tummy was full, most of it was with veggies, so I think I did okay. I can say that this kind of all-day party is the norm in Japan, and there have been times that I am sure I consumed way too many calories for my 125-pound body. Thinking about it, though, laying off the dessert, which I did yesterday is a big help. I always bring brownies, and if I bring them, I eat them, so not bringing them is the best strategy.

I love having parties at my house, too, and I love socializing with my friends. Of course, sometimes I get annoyed that parties last forever, and I just want people to leave so I can get my kids (and myself) to sleep. I hate the massive cleanup that ensues after having a party with ten toddlers, and the mess that is left in the kitchen in the form of dirty dishes and overflowing garbage bags. Although everyone helps with cleanup, there is still quite a bit to do after they all leave. But you know what? As much work as these parties are, as tiring and exhausting as they are, I absolutely love having them, and have never once regretted throwing a party. Relationships and time with friends are much more important than having regular bed times and a clean house. The Japanese may be busy and rushed almost everyday of their lives, but when it comes to home parties, they really know how to chill out and just enjoy being together. I love that about this place. And I love that about these people. It is nice, however, to attend parties every once in a while instead of throwing them. All the fun and fellowship without having the clean up brownie smears on the straw tatami mats! What a deal!

#47 Cherry Blossom Crazy

Every year at the end of March or early April, the Japanese reset their lives. No matter what kind of hardships or tragedies, struggles or frustrations that one has encountered over the past year, people all over Japan are given fresh hope and a new start by a tree—a simple but beautiful white and pink-blossomed cherry tree. This is the *sakura*, the symbol of a fresh start and renewed hope in Japan.

Many Americans, including this one, have very little consciousness of nature. I have no idea the name of any plants, trees or flowers with the exception of the rose, tulip and, umm… that's about it. My first grader comes home with homework where she has to group flowers together and there is no way I can help her. If I don't know something in English, it is a good bet that I will not know it in Japanese either. While most of my friends here are knowledgeable about everything from flowers to trees to insects, I am not; to me, if it is a black bug, it is a cockroach. End of story. I must admit that I admire at times the bond that Japanese people feel with nature, and the emphasis that nature and the changing of the seasons has on Japanese society. There are summer foods like curry and cold noodle salad, and winter foods like boiled veggies, hot pot and cream stew. If you make hot pot in the summer or eat cold noodles in the winter, people may look at you like you are crazy. While I don't really like this part of the culture, I do like how the cherry blossom holds such a special place in the heart of all Japanese people.

People all over the country cannot wait to do *hanami*, or flower viewing, with friends and family. Most people will pack up an extravagant picnic lunch and head to the local area known to have the most beautiful and numerous cherry blossoms. Then, they will chat, eat a lot, take pictures and just enjoy being together eating under the cherry blossom trees. My photographer husband loves this time of year, and takes endless pictures of the *sakura*. I usually just laugh at him, since, having no appreciation of nature, every single cherry blossom tree, every single year looks exactly the same to me. They are pretty, of course, but they all look the same. Riz will quickly rebuke me, telling me that they look nothing alike. Sure, Honey. Whatever.

The Japanese like to go look at stuff. They go look at flowers, fireworks, and my favorite--fireflies. My friends will actually go to a river or some other place known to have lots of fireflies and just look at them. When I was a kid, fireflies were all over my backyard, and my brothers and I would catch them and put them in a Mason jar. So for people to actually go somewhere to look at fireflies was very amusing to me at first. Kind of makes me think of things that I take for granted, though.

There is something about the blooming of the cherry blossoms that brings joy to the Japanese even in the hardest of times. I remember in 2011, the cherry blossoms started blooming not too long after the devastating earthquake and tsunami in Northern Japan. There was something about the *sakura* that lightened the dark mood that had descended on the entire country, something that gave people joy in the midst of the darkness, death and depression. You could almost feel the joy wafting over the land just because of the blooming of this one, simple flower. That is how important the *sakura* is to the Japanese people. It is not just a flower, but it represents a fresh start, hope, joy, and a second chance. I wonder if the *sakura* is one of the main reasons that the new school year in Japan starts in April. It is a chance for all people to have a new start. There is talk all over the country about starting school in the fall like most other countries do, but I personally, don't think that will ever happen. The new start that is represented most perfectly by the *sakura* is too important to the Japanese people, and it is too deeply seared into the national consciousness to ever lead to a nationwide movement to start the school year in September. I don't think it is too much to say that this simple but beautiful flower will control much of the education policy in Japan now and into the future. The *sakura* is a symbol of renewal, and it is currently lifting the moods and renewing the spirits of everyone around me. And, even though there is probably no one in Japan as out of step with nature as I am, it is bringing a spark even into my heart. And yes, I can tell a cherry blossom from a rose and tulip. Even I can do that.

#48 Karaoke-Dokie

When you hear the word "karaoke" what do you think of? Before I came to Japan, my image was probably the same as yours—drunk rednecks in a local bar on a Saturday, lured in by the "karaoke night" sign and the chance to show everyone that yes, they too can be the next American Idol!! One of my friends at this Italian restaurant where I used to work even expressed surprise that there was karaoke in Japan. "Oh, you mean they have karaoke there, too?" she said.

Not only do the Japanese have karaoke, they invented it, they perfected it, and they own it. Legend has it that the karaoke machine was invented in Kobe in 1971[1], but nobody really knows for sure. The word, much to the surprise of Americans who have butchered the pronunciation, is actually pronounced *kara-okay*, or something like that. It is hard to explain in writing because two of the sounds in the word are not found in English. But it is definitely not pronounced *carry-oki.* Many Japanese are

---

[1] http://en.wikipedia.org/wiki/Karaoke.

not even aware that this word comes from the Japanese words *kara* (empty) and *oke* (an abbreviation of the loanword orchestra). So, it means "empty orchestra." Sometimes the origins of words are pretty cool, don't you think?

The Japanese are crazy about karaoke. I have met very few Japanese who cannot carry a tune. Almost everyone I know can sing pretty well, or at least, average. Why is that? I think it is because they are so crazy about karaoke that they go and practice all the time. Most of the time it is a bonding activity with friends, but sometimes people are actually so concerned about showing off their voices when they go to karaoke with friends, that they actually go practice by themselves to get ready in their own little rented karaoke by-the-hour room.

Whereas in the U.S. there are karaoke nights at bars, Japan has popularized the karaoke box, or room. Entire buildings are used only for karaoke, and they are huge. Some of the largest businesses will have 30-50 boxes to be reserved for anywhere from one hour to all night. While there are some karaoke bars where drunk businessmen sing in front of complete strangers, the most popular form of karaoke is the box, where a group of friends, family or colleagues will rent a private room for their singing pleasure. This way, you don't need to be embarrassed about singing in front of strangers, just in front of those you know.

Karaoke is really cheap. I mean, really cheap. The place

we most often go gives discounts to those with children, and it is cheaper actually for everyone to get the drink bar, and all-you-can-drink setup with hot and cold drinks, added to the karaoke fees. Once, I went to karaoke with about eight kids and six adults for an hour, and we paid like, $27 *total* for everyone, and that is including the free drinks. We figured out it is cheaper to go to karaoke for an hour than to the local food court to get a drink. I guess there are so many different karaoke boxes that they are always trying to stay cheaper than the competition. That is fine with me.

The karaoke machines are so complicated these days that one almost needs a manual to operate them. Unless you go with a super tech-savvy teenager, it takes a while to navigate the maze of remote controls, microphones and songbooks in each private room. You can search for a song by title, genre, or artist; you can search for songs in English, Japanese, Korean, Chinese, and Tagalog. There are movie songs, kids songs, top ten songs, new songs, folk songs, animation songs, pop songs, rock songs, medleys, and just about any other genre you can think of. Usually when I go with my Japanese friends, most of whom are my age or older, I am in charge of the remote control because I am more familiar with it than anyone else. However recently, it is getting too complex even for me. Each remote even gives you the option to increase the volume on the music or mic, change the key, stop it in the middle if you are doing terrible, and change the order of the songs after inputting them. Finally, you can even get the machine to score you based on your singing skills, or even tell you how many calories you burned singing each song.

I used to be totally crazy about karaoke, and I credit my frequent visits there with greatly improving my reading skills in Japanese. I remember that I would start off with slow ballads, and then, as my reading speed increased, graduate to hip hop songs. I was totally nuts about Japanese pop music when I first arrived ten years ago, and went to karaoke sometimes once a week. On several occasions I went to all-night karaoke with my students. I knew how to operate the remote control with speed and precision in order to maximize the time, and any slow-moving indecisive friend got pushed way down in the song order. You snooze, you lose. That was my motto. I was one of those who hated giving up the mic to anyone, and probably annoyed others by singing along with their songs, too.

Then came kids. The all-night karaoke was replaced with all-through-the-night nursing; the money I spent on karaoke went to diapers; my two a.m. bedtime became nine p.m. and my constant companions were no longer my students but my babies. Now that my kids are old enough for karaoke, it is they who refuse to relinquish the microphone, and my J-Pop is regularly overruled by Anpanman and nursery rhymes. In case you don't know who Anpanman is, he is the most popular Japanese animation character for kids, a bean paste bread man who gives his head to others to help them, only to get a new head baked by his creator in the bakery. His popularity rivals

Mickey Mouse's, and he has a million songs about him, all of which can be found at karaoke. I am lucky to get even one or two songs in. To make matters worse, since I don't really watch TV all that much or go to karaoke, my knowledge of current songs has gone down the toilet, and I have become one of the old folks who can only sing sons ten years old or so. I have become a karaoke Old Maid.

But that is fine with me. I still love going, and I still love to sing, but now a lot of the joy I used to get singing is being replaced by the joy I get watching my kids sing. I still think that karaoke is one of the coolest things that Japan has given the world. My dreams of becoming a Japanese pop sensation have faded, but I still get a huge thrill singing at karaoke. But it is not as big as the thrill I get watching my kids sing the Anpanman song. Come to think of it, that gives me much more satisfaction than anything else.

#49 Killing Me Softly

After living in Japan for while, the little things that are different from my home country of America started to hit me. In the early days, I focused on the big stuff like differences in food culture, religion, and daily customs, but after ten years, I found myself fascinated by the meticulousness with which Japanese moms eat a hamburger, or the fact that the Japanese earwax has an entirely different consistency than mine does. Like I said, it is the little things. Take for example, TV commercials.

Every year during the Super Bowl, millions and millions of Americans tune in to watch the Super Bowl. While American football is by far the most popular sport in the U.S., I have a sneaking suspicion that many of those tuning in are really there for the commercials, for which some advertisers pay something crazy like a million dollars or something for a 30-second clip. The Super Bowl commercials are legendary, and can be very profitable. It got me thinking about Japanese commercials and what I realized was, everybody is always singing. Doesn't seem to matter what the product is: cars, dishwashing soap, curry. The makers of the commercials obviously think the product will sell better if the actors sing about it. Usually it is pretty cheesy stuff, but I must admit that those little ditties stick in my head more often than not. Of course, Japan is a country that loves cuteness, so the commercials are going to be all cutesy, singing numbers, while American commercials are more likely to be witty (ok, sarcastic), full of inappropriate innuendos, and leaning more towards cool than cute.

Speaking of singing, many electronics stores and home centers have these little theme songs that play over and over and over and over again on the store's loud speakers all day long. I think I would go crazy if I worked in one of those places. My kids were singing the Yamada Denki and Mr. Max store songs not too long after the ABC song. As annoying as they are, I must admit they are catchy, too, but not catchy enough to send me running to Yamada Denki instead of Best Denki because they have a way cooler song.

And then, there is the chanted homework. Mia comes home chanting her multiplication tables so fast that I cannot even understand her. Last year, she was chanting this word play game she learned at school so fast that I only got maybe two of 105 words. All my kids are constantly singing the songs they learn at preschool and elementary school. They even have a sing-songy voice when they are in charge of reporting attendance for their homeroom. In very melodic fashion, they skip down to the principal's office and announce, "Today, Jun Tanaka and Midori Sano are absent, so there are only 17 of us today!" I always wonder why teachers talk to kids in that exaggerated sing-songy voice too, since I once heard at a lecture that speaking slowly and exaggeratedly to kids is a bad idea for their comprehension and development.

Maybe it is not only their endless trips to karaoke, but also all this singing and chanting from childhood that makes the Japanese such good singers. Kinda makes me wonder if singing is not only a God-given gift, but can also be acquired to at least some degree. I mean, if you are singing about electronic stores and dishwashing soap from the age of two, chanting your multiplication tables at seven, and going to karaoke at twelve, odds are you will be able to carry a tune better than most!

Great, now I can't get that stupid Yamada Denki song out of my head...

#50 Dog Days

One day, I was walking in my neighborhood and I saw this lady, probably about 60 years old crossing the street. She was pushing a portable cart, which is used by the elderly as both a walker and as a cart to carry home groceries after shopping. Since this is a walking culture, even the elderly walk everywhere, which is probably one reason Japanese people live forever. Anyway, as I looked closer, it wasn't a shopping cart/walker but a dog stroller. This lady, who looked like she could use a stroller herself, was pushing around this little dog in a stroller. On top of that, it was a sunny day and in order to keep the little guy cool and from getting sunburned, she was covering him with a parasol as she walked. Now, Japanese women very often use parasols during summer, but that was the first time I had ever seen one used on a dog.

Protecting a dog from the sun and taking him for a walk in a stroller seemed a little extreme to me. To be fair, I have never been a dog lover, a trait which goes back to an experience I had in the 6th grade. I broke my leg playing baseball and had a cast up to my knee. One day, I went to play at my friend's house, and his little, stinky-breathed dog licked my toes without ceasing. Since I was in a cast and fairly immobile, I couldn't do much about it. Since then, I have really disliked dogs. The Japanese, however, are crazy about them. Sometimes you will see people taking dogs into malls and restaurants, especially in Tokyo. There is this pet store nearby that even has dog birthday cakes and cupcakes. Dog clothes are all the rage, too, as well as dog strollers. Recently, cat cafes have become popular. Young women go there and hang out with their cats and other cat lovers while enjoying the ambiance of a café. I know that pets are important all over the world, but it seems to me that the Japanese are particularly fond of them.

    They can be pricey, too, especially when they get sick. My friend just paid about $2000 dollars for an MRI and spine operation for her dog. He was even hospitalized for a couple of days. Recently, pet insurance has become available to help defray some of the expenses of pet ownership. I guess when you have a pet for a long time, that pet becomes part of the family and you are willing to pay whatever you have to save him. I had a cat named J.J. when I was growing up. We loved him like crazy, and he ate with us, slept with us, played with us. When he died, we were devastated, but I doubt we would have spent thousands of dollars to save him. I don't know. Maybe I just feel that animals are animals and humans are humans, and it is kind of weird to value an animal like you would value a human. Animal lovers undoubtedly feel differently and that is okay, I just feel that no matter how attached you are to a pet, it is still an animal.

Recently, Japan has experienced a serious birthrate decline, down to 1.39 in 2012. While it is not as low as it has been, it is nowhere near the 2.1 rate to sustain a population, and the population could be down as much as 30% in the next 50 years. This is a very worrying trend, and talking heads all over the country are trying to figure out why Japanese couples aren't having babies and what can be done to reverse this trend. There are a lot of theories out there. It is too expensive to have large families in Japan, especially considering education costs; fathers are often absent and mothers are unwilling to raise more than two children by themselves; more women are working and marrying later; an increase in couples unable to have children.

All these theories are valid and I think together they are contributing to the low birthrate in Japan. Part of me sometimes wonders if maybe, just maybe, the love of pets has something to do with it, too. Maybe some couples are content just having a dog or cat. After all, it is much easier to care for than a baby. Many of my students say that the sacrifice of having children is great, and maybe some people these days, in our self-centered society aren't willing to make it. I think this could also be said of couples all over the world, not just in Japan. Some people are just not willing to give up their comforts and freedom in order to raise children. I mean, children are a huge sacrifice in time, money, and freedom. You can't buy what you want like you used to, and you cannot even watch a movie unless it has a princess in it. Maybe pets have less strings attached than babies. This is just my theory; I am sure lots of people would disagree with me.

Now, I know many couples who were unable to have children and have tried to fill the emotional void with a pet. There is nothing wrong with that, and I admire people who have love to give and want to shower it on a pet if they cannot shower it on a baby. There are also older people who have pets as companions to ease their loneliness. I am not trying to lump all pet owners together. I just wonder if some families figure, well, one kid and a dog is enough. Or, two dogs are easier to care for than a baby. Pets are good and can bring great joy to a family, but I hope that it is never at the expense of knowing the greater joy that having children can bring.

#51 Squatty Potties and Texas Toast

I know. It seems totally random and maybe even a little disgusting to talk about toilets and bread in the same title, but hang with me for a minute; there really is a connection. When I first came to Japan 15 years ago, there were a lot of things that I just didn't get, couldn't figure out, and had no idea how to do. For example, anything that involved communicating with language (I had gestures down pretty well), how to order something I liked at a restaurant, and finding stuff I needed at the supermarket. Other things I learned quickly, like I had to take my shoes off in the house and it is weird to put soy sauce on rice here. There were still other things, however, I figured out way later. I mean like, years later.

This is where I get to the relationship between toilets and bread. Everybody knows that the Asian-style toilet, affectionately known around the world as the "squatty potty" is prevalent all over Japan. While these days it is very rare to see one in a private home, they can still be found in train stations, older restaurants, city offices, and schools, among other places. While most Westerners have a disdain for these toilets, most will agree that if you can keep from peeing on yourself, they are actually more sanitary than Western-style toilets. I also recently read an article that claimed they are better for pooping, as your colon gets all kinked up in a funky way if you use a Western toilet. Apparently, the exit path for feces is much straighter and more direct when squatting over an Asian toilet.

Practicality aside, I hate squatty potties. I am not one of those people who can avoid peeing on themselves when using them, even after 13 years in Japan. My kids have finally conquered their fears after years of me having to hold them up over the squatty potty at some weird angle hoping they don't spray me or pee on their clothes. And while squatty potties may be more hygienic because you are not getting germs on your bottom, they usually stink to high heaven. So, I avoid them when at all possible.

Unfortunately, I couldn't avoid them when I lived in Kobe. Our first apartment had a kind of squatty potty, the kind where you step up to use it after entering the toilet area. We couldn't bear not being able to relax and read while in the comfort room (we are both toilet readers), so we trekked to the local home center to buy this cute little adapter. It was just a plastic toilet top that you placed over the hole in the floor toilet to make it an instant Western toilet. It even came with directions about how to use it. Maybe they were afraid somebody would step up onto it and squat. Bad, but not nearly as bad as someone who did the opposite and tried to sit down on a squatty potty...Now that is disgusting.

For a long time, I wondered why the toilet paper was behind me. That sure is impractical and inconvenient, I thought. Wouldn't it be easier if the toilet paper were in closer reach? Hmm. One day, I was talking to an American friend about this topic, and he informed me that I had been facing the wrong direction. Aha! That made a lot of sense. No wonder I seemed to pee on myself all the time! From that point on, I turned around, the toilet paper was in much better proximity to my squatting self, and I peed on myself with much less frequency (unfortunately not totally eliminating it). So, after a year or so of thinking I was doing something right but actually doing it wrong, I learned an important point about Japanese culture: how to properly use the squatty potty.

And how is that related to bread? Well, I love bread,

especially bread slathered with peanut butter, so that was one of the first things I searched out upon arriving in Japan. Imagine my surprise to find that most loaf bread sold at supermarkets was bigger than Texas toast, being way thicker than my hand and having almost 200 calories a slice. Bread as I knew it was thinly sliced, and anything over 100 calories was considered fattening. It was hard to find bread loaves here with less than six slices (huge), and some even had only four slices (monstrous). But, it was all I could find, so I bought it and made toast in the mornings and ham sandwiches for lunch. It took me a while to figure out that Japanese people only use this kind of bread for toast. For sandwiches, they use much more thinly sliced bread. This sandwich bread is even thinner than that used in the U.S. So, unfortunately for a while I was consuming way too many carbs and calories due to my ignorance of correct Japanese bread usage.

As you can see, some things you learn right away, and for others it takes months, years or even decades. In fact, just recently, after all my time in Japan, I realized something new. When I ask a Japanese person for something, and he says it is difficult, what he really means is that it is impossible. And to think, I had always thought that something difficult could be done--it would just be, well, difficult. It goes to show that no matter how long you live in a new place, you are never finished learning about all the ins and outs of the culture. I am amazed at how many new things I am still learning about Japan. While I am now an expert on squatty potty and loaf bread usage, I cannot help but wonder if there is something out there I have been doing wrong for 13 years, and someone is going to have to the guts to tell me about it one day. I am sure there is, it is just whether or not I will every find out about it or not.

#52 Homeschooling in Japan

My husband is turning into a *kyoiku papa*. In case you have never heard of terms for education--crazy parents in Asia, crazed moms in Japan are called *kyoiku mama* (*education mommy*), and crazed moms in China are called Tiger Moms.

One of the best books I have ever read on the subject was a memoir written by a self-confessed Chinese-American Tiger Mom, appropriately titled *Battle Hymn of a Tiger Mom*. I don't want to ruin it in case you want to read it yourself, but man, she is one wacked out mommy. I have to admit that there are parts of her obsessive personality that I admire, especially her transparancy and honestly in writing the book, and her incredible commitment to her children despite her own busy career. But for the most part, I think she is crazy. My husband is not nearly that bad. While he may have a mild case of education daddy syndrome, his motives are pure and his heart good. He also realizes when it is time to play and take a break. Mainly, he just wants to make sure our American kids can use English properly so they can communicate with their grandparents or be able to function in society if we ever move back. That is a pretty modest but important goal, I think.

A few months ago, Riz ordered some Christian-designed homeschooling curriculum from the United States for all three girls. Since we both work full-time, exclusive homeschooling is not an option. However, part-time homeschooling is. Every day after our oldest gets home from Japanese elementary school, and for several hours again during spring vacation, Riz homeschools Mia not only in English, but also in math, science, Bible, art, and history. Our two youngest are taking a break now, but after the new school year starts, he plans on working with them for an hour or so a day. I guess we have realized that if our kids are going to get a proper English-language education, and more importantly for us, biblical training, it has to come from us. They are not going to get either from the Japanese education system. While the school system here has it's good points, English education is dismal, and doesn't even begin until 5th grade in my city.

Most Japanese will look at you like you are crazy if you tell them you are homeschooling. Most have never even heard of the concept. It is not illegal in Japan like it is in other countries, but because it is so rare here, it is extremely difficult for Japanese parents to get permission from the government to exclusively homeschool their children and be excused from compulsory education. For foreigners like us, getting permission to homeschool is a piece of cake. All we have to do is say that we are taking our kids out of the school system and that is enough.

The main concern that Japanese society has about homeschooled children is their lack of socialization. Unlike in the U.S. where homeschooling is so prevalent, there are few sports leagues or after school activities for homeschooled kids. There are community sports that kids can participate in, but many times they are more time consuming and costly than many parents (like me) want them to be. My American friend who is homeschooling her two children scoffs at this concern and says her kids are socializing just fine, and have plenty of friends their own age to play with.

I think it is just a cultural thing; in Japan education mommies may spend lots of time and money on afterschool activities and study programs, and spend time drilling their children on homework at home, but the main responsibility for educating children falls on the government. I often question whether the government is doing a good enough job because most students have terrible English skills by the time they reach me in university, and many parents feel it is necessary for their children to attend cram schools several nights a week in order for them to get into the high school or university of their choice. I feel that a government that cannot provide a good enough education to get kids into good university is somehow failing the children. It doesn't seem fair that children from families that can afford extra study for their kids should be able to get a leg up on their less fortunate peers.

My homeschooling American friend doesn't spend anything on education except for the $500 per year, per child on the curriculum that she buys online every year. There are no afterschool activities; she plays with them herself. They get all the education they need from her, so there is no need for extra study. And there is plenty of time and opportunity to play with their friends. The elementary school lets the oldest come hang out at recess with kids from her class (she attended one year before switching to homeschooling), and even allows her to participate in Sports Day. That is highly unusual here in Japan. She lucked out. Most schools would not be that accommodating.

I know these kids well. They are really close to my own kids, and I can tell you one thing--they are polite, intelligent, well-behaved and very socially adjusted. I admire what their mommy is doing and sometimes wish that we were able to homeschool our own kids full-time. We would be able to be with them all the time, and save over $600 a month in childcare costs.

But I know that I am not suited to be full-time homeschooling mommy. I don't have the temperament, the passion, or the patience for it. I think my husband could do it—it is right up his alley and he is passionate about it. Maybe in the future if our situation changes it will be both more financially possible and desirable for us to homeschool our kids full-time. But for now, it is fun to watch my oldest memorize Bible verses and learn to read. It melts my heart to see her so excited to read the Bible that she takes it to the table with her to read during lunchtime.

I don't think homeschooling in Japan is impossible or weird. I don't believe that homeschooling will lead to socially ill-adjusted kids. Believe me, there are plenty of social misfits who have gone through the public school system here. But whether parents choose to homeschool or not, ultimately, our kids are our kids, not the school's. We need to be concerned not just about what they know, but about what kind of person they are. Even though Mia has a morals class at school, we are much more responsible for shaping her moral character than the school is. Education is much more than being able to recite multiplication tables, write Chinese characters correctly, or play Beethoven's *Fifth* like a pro on the piano. It is the shaping of a whole person, and there is no one more suited to that than a child's own parents.

#53 Does It Really Cost More?

Okay. So, let's set the record straight. Some things cost an arm and a leg in Japan. For example, getting a driver's license ($3000), a top of the line cantaloupe ($100), and a movie ticket ($18). But I want to dispel the stereotype that living in Japan is crazy expensive compared to living in the United

States. I have actually found that in many ways, it is much cheaper for my family to live here, and the salaries are much higher.

First of all, Japan is a big place (well, kinda. It is still smaller than California). Just like you cannot make a blanket statement that living in the U.S. is expensive, you cannot say that about Japan either. I mean, you can buy a house for $60,000 dollars in Detroit, or the same sized house for $1 million in New York. Likewise, prices in Tokyo, Osaka or other metropolitan areas can be outrageous. My brother lived in one of the ritziest parts of Tokyo for three years, and his monthly rent was $4500 for a modest apartment. Granted, it was very nice and very modern, but $4500??!! That is more than my entire monthly salary. Of course, his company paid for it, not him. But when I tell my friends here in Kitakyushu that my monthly rent for a *two-story house* is $1000, their jaws drop to the floor and they think I am some kind of rich shipping tycoon. In fact, there are very few rentals here in my area for more than $1000 a month. In Norfolk, VA, where I attended graduate school, the housing prices are currently much more expensive. A small ranch house will cost at least $1200 a month to rent. So, I find that housing costs are much cheaper here in Japan than what I experienced in the U.S.

Next, on to food. I must admit that fruits are really expensive here. While I have never bought a $100 melon, I have seen one, and most people I know don't eat melons or strawberries on a regular basis. They are reserved as special treats for parties, birthdays, or other special occasions. When my husband asked me to buy him strawberries on his birthday, my cheap self had to grit my teeth and realize that the least I can do is buy my husband strawberries on his birthday. To be honest, though, the thought of spending $5 on ten strawberries made my stomach turn. Apples cost at least one dollar each, grapes are through the roof expensive, and then there is the mandarin orange—my children's favorite fruit. A bag of ten or so goes for about $4, and they can easily go through a bag in a day. I find myself having to ration them out (one per day for person) to keep me from having a financial panic attack. The only reasonable fruit is bananas, which can be found for about a dollar a bunch, and of course, are even cheaper at Costco.

Unlike in the U.S., chicken is seen as the poor man's meat here, so it is much cheaper than in the U.S. This is good for me because chicken is my favorite meat. Fish is dirt cheap, but I have no idea how to prepare it, so oh well. I guess since it is cheap, healthy and my kids love it that I should make more of an effort to figure it out. Anyway, pork is very popular here and reasonably priced, but beef is very expensive. If you were to have a BBQ here and buy all your beef at a Japanese supermarket, it could cost you a hundred bucks. Even minced beef, which most of the time is a combination of beef and pork, is about three times as expensive as in the U.S. This stinks for me since my kids love tacos so much...

The two areas that save me the most money compared to living in the U.S. are health care and child care. Because health care is socialized for the most part (we do pay a monthly premium and 30% of all medical expenses), it is very reasonable and will never bankrupt you. It cost me only a couple hundred bucks to have a baby, all health care for my kids is free through age 6, and a doctor's visit will only cost $4 or $5. Imagine my sticker shock at having to pay more than $300 for a visit to the emergency room during a visit home to the U.S. That was only for a consultation—no medicine or testing. Not to mention the four hours I had to wait to see the doctor. Health insurance is a huge topic and one of my favorite things about Japan, so if you want to know more, you can read the chapter about health care in my first book, *Driving Me Crazy About It*.

Childcare is also way cheap. I pay about $550 a month for both of my younger girls to be enrolled full-time in a public preschool. That price includes lunch, toilet training, education, and general awesome care and support. To be sure, it is still quite a chunk out of my paycheck and it will be nice to have them in elementary school, but there is no way I would be able to find such reliable care for my kids for such a cheap price in the States. Public schools, however, are a little more expensive than those in the U.S. Elementary school fees are about $50 a month. This fee includes school lunch, textbooks, handouts, and other school materials.

It jumps to over $100 a month in junior high and high

school, but I am not exactly sure why. Students from junior high are also required to buy uniforms, which cost several hundred dollars. And then, of course, there is cram school. Parents who want extra study for their children to get into the best schools may pay a couple hundred dollars a month. University tuition for public institutions is very reasonable, about $5500 a year at my school. Of course, that doesn't include renting an apartment for your child if commuting is not an option. The idea of roommates is unheard of here, and dorms unusual at many campuses, so most parents will pay $500 a month or so on room and board. But more about that in a later chapter.

So what is the deal? Is Japan expensive or not? I would avoid living in Tokyo at all costs if you are on a budget. It will drain you dry. Everything there, from rent to clothing to boxed lunches cost way more than in other areas of Japan. But if you live in a smaller city or even more so in the country, I think you will find Japan to be much cheaper than the U.S. in a lot of ways. So, to sum it up, I am going to include a little chart illustrating just a few things I think are more expensive in Japan (as compared to the U.S.). This is by far not an exhaustive list, and it is only my opinion. Please contact me if you can think of anything else you can add to this list.

More Expensive in Japan	More Expensive in the USA
Driving School	Health care
Fruits and Vegetables	Heated Toilet Seats
City Taxes	Income tax
Primary School Fees (Public)	University Tuition (Public)
Beef	Chicken
Movie Ticket	Root Canals
Gas	Childbirth
Highway tolls	Child care
Pizza Delivery	Japanese Food

#54 Culture of No Moderation

Although I absolutely love the numerous advantages of raising my children here (bilingualism, healthy food, cultural awareness, etc.), there are two aspects of living in Japan that I particularly dislike and I am determined to protect my children from. Both have to do with moderation, or rather, lack thereof. The first one, excessive emphasis on study which manifests itself in a long school year, short breaks, Saturday school and cram school. I have discussed education in detail in other posts, so today I want to focus on one cultural aspect that I think is crazy and even borderline maniacal—excessive practicing for sports.

Last week, I read an article by Jeff Passan at Yahoo! Sports ("*The pitch-count problem: How cultural convictions are ruining Japanese pitchers"*)[2] that made me reflect again on why I dislike so much the way sports are done in Japan. In this article Passan tells the story of Tomohiro Anraku, a 16-year old high school pitcher who recently performed on Japan's greatest baseball stage, the Koshien High School Baseball Tournament. The Japanese are crazy about Koshien like no other sporting event, and it is the dream of every young boy to one day step on the Koshien field. Maybe that is why managers and parents alike lose their heads when making decisions about their players. Anraku threw 772 pitches in one week, started four out of five games, and by the end of the week saw the velocity of his fastball drop from 94 mph to 80 mph. Exhausted with a dead arm, he woefully pitched his team to a 17-1 loss in the final. Not that it mattered that much. To the Japanese, where more is better and less is lazy, the work ethic, self-sacrifice and perseverance this kid showed cemented his name in Koshien history forever.

While most Western baseball analysts will say that this kind of behavior is not only crazy and destructive but borderline abusive, Japanese purists say it is good old fashioned hard work. The over-riding sentiment here is, the more you work, the better you get. It is that simple. No pain, no gain. That is why high school sports clubs practice all year round, every day, every weekend, every holiday. That is why even children's

---

[2] Retrieved April 8, 2013 from http://sports.yahoo.com/news/the-pitch-count-problem--how-cultural-convictions-are-ruining-japanese-pitchers-012016897.html

sports teams practice from morning to evening every weekend and holiday. Practice makes perfect, right? Umm. No. Not in my book, and these are the reasons why.

First of all, call me crazy, but I think that sports should be fun for children. Fun and stress free, not only for children but also for parents. I do not think kids should be in training to become professionals in elementary school. I was so jealous when I visited my brother's family in the U.S. last summer, and I attended a church league soccer game. It's funny that as unpopular as soccer is in the U.S., everybody seems to play it as a kid. Anyway, my brother paid like 50 bucks for each kid (he has a lot of them) for a couple months of games and practice, uniforms, and thermos bottles. The goals were set up with cones, the rules were laxly enforced, and winning was not the goal. I loved it. The kids were learning about cooperation, getting exercise, and most of all, having fun. It is hard to find such a relaxed sports league for kids here. Maybe they are out there, and I just haven't found them yet, but every sports league I know demands an incredibly high level of commitment not only from the kids, but also from their parents. Not only are parents responsible for taking and picking up their kids, but also for preparing *bentos* and other snacks, sometimes for the whole team. The biggest sacrifice that is required, though, is the sacrifice of family time.

Many children in neighborhood sports leagues spend every weekend and holiday away from their families. Since many fathers work anyway in this country, maybe it is not so much of a sacrifice of family time for them, but it is for me. Weekends and holidays, to me, are not a time of public schooling and all day sports events. They are family times. To be sure, I would love to spend Saturday mornings watching my kids play soccer, but unfortunately that is not how it works here. It is not only Saturday morning, but Sundays, too and every holiday. And half the time I might not even be watching, but dropping them off to practice endlessly and then go home, only to pick them up before dinner.

This kind of huge time sacrifice is not one that our family is willing to make. But what if that is what the kids want? Am I going to be the bad guy mom and say no to a sacrifice that the kids want to make? What a hard decision to make here in Japan. Recently, my oldest daughter Mia has been begging me to let her start ballet. I know that real ballet schools here suck all your time and money, not to mention that fact that I don't even want her to start thinking about food, calories and body image at age 7, especially having had struggled with an eating disorder my whole life. Of course, there are the more-laid back, cheaper culture center classes that supposedly have more of a fun atmosphere. Maybe we will check that option out, but really, can we find another $50 to spend on top of the $300 a month we are already spending on swimming and drum lessons?

It all makes me wonder, why do the Japanese think they have to spend such an extraordinary amount of time on everything? Of course, anyone who wants to be a professional at anything must dedicate thousands of hours to master their chosen crafts. I get it. But, really, are 99% of kids involved in various sports and activities around the country ever going to go pro? It seems there is some kind of badge of honor in always being busy, always practicing something, always taking your kids somewhere. There is a joke in the U.S. about mom being a taxi driver, ferrying her kids around to their numerous activities and events, but is it really a joke? Is it good for kids to be so busy, and families to be separated, not only by the necessities of work and school, but then by soccer practice, ballet, piano, or the myriad of other things out there competing for our time and attention? Where is the balance between having well-rounded kids and close-knit families?

And what about Tomohiro Anraku? Will he become the next Nolan Ryan, winning more than 300 games and pitching into his 40s, or will he be more like Daisuke Matsuzaka, another Koshien legend who blew out his arm in his late 20s after a couple stellar major league seasons? I can tell you one thing from personal experience: more is not always better. An exercise addiction that I am only now overcoming exhausted my body, halted my menstrual cycle for two years, and broke down my once healthy body. I erroneaously thought that two hours of working out had to be better than one. But you know what? It isn't. Not for me. It has taken me years to realize that too much of anything, even a good thing like exercise, is bad for you. Just as the mind needs rest from study, the body needs rest from exercise. I can guarantee that a still-growing 16-year boy like Anraku needs to rest his arm a lot more than he did during Koshien.

While there are crazy parents and coaches pushing kids too far all over the world, for some reason, maybe because I live here and am surrounding by it, I think the Japanese are more excessive than most countries. Of course, they would disagree. They would see it as good old fashioned Confucian work ethic, and they probably look at American students and see too much play, not enough structure, and too much free time. To them, maybe American baseball players are gluttonous and lazy. I know that my views will never change a culture, but I can do my part and keep my kids and my family out of the rat race of community sports.

#55 The Cuteness is Killing Me

A couple of years ago, I took two of my Japanese mommy friends with me to Costco. At that time, the one in our neighborhood had not been built yet, so going to the one in Fukuoka was an all-day affair. These lovely ladies had never been to Costco before, and I had more fun watching their reactions to the huge sizes of everything than actually shopping myself. The funniest thing was the first time they saw baby carrots. Baby carrots, while being a common snack food in the

U.S., are not seen at Japanese supermarkets. My friends took one look at these carrots and shrieked, "Ahh!! *Kawaii!*!" (Oh my goodness, they are so cute!) I must admit that I had never in my life heard baby carrots referred to as cute before. This exclamation was just another reminder to me that in Japan, all that really matters after all, is cuteness.

Now, I like cute cuddly babies, little kittens, and other normal "cute" stuff, but the cuteness obsession in Japan is way over the top for me. For starters, everybody here seems to love Mickey Mouse, his wife, and all the other Disney characters. I mean everyone. You can go to Disneyland and see a 20-year old guy squealing about posing with Mickey, and adults everywhere buying up Disney stuff to put on their car dashboards, cell phones, or to decorate their houses. Most of my adult female students have really cute pencil cases, key chains, and bags, many of them of a Disney hero or some other cute character. Now, when I was a kid I probably liked stuff like that, and my own daughters squeal upon seeing Mickey, Minnie or Anpanman. However, as an adult, I have zero interest in Disney or any other character.

Maybe I am a cold cynic who has lost the imagination of my childhood, but the only reason I go to Disneyland is because I love my kids, and it makes them happy. I mean, I absolutely hate that place. We have been to Tokyo Disneyland twice, and I absolutely can't stand waiting in line for everything from rides to popcorn, and I hate paying out of the nose for food, drinks and the same souvenirs they have in the 100 yen shop. Besides, the rides aren't even fun or scary. I am a roller coaster junkie, not at all moved by all the magical rides or parades that are Disneyland. Give me the 17-roller coaster paradise of Magic Mountain any day. I don't think every adult American is as cynical as I am, but I don't think they are still into the cuteness of Disney and other characters upon entering adulthood like the Japanese are.

Cars that are cute sell well, too. Little girly cars with boxy shapes and feminine colors like pink, green and yellow sell well here. My kids, who I think are very cute in any language (okay, I am biased!) are constantly barraged with the Japanese "*kawaii*!!" every time we go out in public. Female students are always telling each other how cute their shoes, clothes or accessories are on any given day. Even metrosexual guys are "*kawaii*," as it seems that maybe it is more of a complement to be 'cute' than to be 'handsome' or 'good-looking.' The other day I was bemoaning the increase of girly guys in Japan, watching this famous girly guy singer on TV with a 56-year old female friend. Her response, "Oh, but he is so cute!" Call me crazy, but it is weird to refer to a guy in his mid-to late 20s as cute. Personally, I don't like it when people tell me I look cute. I would rather be 'cool' or 'fashionable.' Cute is definitely not what I am aiming for when I get dressed in the mornings.

Finally, when using English, Japanese people sometimes are confused by how to use 'cute' 'pretty' and 'cool' It is weird when people come up and touch my little kids and say, "Oh they are so pretty!" I don't know, maybe it is just me. A toddler is more cute than pretty. And once, one of my husband's male students was commenting on a picture of my husband on Facebook. He posted, "Oh man. You are cute." My husband promptly responded, "You never tell a guy he is cute. Never." I wanted to add that you never call a guy cute especially on Facebook.

As much as I dislike it, I think cute is here to stay in Japan. Maybe I will suck it up and take my kids to Disneyland every few years, pay ten bucks for Mickey Mouse pancakes and take endless pictures of a waving Minnie Mouse at the daily parade, but secretly I am waiting for the day the kids are big enough to ride the scary roller coasters at Magic Mountain with me. Yep, I am definitely way more into cool than cute.

#56 Volunteer...or ELSE!!

It's that time of year again, the time when massive trees are killed all over Japan to support the paperwork-heavy monstrosity of PTA elections in public schools all over Japan. My oldest Mia hadn't been in school two days before the first form came home, and I must admit that I still don't really understand it. From what I can tell, they will elect by lottery two representatives from each class. Unfortunately, I do not seem to have met the requirements to be exempt from the lottery process, so since there are 33 kids in Mia's class, I have a little less than a 10% chance of having the misfortune of being chosen. However, we do get the option of letting them know if we want to do it or not. The three choices were 1) I want to do it. 2) I will do it if there is nobody else to do it. 3) I do not want to do it. Despite having a little say in the matter, I am not really sure what will happen if 33 moms and 33 dads in her class all don't want to do it.

Well, now I do. The election day has come and gone, and let me tell you, it is a totally ridiculous system. Of all the moms and dads in the class, only eight of us were not exempt from duty. Apparently, full-time working moms are not exempt; only full-time working moms whose kids are not in preschool but at home are exempt. Of course, how can a full-time working mom NOT put her kids in preschool, unless the kids stay at grandma's house? In which case, a mom lucky enough to have grandma's help gets out of it, but a mom struggling on her own doesn't. Really fair.

So anyway, here I am with five other moms (two were skipping out), and I realized something this day: I am definitely not the only one who dislikes the PTA. This one other mom was complaining like crazy about not having time and having small kids to look after. The others were silently looking down, just letting me and this other mom doing all the whining. I asked about the duties of the class PTA representatives, and I was told it's not that bad; all I have to do is take notes at the occasional class meeting, and count the Bell Mark coupons (the equivalent of Campbell soup labels) once a month. The day is set, so there is no flexibility, but you don't have to go every month if you can't.

One mom volunteered, but that was it. Since two people were needed, it was time to draw straws. As much as I hate the PTA system, I do feel like I have been blessed with a very flexible job and much more freedom that most moms. So I found myself feeling so sorry for these other moms that I thought maybe I should volunteer. What I decided was that if this really stressed mom drew the unlucky straw that I would do it for her. Crazy since I loathe the whole thing, but I felt like God was calling me to do it. Well, turns out that neither of us drew the unlucky straw, but one of the mommies who wasn't there got chosen in her absence. I found myself nauseated by the whole thing, but I told the leaders that I would do it if that lady wasn't willing to serve.

Here is what makes me so mad. This is a mandatory system. You cannot get exempt unless you have kids at home or are on some other committee. You are working full-time. And yet, this mandatory job entails coming to the school once a month **ON A WEEKDAY DURING THE DAY** to count soup labels (Did you notice now I capitalized, bolded and underlined that to emphasize the ridiculousness of it all?) It is, to me, totally a rights issue. Maybe I wouldn't have such a beef with it if it was at night, but it isn't. I totally found myself feeling sorry for all the hard-working moms who are probably much more stressed than I am having the additional burden of mandatory PTA service put onto their plates. Anyway, I have yet to hear whether I have to do it or not.

The letter Mia brought home stated that moms (or dads) are expected to serve on the PTA at least once for each child. Since I have three kids, that means three years of slavery, uh, I mean service for me. The class representative PTA, and the school PTA is different. If you serve on one you are exempt for three years, but not exempt from the other. And, if you have another child enter the school, your exemption is gone again. So, for me with three girls each two years apart, there is no exemption in sight.

The PTA is not voluntary and anyone who thinks it is is crazy. It is the duty of all parents. There is an incredible sense of community duty here, much more so than in the United States. Anyone in a community, be it a school community or a neighborhood community, is expected to pull his or her weight as a member of that community. Which, in theory is not a bad idea, but there are two things in particular I don't like. First, although serving on committees is supposedly voluntary, it is not. The only thing you can volunteer for is your particular role or maybe, the time when you serve. Eventually, your turn will come, and if you don't take it, you are looked down upon as a bad member of that community. It doesn't really matter if you are working or busy. It is assumed in this work-crazy country that everyone is busy and working so that is not an excuse.

The other thing is, I feel that a lot of the stuff that is done on the committees is just making extra work. There are committees for committees. You should have seen the organization chart that came home for the PTA. I felt like I was looking at the cabinet and various departmental duties of a small country, not that of a public elementary school.

As I was looking at all the stuff that the PTA does, I started thinking, "Uh, and what exactly does the school take responsibility for? And if the parents are doing so much, why are the teachers always having nervous breakdowns and working until 8:00 at night?" I am not kidding. Teachers here have nervous breakdowns all the time. It seems almost as common as a cold.

The Japanese obsession with committees is legendary. Not only are there millions of committees at my university, there are several subcommittees within the committees. There is not only a neighborhood association, but a block association, and a block children's association. Granted, these groups do great things for the kids for which I am grateful, but sometimes I wonder if they do not do too much. Maybe I am kinda of *laissez-faire* in this respect, but is all this stuff really necessary? While I appreciate the strawberry picking trips and fishing expeditions the kids' association provides, I can take my kids to those places myself (well, the strawberry picking anyway). And while I recognize the need for traffic guards in the morning and afternoons to protect the kids walking to and from school, does the PTA really need to put out a newspaper with pictures so dark that you cannot see them? Sometimes I just feel like there is too much excess. Is it possible for something to be good, but excessive and unnecessary at the same time?

So, it comes down to this. Sometimes doing all this extra stuff, while it may be good, can take you away from doing other good stuff. Time is limited, and you cannot do everything you want to do. Teachers who stay late at school every night and travel on weekends coaching sports teams probably do so at the expense of time with their own kids; community service is good, but what are you sacrificing your own family for the sake of others? If many of these committees like the PTA were not so time consuming (mothers are expected to go to school at least one day a week), maybe I would be more willing to join; maybe if it really was voluntary instead of mandatory, this rebellious American heart wouldn't be so reluctant. Or maybe I am just being selfish, unwilling to do my part.

This is the conundrum of the working mother. How do you work, take care of your kids, cook healthy meals, take care of yourself, and carry out your civic duty serving on a myriad of different committees? Since time is limited, at some point, you have to make a choice. For now, I am choosing to be home with my family in the evenings after I come home from work. I am not unwilling to serve, but can I please serve at something I am gifted at and on my time schedule? Why does everyone have to do the same stuff? Couldn't my skills as a bilingual resident be put to much better use than counting soup labels? If the school asked me to translate documents or interpret for the numerous non-Japanese speaking parents at the school, I would love to do it; if they asked me to teach English occasionally, I would do that too. But the mandatory volunteerism grates at me like nothing else has since I came to Japan. I don't know what is going to happen with the PTA. If I get chosen, I will do it. Maybe I can change something in the process. After all, I love this country and have chosen to live here. Japan has been gracious hosts to my family. 95% of the time it is "When in Rome..." But not this time.

I ended up not having to serve as PTA class representative this year since the lady chosen by lottery agreed to do it. So my rebellion begins again next year...

#57 IV, please

Being a total expert on the Japanese health care system after 13 years here and numerous health scares, I thought I would take some time to reflect on the major differences I see in how problems are treated here and in the U.S. So, let us begin.

First, Japanese doctors dole out medicine like candy, but don't expect to get more than a few days worth. It is not uncommon to go in for a cold or something, and come out with only a three day supply of five or six different kinds of medicine, all of which not only taste like candy, but also have about the same medicinal value of candy on this strangely-built Western body of mine. The same medicine which works wonders on a Japanese friend's cold doesn't do anything for me; a powerful pain medication that can knock a friend out cold can keep me up at night (maybe that is a little exaggeration, but I have yet to find a medication here that makes me drowsy). In fact, the only time in 13 years I have ever felt any strong effect from medication is when I took some medicine to stop premature contractions when I was pregnant. It gave me terrible heart palpitations and made me feel like I was going to pass out. I wish my doctor had informed me that might happen. I have also found a headache medicine that works wonders on me. Recently, doctors have been able to give out doses for a longer period of time, but many still feel more comfortable seeing you every couple of days to make sure you are doing okay.

The biggest difference I have found is is at the ENTs. They love to have patients wash their noses for sinus infections and colds. I admit that at first I found the prospect of squirting water up my nose and then back out again pretty disgusting, like the boys who would hurl hockers out of their noses in junior high. But believe it or not, it actually really makes you feel better. ENTs particularly like you to pay a visit every few days for eternity to keep an eye on you. Many are reluctant to give out antibiotics, and prefer the slow boat to health. Patients, too, often prefer the slower, more natural path to healing. One of my friends has been visiting a clinic for two or three years to treat an ingrown toenail, choosing that over just getting it removed and being done with it. She told me she feels slower is better.

One thing that really surprised me was IV usage. The only time I ever saw IVs used in the U.S. (never on me) was in the ER on TV or when someone was deathly ill, clinging to life. Here, IVs are used as a normal course of treatment--especially to speed recovery or to hydrate someone dealing with high fever or diarrhea. When I was pregnant with Abby, I had one sinus infection after another, and finally, went to the OB/GYN clinic at 10 pm one evening with a high fever and a splitting headache. They did an antibiotic IV right away, and two hours later I felt like a new woman. After being warned that coming in after hours was going to cost me an arm and a leg, I went home not caring because I felt like a million bucks. I think I paid 35 dollars for that IV. Maybe a fingernail, but not an arm and a leg.

I had an IV for viral meningitis, too, and my husband had one for a high fever. My kids get them whenever they are fighting a particularly bad case of diarrhea, and almost everyone I know has had one at one time or another. I love this about Japan. It is almost like you can feel the healing powers flowing into your body. I think this is one of my favorite treatments in Japan, after nose washing of course.

And finally, there is the most shocking one of all, the prevalent enema and suppository usage. I remember when I first came to Japan, I was teaching kids English and one little guy came up behind me and acted like he was sticking something up my butt. What the heck? I thought. Where are these little dudes learning this stuff? Well, it turns out that Japanese people are very quick to stick various things up the butt to bring about faster healing. It starts at birth where cotton swabs with baby oil are inserted up there to cure constipation; as they get older, fever-reducing enemas are used as the best way to bring a fever down fast.

Even adults endure more enemas than in the U.S., with them regularly being used in childbirth and often before colonoscopies. I remember once when I was in labor with Abby, my husband had a 104 degree fever that wouldn't come down even with an IV drip. Because we were so close to the staff at the hospital, they just put him in a bed next to mine, and he thus became the first male patient in the history of the hospital. Finally, after a fruitless day of treatment, the doctor looked at the midwives and said, "I think we need to give him the enema." They quickly responded, "Um. We're not gonna do it. Go right ahead, doctor." Luckily, it was a moot point as the fever broke soon after this, and I had the baby the next day. My lucky husband both avoided the enema, and was conscious for the birth of his second child. A good day.

For the most part, while I am not crazy about commuting to the hospital, there are a lot of wacky treatments here that I actually like. If you have never washed your nose, I highly recommend it. You will never use nasal spray again.

#58 Election Noise

I grew up in a very politically-minded family. My dad was always talking about politics, and quizzing me about politics for my high school quiz bowl team, so I had a lot of exposure to it as a kid. Like most Americans, I get fed up with the do-nothing politicians and political gridlock, but the whole process still interests me, although here I must confess that I have not voted in the last two political elections. One reason is just because voting absentee is a pain in the neck, and I never got around to it. The main reason, though, is that I never really felt strongly or passionate about any of the candidates. I know, I know. You are probably saying that doesn't matter, that it is my civic duty to vote anyway. You are probably right, but I often find myself in the conundrum that I cannot agree with either candidate and their stances on moral or social issues.

Even though I have been an apathetic non-voter at times, I still find the political system interesting and important, and despite the number of crooks in Washington, I still believe there are some good people there who genuinely want to change things. I am an optimist. One thing that surprised me coming here is the total apathy, and even distaste for politics among the common Japanese person. The voter turnout in 2012 was 59.32 %, the lowest in history, down from a peak of 76.98 % in 1958.[3] Young people, in particular are apathetic and even hostile at times. When I asked students to tell me their opinion of politicians in class one day, almost all of them responded negatively, citing reasons such as dishonesty, greed and selfishness.

One reason may be the constant changing of government in Japan. I must admit to being a little ignorant on the issue, but it is similar to the parliamentary system in England. The leader of the ruling party is chosen as the Prime Minister. It seems that Prime Ministers change so often I can't even keep up with it. There have only been two since I have been here that have been able to sustain any amount of popularity and public trust--Keizo Obuchi and Juichiro Koizumi, although the current Prime Minister Shinzo Abe is generating a following with his "*Abe-nomics*," a radical plan to resuscitate the

---

[3] Retrieved April 12, 2003 from http://www.idea.int/vt.countryview.cfm?id=114

ailing Japanese economy. Both Obuchi and Koizumi had colorful personalities and tended to buck the cultural trends in politics, and the public really admired them for it. Others have come and gone, and there have been 17 administration changes since 1989, a period of only 23 years.[4] In addition to the national elections, there are also local elections, and it seems to me like there is always some sort of election going on. One thing that is bound to accompany an election in Japan is noise pollution--a lot of it.

For some reason, Japanese politicians think that if they drive around blasting their political propaganda from a megaphone in a van with their picture plastered on the side, the public may decide to vote for them. I would love to see some research on how effective this strategy really is. They must think it works, because they all do it. It is insanely loud and annoying. This kind of thing would never fly in the U.S., as people would scream noise pollution and call the cops within five minutes. Japanese people, though, seem to accept it as an inevitable aspect of the political campaigns.

In addition to the noisy campaigning, they also make obnoxiously loud speeches in front of train stations, and stand in random places waving at passersby trying to garner a few extra votes. I will never forget one guy whose campaigning strategies really made me laugh.

---

[4] Retrieved April 12, 2013 from http://en.wikipedia.org/wiki/List_of_Prime_Ministers_of_Japan

It was local election time, and this guy seemed to really want to win. He often stood alone on the corner of a busy intersection waving and holding this huge caricature drawing of his face. It was comical. Another time, his staff was circling around the intersection on bicycles draped in banners with this candidate's name written on it. The candidate was also circling, but attached to his bike was this huge flag that said *"honnin,"* which translated means, "It's me. I am the guy." Cracked me up so bad that I started laughing out loud.

I wonder if the Japanese apathy towards politics will continue as the economic recession shows little sign of abating. I wonder if they will ever stand up and complain about the noise. Who knows? Maybe it doesn't even bother them. Maybe they have learned to tune it out better than the foreign population has. Maybe it is all they have ever known, so if they ever went to the U.S. they would marvel at the silence...

#59 The Westernizing of Japan

Japan is an island nation, and was closed mostly to the outside world until 1868 when Commodore Perry sailed into Tokyo Bay, an event that ushered in the Meiji Restoration and opening Japan to the outside world. From that point on, Japan has been devouring anything Western at an amazing rate. In only 150 years, Western things, from clothing to food to music to movies, have come to dominate Japanese culture. In addition, you will find it almost impossible to have a conversation in Japanese void of loanwords borrowed from Western languages.

While I say "Western," it is much more honest to say that Japan is obsessed with America. Young people love Hollywood movies, hamburgers, Coke, hip hop, and blue jeans. Many Japanese naively assume that any white person is American, much to the chagrin and annoyance of my Canadian and British friends. While the adaptation of things Western, in particular the Western diet, is not always a good thing, I am more worried about the Americanization of Japanese things.

For example, sushi. Most sushi purists view sushi as a dish in which raw fish is served on top of white rice. America, like all countries seeking to change an ethnic dish to make it friendly to their own palettes, has decided that sushi is rice and pretty much anything. Thus came the advent of California rolls, spicy tuna tempura rolls (apparently frying fish and covering it in sauce and breading kills the fishy taste), and pretty much any other Western-friendly food on rice you can think of. Although sushi purists are horrified, recently, cheap Japanese sushi restaurants have begun to serve hot dog sushi, hamburger sushi, and deep-fried pork cutlet sushi. In addition, they will put just about any sauce imaginable on top, from mayonnaise to ketchup to teriyaki sauce. The idea of meat-based sushi used to be unheard of here. Of course, Japanese kids, who are being exposed now more than ever to Western food, love this kind of sushi, so why not keep selling it if it is profitable? Many of my university students even confess to liking Western food more than Japanese food.

In addition to food, the language is also becoming Westernized. While it is inevitable that a language must borrow words for which there is no native equivalent (in particular technology terms), Japanese has even been borrowing words when there is already a perfectly good Japanese word. For example, *ringo juusu* has become *appuru juusu* (apple juice), and *yoyaku* has become *apo* (appointment). Japanese words for colors are routinely replaced by English equivalents, as are words for fruits, vegetables, and clothing.

Even the traditional Japanese calendar, which marks time not by the western calendar but by the reign of the emperor is slowly changing. Up until now, most government offices and official documents would ask people to write the year based on the reign of the emperor. For example, it is now the 25th year of the Heisei period (meaning the current emperor has been on the throne 25 years), and my oldest daughter was born in Heisei 17. Recently, however, many forms have been asking for the date according to the Western calendar. My university is still very traditional and uses the Heisei terminology for all official documents, but the local city office will sometimes use the western calendar. It can be a little confusing using both, and sometimes I feel Japan is a country caught in the middle, trying to preserve traditional culture yet be relevant in today's increasingly globalized society.

So, is all this bad? Good? Or just inevitable? Personally, it makes me kind of sad, especially the direction that the language is going. I love the Japanese language, and I think that when spoken correctly, it is one of the most beautiful, poetic languages in the world. There is absolutely no value in replacing a native word with an English word. I think people do it just to sound cool or sophisticated. While hamburger sushi is helpful when my very American mother visits, part of me thinks that if I want to eat a hamburger I can go to McDonalds. Although I don't really like sushi, I can get by on traditional non-fish sushi like cucumber rolls or egg sushi.

Taking in the food culture and entertainment culture of other countries is the bi-product of globalization and inevitable in today's world. Currently, American pop culture is dominating the world, and that culture is what most young Japanese long for. I just hope that Japan is able to preserve the part of their culture that makes it so special, and that makes it a popular tourist destination for people all over the world. I am going to be totally worried if I ever see a girl wearing a kimono and blue jeans. Drinking a coke. While eating hot dog sushi. I hope I never see that.

#60 Say Cheese

My husband, Riz, is a very talented photographer. Maybe I am a little biased because he is my Honey and I love him, but he really is a great photographer, almost entirely self taught, and I couldn't be more proud of him. Because I recognize his high skill level, and ability to take photos that many Japanese photographers don't even dream of (again, maybe I am biased), it pains me to see him struggle to get his potential clients to see that he is worth what he is charging. I think he is worth way more than he is charging, but at this point, because the Japanese don't value photography as much as those in the West, it is impractical for him to seek what he is actually worth.

Why are the Japanese just not that into pictures? I mean, if you think about it, what is one of the biggest stereotypes about the Japanese promulgated by the American media and Hollywood movies? That's right—it's the Japanese tourist with the camera hung around his neck. We always thought this meant the Japanese love pictures, and to some extent they do, but there are a couple reasons they are not into hiring professional photographers.

First, they are by nature a shy and humble people. I know, I know. This is a blatant stereotype and I am perpetuating it, but it is true when it comes to photographs, especially compared to the showy, outgoing American persona (I know. Another stereotype.) The Japanese, being more reserved, are not used to decorating their desks, tables, walls, and every other empty space known to man with photographs like their more showy American counterparts. While I have pictures of my family and students everywhere you look in my office, none of my Japanese colleagues do; I have never seen a Japanese worker with a family picture on his desk. Maybe it is the cultural expectation to separate work and family here. Work is work, and family is family, and never the twain shall meet. That is why families are rarely invited to company parties or events. It is seen as prideful here to show off pictures of your wife and children, and usually, they will only show you a picture when asked. In fact, even when you visit a home, it is unusual to see many family pictures anywhere. Occasionally there will be a picture of an important life event, for example Mommy and Daddy with their son at the school entrance ceremony, but mostly the walls are bare. I just recently saw a wedding picture on display at a friend's house. That was the first time I ever saw that.

However, photo studios are everywhere here, so what do they do with all those pictures? Well, from my experience, they put them in albums on a shelf, or in a small cardboard case called a *daishi* in their kitchen drawer. When people come over for a party or dinner and ask to see them, they will bring the photos out, but they are way too embarrassed to keep them out on display all the time for anyone from the insurance guy to their kid's first grade teacher to see.

So what about these photo studios? These places offer cookie cutter poses, and cookie cutter pictures. The prices are exorbitant—between 30 and 60 dollars for one 5x7 or 8x10 picture--and they do not do any photo editing or provide the data to the customers. So why do Japanese people pay through the nose for something like this, but balk when my husband gives his much more reasonable prices for way more services? Well, I think it is a couple of things. First of all, photo studios are familiar. They are all most Japanese have ever known, and they are predictable. They know the prices are crazy, but since they so rarely venture to the studio for professional shots, they don't mind paying an arm and a leg on occasion. Also, these photo studios do everything for the client--from the makeup to providing the clothing and props--so the customer does not have to think of or plan anything. It is simple, and they can be in and out in an hour or two.

The lack or originality that is found in the posing and props goes along with the Japanese tendency to not want to stick out. Most people take the same kind of picture in the same pose with the same cheesy flowers or throne-looking chair in the background. Once, before my husband had much confidence, we took our girls to a photo studio. They kept trying to put these garish flowers and an over-the-top chair in the picture. I just wanted a simple while rug with a simple background and no chair, so I asked them to please remove the props. They looked at me like I was crazy, "Why?" they asked. I was blunt, maybe too blunt, but oh well. I am my mother's daughter. I simply stated, "Because I don't like them." Okay. Maybe that was a little impolite, but I could tell from her reaction that not many Japanese customers make requests about the props and backgrounds.

Japanese are also not used to lifestyle photography, which is the trend now in the U.S. Unlike in studio photography, the lifestyle photographer goes with the clients to the location or locations of their choice and spends a couple hours photographing them in a natural, casual environment. This is very rare in Japan, and because of the time required for actually going with the couple and for editing, Riz charges an initial shooting fee in addition to the photo packages which include albums, wall canvases, slideshows and data. Because at studios there is only one flat fee (be it outrageous) for the photos, initially his shooting fee seems expensive to them. They do not have the experience with lifestyle photography to know that, unlike studios, he spends hours and hours editing the pictures and designing the album templates. However, I can tell you that, without exception so far, every one of his clients has been 100% satisfied with his work. While they may hesitate or balk upon hearing the initial fees, they are always satisfied by what they get for it, which is an album or slideshow design that they have never seen before in Japan. One client who started out wanting not to spend much money at all ended up joyfully paying four times what she had originally budgeted, and even paid to bring him to Guam for her location wedding.

The earthquake and tsunami of 2011 helped people to realize more than ever the value of photography, and recently, Japanese people have started to gain more interest in preserving memories better through pictures. I mean, if you think about it, what is the only thing that remains after a wedding? The presents all break after time. The flowers wilt. The food is eaten. The wedding dress becomes too small to even think about getting into after kids. The pictures are the only things that remain unchanged, the only things that don't fade or break after time. Why would you spend more money on flowers which will only wilt, than on pictures, which will last a lifetime?

I am so glad that Riz is doing what he can to impart the value of photography to the Japanese people. After all, no matter where you live or what language you speak, everyone loves their families and friends and wants to remember the good times with them. It is also pretty cool that I have a live-in photographer to document our own family through the years. My kids are so used to posing for him that they could instantly become professional models. I used to get annoyed with him for taking his camera everywhere—the park, the supermarket, the library—but not anymore. It is those everyday shots, not the big occasions, that make the best memories for me. Okay, maybe he does overdo it a little. I mean, how many shots of my daughter going down the same slide do we really need? That being said, I would rather have way too many pictures than way too few any day. So, what I really want to say is, "Keep shooting, Honey! I am so proud of you."

#61 Crazy Rock Climbing Mama

My friends here must look at me and think I am crazy. I am a full-time working mom like many of my friends, but unlike them, I also do a lot of crazy things in my free time. Like leaving my kids with my husband for three days to climb Mt. Fuji with my brother in 2010. Or like going with a church friend up to northern Japan to volunteer after the earthquake and tsunami. I love my kids, and my husband, but I also have an identity that I don't want to lose. There is no reason that I cannot continue to do the same things after having kids that I did before having them. Of course, I realize that there are sacrifices to be made, and there are times when I have to sacrifice my desires for the sake of my family, and I will do that joyfully. But I don't want to sacrifice everything I did and who I was before kids for the sake of my new role as a mother, and it makes me sad when I see women here who do.

Of course, I have a huge advantage that many of my friends don't: an incredibly supportive and helpful husband with a flexible work schedule. His support and encouragement make it possible for me to continue to do things that I love. I don't have many friends who have ever left their kids with their husband in order to go somewhere on their own or with a friend; I have done it several times. Sometimes I wonder if it is that their husbands don't want to take care of the kids, or if they don't trust their husbands to take care of them. Moms are so used to taking care of the kids alone, and the fathers have so little experience, the moms seem to like to keep control and are afraid to leave their kids with their inexperienced husbands. I trust my husband 100%. He is a great father, and I have no doubt that he can take care of them. He may feed them weird stuff like popcorn for breakfast (he did this just last week!), and dress them funny, but they will be alive at the end of the day. That is enough for me. A couple of months ago, one of my good friends had her second child, and her husband took care of their 3-year old for about a week while she was hospitalized. It was so cute to see her one morning with her hair sticking up and food all over her face. She was alive and she was happy, though. That is good enough.

I want to do all kinds of crazy things. I want to learn boxing. No sissy exercises like walking and swimming for me! I want to go bouldering every now and then at the local rock climbing wall. I finally found a mommy friend, Yoshiko, who would try it with me and she loved it! It took me 10 years, but I finally found one. I love carrying around my kids in my hiking backpack (although the last one is almost too big now) and carrying them on my shoulders, neither of which I have ever seen a Japanese mother do. I wonder if it is because they don't have the strength, or because that is just not something Japanese mommies do here.

Of course, there are a lot of things I do differently that I am not too proud of. I am a terrible cook, and feed my kids Costco hotdogs a little too often. I am often jealous of my mommy friends, not only for their cooking ability, but their love of it as well. I just cannot find the enthusiasm or excitement for it. They also selflessly sacrifice their time and energy every day to ferry their kids around to this activity after that, and then come home and prepare a delicious dinner even though they are exhausted. Japanese moms give and give to their kids. Sometimes, I feel very selfish with my time, telling my kids no when I know I should be saying yes. Some of my friends can make their kids' clothes, and I can only sew on a button. But you know what? My kids don't care at all about that. In fact, they are probably so impressed by my button-sewing ability that they make sure to tell all their friends and teachers about it.

The moral of the story is, be who you are, and don't apologize for it. While I will never fit into the mold of the Japanese mommy, I still have great respect for my friends who do. They are doing what they feel they should, and that is okay. I secretly wish, though, that one day they would do something crazy and out of the ordinary with me. Come on, Moms! Skip bath time tonight! The kids don't smell THAT bad. Leave the kids with Daddy or Grandma and come rock climbing with me!

#62 Excuse Me, Your Onion is Falling Out...

99% of the time, the Japanese are the kindest, most polite, self-sacrificing people in the world. They will go out of their way to help you, treat you better than they treat themselves, and even give you the shirt off their back if you ask for it. That remaining 1% percent, though, oh boy. You better watch out. I have found that on any occasion involving a sale, discount, or any other event that will lead these frugal people to save money, they can be cutthroat and downright violent. So, I will use two events at my local supermarket to illustrate my point.

The third Saturday of every month is all-the-fruit-and-veggies-you-can-stuff-into-a-bag day. A huge array of healthy goodies is stocked in the entranceway of the supermarket, and customers can fill up a pretty good sized plastic bag with whatever they want for 200 yen. The supermarket opens at 9:30, but radical savers start lining up at 8:45, getting all the vegetables into their carts ready to rush right in to pay when the store opens. All the best stuff is gone by the time the store opens, and by 10:00, almost everything is gone except for a few stray peanuts and puny oranges.

I am trying to save some money on food these days, but not to the point of risking not only my health but my sanity. It is like a battle zone in there, and being a country girl, I absolutely hate crowds. It has gotten worse over the years, and now when

I go to Costco on Sundays I feel like I am going to suffocate (Don't go to Costco on Sundays, Anne. Duh). My hatred of crowds reached its tipping point about five years ago, when I went to a fireworks festival in my city and for the first time, understood how people could get trampled to death at a soccer game. I have avoided crowds like the plague since then, so I think I will just pay a little more for my veggies, thank you very much.

But the helpfulness of Japanese people won't let you sometimes. Once, before this once-a-month extravaganza got so popular, I had filled my bag and was happily off to the register. This lady, maybe 70 years old or so, stopped me. She said, "No! No No! What are you doing? You can get SOOO much more into your bag than that!" She proceeded to grab my bag from me, rearrange the contents (apparently the key is in standing up the carrots and filling in the gaps with peanuts), and put approximately 40% more veggies into my bag. I thanked her, wondering how long she must have thought about it to come up with a strategy like that. As long as the contents are not falling out it is allowed, so most people balance their overflowing bags until they get to the register.

The other place in the supermarket where your life is put at risk is the pre-made *bento* and sushi section. At around 7 pm every evening, everything goes half price. I have a friend on the inside, a *bento* maker, who usually will give me inside information as to when the *bentos* will go half price. At times when work is really busy (or I just don't feel like cooking, which is like, everyday), these half-price *bentos* are crucial to our health and budget, so this insider info really comes in handy. Customers here, too, put what they want into their carts and wait for the employees to come out and slap that wonderful half-price sticker on. The sushi and sashimi area is particularly dangerous, as that normally expensive splurge becomes reasonable for any family after seven p.m. Enter there at your own risk.

These two areas become virtually impassable as frugal retirees battle it out with poor graduate students for the best stuff. It is almost as bad as the meat section at Costco when there are free samples on Sundays. This is the one time when the normally polite Japanese lose all civility in the quest to save a couple hundred yen. I heard someone say once that the reason Japanese can be so rough sometimes, pushing others around to get on the train and bargains at the shopping mall, is because they don't know you. You are in the outer circle, or the *soto*. They would never act like that once they got to know you.

So, anyway, these days I have been cooking more and avoiding the half-price *bentos* as much as possible. As for the once-a-month fill your bag veggie event, I thought about entering the fray today, but just for a minute. I gave up and asked Riz to take a picture instead. That was much more fun. And safer. Although Riz did get a few suspicious glances and one lady wanted to know who this crazy foreigner taking a picture of her veggies was. Maybe it is not all that much safer after all...

#63 Please Don't Call on Me

This past Saturday, we participated in a class observation day at my oldest daughter's elementary school. Parents are invited to come and see what is going on at school, checking out stuff like what the teacher is like, the classroom atmosphere, their own child's interaction with other students, class content, etc. One thing that really struck me was the exuberance of the students, especially when it came to volunteering for things.

I teach in a university, and let tell you one of the first things I learned after coming here: Japanese university students very rarely volunteer in class. I learned early on that if I just asked a generic question to the class, I would not get an answer like I would if I were teaching in America. Volunteering in class is common not only in U.S. universities, but also among international students from certain outgoing countries (Saudi Arabia, Mexico, etc.). My students who study in the States all tell me how shocked and intimidated they are when they see their fellow classmates volunteering like crazy. They are both impressed by their classmates, and terrified that the same may be expected of them. Despite having the same English level as their talkative classmates (as evidenced by placement test results), these students are convinced that everybody in the class speaks English better than they do.

Many Japanese students are shy and have a debilitating fear of failure, which leads many of them to sit in silence in classes not only in Japan, but overseas as well. But without fail, every one of my students who studies abroad, even if for only a month, comes back not only a better English speaker but way more confident and way more eager to talk in class. I couldn't be prouder of these guys. However, the majority of students who don't study abroad are much more comfortable with silence.

I wonder when this tight-lipped phenomenon begins. It is certainly not that way in preschool and elementary school, when kids are tripping over themselves trying to get called on by the teacher. When I watched my daughter's class, at least half the students would raise their hands for each question, hoping to get called on by the teacher. Of course, there are always shy students at any age who try to avoid eye contact at all costs, knowing that eye contact with the teacher almost inevitably leads to being called on. University students have perfected the art of avoiding eye contact. Of course, that doesn't work at all in my classes, as I call on them anyway.

Although it was more than 10 years ago, I still remember the terrible feeling I had after my first class teaching in university. I felt like I was the worst teacher ever. None of my jokes got a laugh; none of my games seemed to be any fun; and none of my questions were answered. Now, ten years later and ten times wiser, I have learned that I am not the worst teacher in the world, and that my students actually like me. The key to having success in Japan is group work, and encouraging students to answer questions even if they don't want to. I don't really ask for volunteers that much anymore. Well, to be honest, I do sometimes. Part of my idealistic self is still hoping against hope that maybe this year is different, maybe I will have some students who will break the mold and volunteer. And, you know what? Sometimes I do. It is rare, but sometimes I do get a student or two who will volunteer answers without being called on. And those students always make me just a little happier that day.

Every year I teach my students that in English class, you cannot be passive. As much as you may dislike English, you have to talk, and you have to participate. If they were to ever go abroad, they would be shocked like countless exchange students before them by the level of participation in classes by students from other countries. I figure it is part of my job not only to teach language, but also culture, and part of learning culture is learning to be active. After my first class of getting blank stares for every question I asked, I learned to teach all my classes that it is extremely rude to not answer a direct question, even if it is one given collectively to a class. I told them, "You have to give some kind of response. A nod yes, a shake of the head no, a verbal yes, a verbal no. Anything. You cannot tilt your head to the right and say nothing."

Of course, they are not meaning to be rude. In fact, my students are wonderful kids with vibrant personalities. It is just that in Japanese, when someone asks if they understand, it is more of a rhetorical question; the speaker is not really expecting a response. Most Japanese classes are lecture-style, and the students are supposed to listen and be quiet, just taking in the teacher's infinite knowledge. Well, I do not have infinite knowledge, and I don't want a class of quiet students. I would much rather teach loud, and even boisterous (not obnoxious, though; have little patience for them) students over passive students any day. And another thing. I do not have infinite knowledge. Although many in Japan may think that teachers know everything, I don't. I make mistakes. I sometimes get a question for which I do not know the answer, and that is okay. I tell them I will look into it and get back to them. Maybe if my students see that I am human and approachable, it will break down the wall between teachers and students so prevalent in Japan, and maybe, just maybe, they will feel more comfortable talking in my class.

So, if elementary students are crazy about participating in class, and university students hate it, something must happen in junior high and high school to suck the adventurous spirit right out of students. I am not an education expert, but I would guess it is the shift to rote learning, test preparation and cram schools that are so much a part of life during those years. I wonder, looking at my daughter who is already a little shy, what she will be like when she gets to university. If I have anything to do with it, she will be a confident, bold learner not afraid to make mistakes. If I have anything to do with it, my students will be, too, after a year of relentless questioning from me. There is nowhere for them to hide since I am so good at remembering names…

#64 Did You Know.....

Today I was thinking about what to write about and a bunch of random thoughts popped into my head, so today is a day for random Japanese trivia. Here goes. Did you know...

•Japanese people don't eat the apple peels and grape skins. As for grapes, they have refined the art of putting it into their mouths, sucking out the grape, and gracefully spitting out the skin and seeds into a bowl.

•They never pick up a hamburger and eat it; it always stays in the wrapper to keep their fingers from getting dirty.

•At parties, they will open a bag of chips in the middle instead of at the top for easier group access.

- In Japan, you always must take a sip of your drink after the toast before setting it down.

- There are house slippers and toilet slippers. Many a foreigner has embarrassed himself by wearing the toilet slippers out into the living room. Neither are to be worn on straw tatami mats.

- There is a correct stroke order for writing kanji (Chinese characters) but these days young people don't really follow it. I do, though. Looks prettier.

- It's okay for girls to wear shorts in winter (fashion), but wearing a short-sleeved shirt is unacceptable (crazy).

- They get on and off a bike differently than I do. But I can't explain how.

- Never call yourself *-san*. For example, Anne-*san*. This is a term of respect reserved for other people.

- Despite the stereotypes, most Japanese don't know karate, and eating sushi is a luxury.

- I have never seen a Japanese steakhouse in Japan.

- Or a California roll.

- My feet are too big (U.S. size 9) to buy shoes in regular sizes.

- Japanese decide everything from where to eat to who gets to take a university class using rock-paper-scissors.

- Dyslexia is virtually unknown here due to to writing system.

- Stomach cancer is much more common than colon cancer.

- Eating raw horse is a delicacy, but a raw carrot is barbaric.

- Girls shoot with two hands in basketball.

- You can buy beer, batteries and eggs in vending machines.

- They call Baskin-Robbins "31," and Kentucky Fried Chicken "Kentucky."

- Kids (oh, okay, I do too) eat seaweed like American kids eat chips.

- There is a sports drink called *Pocari Sweat*, a car named *Naked*, and a drink called *Pungency*.

- Most regular workers get twice a year bonuses amounting to two months salary.

- They count starting with their thumb, whereas we start with our forefinger.

- The Japanese gesture for "Come here" means "Go away" in America.

- Some people even bow when talking on the phone.

- Parking tickets will cost you between $100 and $200.

- Speeding tickets even more than that.

- Many Japanese have flaky white earwax, not the yellow sticky stuff I have.

- Most Japanese moms adhere to attachment parenting, sleeping with their kids at night and nursing on demand.

- Blowing your nose in public is rude.

- So is walking with your hands in your pocket.

- And eating on the train or while walking.

- PDA is very taboo.

That's all for now. Now you are a little smarter.

#65 Love Shack

You can spot them in an instant. The loud, colorful facades. The windowless exterior. The cheesy names like "Hotel Harmony" or "Apple Hotel." The hidden entrances. Yes, the love hotel is one of the most secretive things in Japan that everyone knows about. As you might have guessed, a love hotel is one of those by-the-hour kind of hotels, where people don't go for the continentals breakfasts...

In the U.S. these pay-by-the-hour hotels are notoriously seedy, and no self-respecting person would go to one. They are most commonly frequented by prostitutes, drug dealers, or husbands cheating on their wives (or vice versa). Not so in Japan. While, of course, they are frequented by people for not-so-ethical behavior, they are also used by husbands and wives trying to enjoy both a little privacy and a little space, cramped by living daily with three kids in four rooms. Some of my very respectable friends tell me that they have visited a love hotel from time to time to just get away from the crowded house. They are usually very clean and spacious (so I have heard. I have never been. Really). They also have the reputation for having top-of-the-line karaoke systems and hot tubs.

Although I have never been to one, I hear you drive in through a secluded entrance and park in a lot where no roaming eye will be able to see your car. Then you can pay for your room by purchasing your ticket from a machine, or paying a faceless employee through a blinded window, an employee who you will never see and will never see you. Privacy and remaining anonymous are the keys here, and most of the time patrons will never encounter another human during their stay.

Korea has love hotels, too, as we unfortunately found out unwittingly last summer. We had a layover in Seoul on our way back home, and we forgot to book a hotel until the last minute. So, Riz searched online for a hotel, and there was a nice enough looking one close to the airport for a reasonable price. We learned soon after checking in that it was not the kind of family-friendly hotel that we had expected. For starters, there were certain toiletry items not normally included in the room amenities, if you catch my drift. There were crazy red and green lights over the bed and mirrors on the ceiling surrounded with what looked like popped balloons. The hot tub was heart-shaped, and my pure and naive kids thought this was the coolest thing ever. The soap in the shower was used, and there was hairspray and other weird stuff on the dresser. To top it off, the floor felt greasy and yucky.

The worst part of the experience came when my kids turned on the TV looking for the Disney Channel. Umm. That is not what we found...Note to self. Don't let your kids touch the remote control next time you find yourself in a love hotel in Korea. Another note to self. Don't let Riz book a hotel again. To be fair to him, I looked at the website, too, and it was a pretty harmless looking hotel. The only good part of the experience was the free ice cream, popcorn and water in the lobby.

So, the moral of the story is, if you ever come to Japan or go to Korea, look for a hotel named "Marriott" or "Hilton" or, if you are financially challenged, "Comfort Inn." Definitely avoid one with no windows and with a fruit in the name...

#66 Slipper-y Slope

I know it seems like I write about toilets a lot, but, hey, Japan just gives me so much good material! The other day I had an epiphany about toilet slippers, and I just couldn't resist writing about it.

Most people know that in Japan, people remove their shoes before entering a house. If you think about it, this is a pretty good idea, as your shoes are filthy and being barefoot is much more comfortable anyway. Of course, one must pay extra attention to foot odor and the presence of holes in the socks, which I have heard is considered bad manners here.

Most people will provide slippers for guests who enter their homes, although we don't. I have a fundamental dislike of slippers. They are usually too small or too slippery, and I am just a barefoot kind of girl. In the summer, my kids and I usually go barefoot outside in our yard or in the park. I love the feel of the grass between my toes in summer. Japanese people don't go barefoot nearly as much as we do, probably because when they go home, going inside with dirty feet is just as bad as wearing shoes. Sometimes people are shocked by our bare feet. The other day in the park this kid said, "Hey. There is a foreigner. And, what's more, she is barefoot." Love it.

Some buildings require you to take your shoes off and wear slippers and others don't. In some bathrooms you have to take your shoes off and change into toilet slippers, and in others you don't. There is really no rhyme or reason as far as I can tell; seems like it just depends of what the owner of the place wants. Toilet slippers seem even smaller than house slippers...

Anyway, the other day we were at this really nice community center and it had a clean, modern bathroom. We went with the neighborhood kids' association, and after a long morning outside strawberry picking and playing in the park, everyone went inside to use the bathroom and wash their hands before having lunch. There was a long line, which I figured was because there were so many of us. We had to all take our shoes off about twenty yards before the bathroom. It is a little strange that in such a modern bathroom people are required to take off their shoes; it is much more common in older bathrooms with concrete floors.

When it was my turn and I went inside, I realized there were about 20 stalls, but that they were not being used; people were still in line. Then it hit me. Although there were 20 stalls, there were only five pairs of slippers, and there was no way a Japanese person was going to enter the bathroom with no slippers on. Even though the toilet was modern and the floor was clean, it was unthinkable for them to use a toilet without slippers. I guess I can see the point; maybe it is a little gross to walk around the toilet in your socks and bare feet, but it was a Western bathroom with no squatty potties. Now, even I would not think about using a squatty potty without slippers; the possibility of errant pee is too high. But I might have entered a nice clean bathroom in my bare feet. But this is one of those times in Japan you have to think not only about what bothers you, but what effect it may have on others around you. If I had used the toilet without slippers, it would have horrified those around me, and maybe mentally scarred them for life. So, in cases like this, even though it wouldn't bother me, it would bother others, so I do as the Japanese do.

I wonder why that community center doesn't provide more slippers. At any given time, there are 15 stalls not in use. Seems kind of wasteful to me. Better yet, they could let people wear their shoes inside. I wonder which option Japanese people would prefer. To me, taking off my shoes is a pain in the neck, but maybe they don't want to soil their shoes with bathroom germs.

It is amazing I have lived here for thirteen years, and this is the first time I have thought about this. Learning how to live in another culture is definitely a lifelong endeavor.

#67 Hee Hee Hee

Welcome to Japan, the land of the laughing! While you may have a stereotype of the Japanese as a serious, hardworking people, they are actually some of the giggliest, most laughing people I have ever met. The only difference, is, they laugh at weird times. At least, that's what I think.

Yesterday my husband and I were walking on campus and we saw two female students with their backs turned to us. When I recognized one of them, I waved and said 'hi,' and both of them immediately broke out in laughter. I am pretty sure that saying 'hi' isn't all that funny, and I wasn't dressed like a clown (although I was wearing flip flops in April. Maybe that was it). Riz and I started wondering why Japanese people always laugh when they see us. It can kind of give you a complex if you don't understand this place. This kind of laugh can be termed the embarrassed/shy laugh as far as I understand it. But I don't really understand it, so that is my best guess. When they are shy or don't really know what to do, they laugh. Like, "Oh, I am sick and have to be hospitalized." "Oh really. Hee Hee. That's too bad. Hee Hee."

I know all people, even Americans at times, give a nervous laugh when they are uncomfortable and don't know what to say. I am sure everyone has been horrified at laughing nervously upon hearing of a tragedy or death or something, but the Japanese seem to do it more often than most. I know that death or tragedy, or on a lighter note, seeing their English teacher in flip flops isn't really a funny thing, but laughing is just a human response sometimes to cover up nervousness or discomfort.

While we are on the topic of humor, I must admit that I don't get Japanese humor at all. Many Japanese comedians have weird English names that don't make any sense at all, and the jokes don't even seem funny to me. There is this one guy, Hard Gay (yes, that is really his stage name) who dresses in tight, black leather and acts gay even though he isn't. Here, a straight guy acting gay is funny. Now, mind you, he is not making fun of gay people; this Hard Gay guy is really trying to mimic gay behavior, fashion and talk, all while not making fun of it at all. My male students sometimes act gay for a laugh, and two guys even kissed in class once during a role play activity. In Japan, slapstick comedy is king.

I have never liked slapstick comedy. I was never a big fan of Naked Gun, Police Academy, and the mother of all slapstick comedy, Monty Python. I prefer witty, creative humor like improv, and while I hate it when people are sarcastic to me, sarcasm in comedy is great. Sarcasm is virtually unheard of in Japan. It is amazing to this American that an entire culture can interact with each other on a daily basis without a hint of sarcasm. There doesn't even seem to be the equivalent of 'duh' here. It's too bad.

Acting stupid and outrageous seems to be the key to humor here--doing stuff that a normally reserved Japanese person wouldn't do. They like to make fun of themselves, too, particularly their poor English ability. I admit that I have seen some funny Japanese skits on this topic, and those crack me up.

Many Japanese, especially women, laugh in a very quaint and respectful manner, often covering their mouths in humility. It is really rare to see a Japanese person give a rip roaring, knee-slapping laugh. I have one friend here who laughs like that and I love her. In fact, it is both so unusual and so appealing that her laugh is one of the first things people mention when talking about her. Most laughs are of the hee hee hee variety. I really love a Japanese who can put off the restraint for a while and give a good guffaw. Young people are changing and losing some of the restraint of the older generations, causing them to really give some rip roaring laughs at times. Maybe the freedom to really laugh is one of the more subtle ways that young people are changing in Japan.

#68 On the Radar

Recently in the U.S., gay marriage has been a hot button topic. Since President Obama came out (no pun intended) in support of gay marriage last year, it has been moving higher and higher up the political agenda, and more and more politicians, actors and public figures have come out in support of it. In addition, the public support for gay marriage has dramatically increased in recent years. Just yesterday, Jason Collins came out of the closet as the first openly gay active athlete in American professional sports. Everybody and their brother seems to have something to say about it on Facebook, and tolerance is the word of the day, unless you are opposed to gay marriage, in which case you are not tolerated.

When I was a kid, say 30 years ago or so, this was not even a blip on the radar. Being gay was still taboo, and most people tried to hide the fact. The hot topics back then were abortion and nuclear weapons. It seems these days that neither of these things is talked about all that much anymore. These days, most of the media attention is on the economy, the war on terrorism, and the fight to legalize gay marriage.

Being an evangelical Christian, I don't think the gay lifestyle is what God has intended for humanity. If you don't agree with me, that is fine. But let me have my opinion, please. I am not an intolerant bigot. I do not hate gay people. I love them and respect them as God does, and I condemn Westboro

Baptist Church and any like them who preach the un-Christian message of hate. I have gay friends and their sexuality does not influence in the least how I treat them or love them. But honestly, I get irritated by the double standard that is our country's view on this issue. You can believe what you want as long as you support the gay lifestyle. Just yesterday, pro athletes like Kobe Bryant and Steve Nash were tweeting support for Collins' courageous behavior, while ESPN analyst Chris Broussard was lambasted for calling homosexual behavior "open rebellion against God" in response to someone asking him his opinion on the issue. I can't understand why he gets condemned for staying true to his beliefs after someone asked him a question.

In Japan, the issue of gay rights is not even on the radar. It is never talked about. I have never once in thirteen years here heard any conversation about gay marriage. The only time you ever hear homosexuality talked about is on variety shows, and by comedians. Gays are parodied, but with no malice whatsoever. From what I can tell from personal conversations, most people accept homosexual behavior as natural, and don't have any negative opinions about it. There is most definitely not the polarization that you find in the U.S. on this issue, or any other issue involving morality for that matter. Abortion is both legal and socially accepted, and abortions are performed here in regular maternity hospitals that also deliver babies. While many individuals feel something is not right about it and would not choose to have an abortion on their own, they seldom condemn those who do.

Being a non-religious society probably has a lot to do with the acceptance of most kinds of lifestyles here. When I say acceptance, let me clarify that most people don't have a moral problem with homosexuality or abortion, but both seem to still be shameful enough for people to feel compelled to hide it from those around them. Many gays stay in the closet here, and many people hide the fact that they have had an abortion. In a culture that values conformity, any differences in behavior, even if morally acceptable, are shunned. Seems like a contradiction, doesn't it?

I don't know if gay marriage will ever be on the radar here. Being a semi-socialistic state, many benefits are tied to one's marital status. Legalizing gay marriage would drastically alter the social welfare landscape here. And despite the moral acceptance of this behavior and the belief of many Japanese that gays are born that way, it is still a traditional society with a very traditional views of marriage and family.

And what are the hot button topics in Japan? Right now, exciting stuff, really. The consumption tax being raised from 5% to 10% has society up in arms. The horrible behavior of American servicemen stationed in Okinawa, fear of crazy North Korean leaders and their missiles, and the 20-year recession are at the forefront of everyone's minds here. The only moral issues that ever come up are the huge bullying problem in public schools, and the increase in cheating on college entrance exams. It fascinates me how defining issues in some cultures aren't even on the radar in others.

Well, anyway that's my take on this issue. I gotta go now check the news and see if that ESPN guy has gotten fired yet...

*ESPN issued a 'tepid' apology (meaning, we will apologize but we don't really mean it) for Chris Broussard's comments, and the controversy blew away. Surprisingly, he kept his job.[5]

#69 Japanese English Quiz

How well do you know Japanese English? Look at the following words and see if you can figure out the authentic English equivalent. (answers in the back of the book on pages 372-373). Here is an example:

ex. baby car (Japanese English) = stroller (English)

1. ending note

2. running machine

---

[5] http://www.sportsbusinessdaily.com/Daily/Issues/2013/04/30/Media/Collins-media.aspx

3. cunning

4. doctor stop

5. idling stop

6. soft cream

7. short cut

8. cooler box

9. best ten

10. ice candy

11. salaryman

12. mother bag

13. child seat

14. skinship

15. nighter

16. silver seat

17. one piece

18. trainer

19. don't mind

20. blind touch

#70 Country Girl

When I first found out that I was moving to the city of Kitakyushu, I didn't really know much about it except that it was the sister city of my city of Norfolk, VA. When I was in graduate school there at Old Dominion University, I met a lot of international students studying short-term from Kitakyushu. After getting hired at my current job, I contacted one of my friends and asked her what kind of place I was going to be working at. She wasn't familiar with my university because it was new; it had only been built three years before. She went to check it out, and the next time I talked to her, she said, "Oh my goodness! It is soooo country!!" Now, being from the country myself, I have a a very clear idea of what the word "country" means. It means cows, pigs, and lots of grass. Lots of grass. And no stores or restaurants except a diner or a 7-11.

So, when I came to Kitakyushu in March 2003, imagine my surprise at seeing that it wasn't at all what I had imagined. There was a post office nearby, a bank, supermarkets, and even a huge university hospital. Just a twenty-minute train ride away was the hub of the city bustling with activity, and 40 minutes away is Fukuoka city, the biggest city in Kyushu with five million people.

And, by the way, how can you call a city of one million people like Kitakyushu country anyway? Sure, it is such a big place that some stretches of it can be considered country, but it is nothing like the image of country that I have as an American. Then it hit me. In Japan, a place must be country if there is no train station within walking distance. Because my university was a 20-minute bus ride from the closest train station, and therefore, civilization, it must be country!

To be fair, it was a lot more remote in 2003 than it is now. There was no Costco right around the corner, the closest supermarket was a 20-minute walk away, and there were few clinics, drug stores or much of anything else. But there were definitely no cows in sight.

However, the other day when I was biking to the beach, which is about a 30-minute ride away, as soon as I crested a certain hill, there it was in front a me: a swath of land so green and deserted that it would be called country even by American standards. I realized that just five-minutes away from my school, even though my school is surrounded by busting activity, is the the country. And then I saw a pig inside a fence by the road, and this realization was again confirmed. Yep. I live in the country. It may be hiding behind Costco and a new bank, but the country is still there right under the surface. And the train station is still 20 minutes away. And my colleague saw a wolf on campus the other day.

#71 Who Needs Disneyland?

Most parents know that once you have kids, the most frequent weekend/holiday destination is the park. Whereas in the pre-child days, you and your spouse may have strolled hand and hand in a shopping mall, breaking for a vanilla mocha and scone, after children you find yourself burning way more calories than you take in from chasing the kids around the park (anyone else's kids think that almost-40-year old moms just can't wait to play tag with them?), and from my experience, often spending far less money. My city of Kitakyushu is the place to be if you are looking for cheap, outdoor family entertainment.

This past weekend was Golden Week, a mysteriously named four, sometimes five-day holiday in early May. One aspect of my personality that has gotten worse and worse since having kids is my absolutely hatred, almost terror of crowds. I often find myself tempted to run people over with my cart on a Sunday at Costco. So, since the rest of the country is also off from work during Golden Week, you can probably guess that almost anywhere you go is going to be crowded. My fear of crowds, coupled with our recent efforts at saving money, meant that there was no way in a million years we would go to Disneyland or any other faraway, people-infested destination this holiday. Nope. We were planning on avoiding amusement parks, shopping malls, museums, and aquariums. So, what is left, you may say? Parks. Mountains. Bike riding. Good, cheap outdoor family fun.

I have found that I can usually handle outdoor crowds much better than indoor crowds (except festival crowds. I cannot handle them). This year, we were blessed with great weather so we spent the entire four days outside all day long. We visited more parks than I can remember, rode bicycles, climbed a mountain, had a BBQ and even played very short games of tag. Have I mentioned how I hate tag?

The park system in my city of Kitakyushu is awesome. There are great neighborhood parks everywhere, and a huge public park called Green Park, where everything is either free or dirt cheap. We decided to go to Green Park on the last day of the holiday yesterday, but I was a little nervous about probable Golden Week crowds. But even though we had to use a parking lot in the nose bleed section, the attractions were not that bad at all. We rented tandem bikes for us, Abby and Emmy, and Mia rode on her own. This unlimited usage was only $12 total for all of us. Mia was so excited for her first solo trip with the family, as she just recently graduated from riding with us on the tandem bike to riding on her own.

What a view. We rode about 6 km around a beautiful lake through a mountain path. The kids absolutely loved it, and we got in a good workout. Then we went to ride these crazy bikes. There were ones you moved by jumping up and down on this lever-looking thing; there were ones that had a coffee cup like you see at amusement parks attached to the front while two people pedaled; there were ones that looked like race cars. The kids giggled the whole time, all for a mere additional $12.

Lastly, we went to the kids' favorite park in Kokura, about 30 minutes away. They took their grass sleds and gleefully sledded down over and over and over and over. And over. I tried once, and fell off and skinned my elbow trying to avoid crashing into Abby. Maybe I should leave this fun stuff to the kids. Nah. I would rather keep hurting my aging self.

The rides and play area there are amazing. There are huge play sets with rock climbing walls, rope jungle gyms and endless slides and sandboxes. This park was best of all, FREE!! The kids amazed me with their boundless energy. When we ran out of tea and water, and my cheap self refused to buy more, we packed it in, and headed to the nearest restaurant to share (again, I am cheap) a hot fudge sundae. Sweet ending to a sweet adventure.

I came home exhausted, too exhausted to cook, so I found myself ruining our cheap fun by getting take out. But you know what? It wasn't ruined, because we don't do it all that often and the kids loved it. I would much rather spend my time with them than rushing home to make dinner. So we got home, gave the kids a bath and watched some TV while eating dinner.

This Golden Week we didn't spend a second in a shopping mall. And we didn't go anywhere kids dream about like Disneyland. We didn't need to. We have each other, and spent four whole days being together, so it didn't matter at all what we did. I read somewhere that kids remember the daily stuff they do with their parents much more than the big trips. That is true about my own life, and I hope it is true about my kids' life as well. I had one of the best Golden Weeks ever this year. I do however, need another vacation to recover from the fatigue. Working is much easier, but playing with the kids is much more fulfilling.

#72 Caught Between Cultures

Last summer, my family returned the the States for the first time in two years. Before we had kids, we went home at least once a year, but the bigger our family got, the more expensive going home got, so now, it is only once every two years. Just the airplane tickets alone for five people cost over $7000 (in a good year. The time before that, it was $8000!) We really look forward to these visits home, and try to expose our kids as much as possible to American culture.

Since my kids were born in Japan, there is a lot they don't know about American culture and a lot of things that I experienced as a child that they never will. They may never play recreation league softball, join a gymnastics class, go on a hayride in the fall, or roast marshmallows over a campfire. Since these were some of my best memories of childhood, it was makes me sad that my kids may never have these experiences. Of course, they are having an amazing cultural experience that most American kids can only dream of. They are entirely bilingual, they can use chopsticks like pros, they have travelled all over Japan, and they have had the chance to be blessed by the wonderful Japanese people just like we have. We love living here, but we also love our native country, so every time we go back we do everything we can to give our kids experiences that they can't have in Japan.

We did a lot last summer. We took a road trip to South Dakota and saw Mount Rushmore and Crazy Horse; we took them to their first corn maze (mine too!) where they got to romp around in a pumpkin field afterwards; we visited New York City and the American Girl Doll store (maybe that was a mistake), ate roasted peanuts on the street and strolled in Central Park. We went to the Illinois State Fair where they petted farm animals and ate Fried Snickers for the first time. We also visited their cousins' elementary school and school carnival. It was a magical time for them and for us. I felt like we were giving them just a little taste of what childhood would be like for them in America.

Of course, they had a great time and started talking about wanting to move back to America some day. We had to bring them back to reality and inform them that, if we did move back, our family must engage in the bothersome tasks of working and going to school. Oh, they said. They realized that life would not be one fun road trip after another, and that french fries and ice cream would not be on the daily menu if we actually lived here. They would have to go to school, just like they do in Japan, not go to water parks and play areas every day.

I must say, though, that it warms my heart that the kids love America so much. I am not one of those foreigners who moves to a new country, and assimilates so much that they start bad mouthing their home country. I love Japan and love living here, but I also love my home country. I truly think I love them the same, but in different ways, and that I could happily live in either place (provided there was a Japanese community for me to interact with in the States!) I want my kids to have a clear identity, to realize that while Japan is their home, they are American. It is crucial to us that they understand American culture and history. My husband loved visiting Abraham Lincoln's home in Springfield, Illinois and teaching my kids American history. We loved watching a movie about Lincoln's life and buying some kids' books and place mats about American presidents. I never want my kids to forget where they came from, even if we live in Japan our whole lives.

That being said, they are very comfortable in Japan. They speak Japanese better than English. They like Japanese food better than American food. Every time we go back, they long to eat rice and complain about the constant pizza, sandwiches and pasta. Although they are getting better about eating American food, for a while there they were losing weight every time we went back. I still remember the time we found a Vietnamese noodle restaurant and they scarfed down the food like they hadn't eaten for a week. I guess I shouldn't complain that they would rather eat fermented soy beans, rice and fish than pizza and hamburgers.

Once thing they do love, though, is American junk food. I think there was a stretch during which they were eating Doritos and candy everyday. I think my mom is the only American on earth who doesn't like Doritos. They are by far and away the number one chip choice for everyone in my family. That is a far cry from the seaweed and dried fish they snack on in Japan. I realized one day that the kids were eating too many desserts when one of them said, "Hey, mommy, we haven't had dessert yet." I realized they were expecting it after every meal. Uh. Not good.

Another thing they really loved was the disgusting American all-you-can-eat buffet. We have buffets in Japan, but the choices are much healthier, much more limited, and the desserts not nearly as sweet. While I used to love these places, my Japanese self and aging stomach just can't handle them like

I used to. I am bothered by people filling their plates high with fried everything, even though there are definitely healthy options in places like those. I guess people don't really go to a buffet to eat healthy, though. I try to eat well there, but I still feel gross when I leave because the dessert bar gets me every time. While I am not a fan, my kids love these places. They love being able to get whatever they want and having so many different choices, and as a parent it is nice to not have to fight the battle of getting my kids to eat for at least one meal.

Without fail, every time we go back, when we are approaching the end of our time, we all start longing to go home, for that is what Japan is to our entire family. We love seeing family, friends and experiencing American culture, but that is not our home or where we have made so many memories as a family. So, for the sake of our waistlines and my kids' Japanese, going back at the end of our two months is always a good thing. It is interesting how you can feel both comfortable and uncomfortable in a place at the same time. I don't ever really feel 100% at home in the U.S. or in Japan, but I feel 100% happy in both. I think the main reason for this is not where I am, but who I am with. With my family, I can be happy anywhere.

I was just approved for a one year sabbatical in the United States beginning in the Fall of 2014. So, the Crescinis are going to America. Maybe my kids will get those gymnastics lessons after all.

#73 Fattening Festival Food

Last summer when we visited the U.S. as a family, I visited my first ever State Fair. I had always wanted to go to one, especially recently, as I had heard of all the crazy fried stuff that you could get there. I had heard of fried Oreos, fried Twinkies, friend Snickers, fried butter, and even fried Coke. I only got a chance to try the fried Snickers and fried Coke, and while the Snickers was awesome, the Coke was weird. All those calorie bombs are in addition to the regular festival fare of funnel cakes, caramel popcorn, hot dogs, pizza, and shaved ice. We also ate lots of ethnic foods like Indian and Mexican, and left with happy hearts but a really heavy tummy.

In Japan, festivals are the main summer events, and people everywhere look forward to them for months. Young women and little children dress up in summer kimonos, and people head to the festivals to participate in summer games, eat festival food and see traditional and modern dancing. Festival food in Japan is almost the same at every festival all over Japan, but very different from festival food in the States.

Grilled *yakitori* is one of the most popular and probably the healthiest festival food. This chicken-on-a-stick is my husband's favorite, although not mine because it is one of the priciest of the festival fare with the longest lines. Curry and rice is always popular, as Japanese people love to eat spicy food in summer to work up a good sweat. *Okonomiyaki* pancakes, footlong hot dogs, french fries and *yakisoba* noodles can be found at any festival in Japan.

There are also plenty of sweets, like cotton candy and bean paste filled pancakes. My favorite festival food is Japanese shaved ice. Japanese shaved ice is way better than American snow cones, as the ice is shaved much finer and the syrups much more delicious. Sometimes you can even find it topped with condensed milk to make it even better. My kids are absolutely crazy about this shaved ice, called *kakigori* in Japanese. They would choose this over ice cream if given a choice, and they would eat it all day, everyday if I let them. My friend has an industrial-sized shaved ice machine that she lends out to various groups for festivals and other events. Once, after borrowing it for a summer camp, she let us keep it in our house for the rest of the summer. The kids were in sugar heaven.

My university holds a school festival every fall, and the foods found there offer way much more variety than the average summer festival. The students work hard every year to come up with some interesting culinary creations, while still making enough of a profit for their sports club or class. The sheer number of food stalls makes for amazing variety. I bet there are 40 or 50 different groups selling different foods. The best part is being able to taste the myriad of ethnic foods prepared by the international student body at my university. We get to try Indonesian food, Vietnamese food, Korean food, and Chinese food. Students usually sell tickets for cheaper in advance, and I find myself spending thousands of yen on these tickets. Not that I plan on eating all that food myself, but I want to to support them as their teacher. I usually end up giving a lot of them away to friends, using some of them, and probably losing more than I wish to admit. I always find one or two AFTER the festival is over.

Although festival food is much healthier in Japan than in the U.S, it is still pretty high calorie, greasy, processed, and most people eat way to much of it. Personally, I am not a big fan of festival food, but I still like to go to take in the atmosphere. Even though most festivals in Japan have many of the same events and most of the same foods, it is still a great place to tap into the heart of Japan.

#74 Baseball, Baby!

Everybody knows that baseball is America's national pastime. Yeah, I know. The NFL and NBA are much larger money making machines, much flashier and have a lot more viewers than baseball. I don't care about any of that; baseball is the soul of America, and it captures the hearts of young children like no other, just like it did mine when I was growing up as a young kid in Southwest Virginia. My dad is from Iowa, and has been a rabid St. Louis Cardinals fan his whole life. Of course, he passed on this love of baseball and of the Cards to my two brothers and I. Thank God he is not a Cubs fan, like my husband, who deviously concealed this fact until after our wedding day.

My childhood was all about backyard baseball games, and family vacations to different ballparks to watch Major League games in the summer. We never really went anywhere else; we visited Grandma and we saw baseball games—at the same time if possible. I never went to Disneyland or Disney World, I never flew on an airplane, and I never went camping. But you know what? I didn't care a bit. To me, those magical trips to Busch Stadium, the sea of Cardinal red everywhere, and the $5.00 hotdogs were all I needed then. Baseball and family made for a perfect summer.

My only two childhood injuries occurred while playing baseball. When I was in the sixth grade, I broke my leg sliding into home plate while playing with my Dad and younger brother, David. We argued the whole way to the hospital about whether I was safe or out. In fact, we argued for the next ten years or so, until on my wedding day as I got ready to walk down the aisle, he finally admitted what I had known all along--that I was indeed safe. The other injury was when my older brother's faulty outfield play resulted in him missing an easy fly ball, which then soared over his glove and scored a direct hit on my forehead. Emergency room trip #2.

The backyard games, which occurred everyday during summer, were the highlight of my childhood. Most of the neighborhood kids would come over. The neighborhood kids were 90% boys, so I just joined in and became one of the biggest tomboys you will ever see. I still hate to wear dresses and makeup, even to this day. My dad was the permanent pitcher for both teams. I will never forget the big tree that marked second base and how nostalgic it was when mom and dad had to get it cut down a couple of years ago. It is weird looking out and seeing second base gone.

So, you can see I am crazy about baseball. I love playing it, watching it, breathing it. The first thing I asked my doctor after giving birth to Mia was how soon I could visit the batting cages; my husband proposed to me by throwing the ring box to me during a game of morning catch, and when I return to the States, my family still tries to take our family trips to the nearest baseball stadium, even all these years later.

I would love to pass on my love of baseball to my kids. When we go back to the U.S. we take them to see some games and try to explain the rules to them. My middle girl, Abby, loves to play catch and is a hitting machine. My oldest Mia is really athletic, but she would rather just climb around on a jungle gym or ride her bike. She is not into ball sports at all. My youngest Emmy is only four, so it is too early to tell with her. So, it seems that Abby has the best chance of picking up our love of baseball.

That being said, thank God that I did not give birth to a boy. The reason I am saying that is, that boy may have grown up and decided to play baseball here, one of the most popular and honorable things for a kid to do in Japan, but the biggest time sucker and stress-giver to the poor creature called Japanese baseball mom. While I have no personal experience with this since I have only girls, I have read some books and heard stories of baseball moms. I know the pressure on the moms to make snacks and lunches not only for her kids, but for the entire team on occasion. I personally see the moms dropping off their kids before seven a.m. on Saturdays, Sundays and holidays at the local field. The other day I saw the moms sitting in the shade under a tent during practice at 6 pm on a Saturday night. The kids had probably been there all day, practicing from morning to evening as they often do on weekends. What about the moms? I wondered if they had been there all day, too. I wonder how much family time and family vacations they have sacrificed to baseball.

These kids sure were skillful. I was shocked that kids this young could be so good. My husband pointed out that they are bound to become good if they practice all day long. I was watching a coach work with the players on fielding practice, hitting grounders to the infielders and outfielders. Once, after the center fielder caught the ball on a hop and relayed it home, the coach had some words of advice. The player took off his hat, snapped to attention, and responded "*Hai. Hai. Hai*" to everything the coach said. I felt as if I was watching a solider receiving instruction from his commanding officer, not a twelve-year old kid playing baseball. But I don't think this is bad at all. Kids need to learn discipline and respect, and playing a team sport, especially one as revered in Japan as baseball, can instill those qualities in kids. I can often tell as a teacher which of my students played team sports by the way they talk to me and act in class.

When practice was finally over, the players raked the dirt, which is always done at the close of practice to show respect for the field and to leave it in better condition than it was in when they came. The thing that still shocks me now, even though I have seen it many times, is the way players bow to the field as they exit through the outfield grass. Players take off their hats, turn around, and bow. Moms, who have been both watching and helping clean up, bow, too. Baseball, and the field on which it is played, is so revered here it has almost received godlike status.

Part of me admires the discipline, respect and hard work of both kids and parents involved in baseball in Japan. And part of me wishes it could be just a little bit less intense and a little more relaxing and enjoyable. I wonder if Japanese kids put together pick up games in the park like my family did in my backyard as a kid. Maybe, but I have not seen it very often. Any time I see a game here, it is a community team having an official practice. Just like in everything else, the Japanese practice and play baseball with the same effort, hard work and precision with which they conduct so many other areas of their lives. I am still not sure if I like it or not.

#75 Fat Americans

Last week in my classes, I did a lesson on stereotypes. When I asked my students about their stereotypes of America, most of them had to do with food. For example, "Americans eat hamburgers everyday," "Americans are fat," "American food is big," "Americans love fast food." I realized that while most Japanese love America and long for many things American, they also think we are big, fat overindulgent slobs with no self-control. Well, maybe not that bad, but there is an overriding stereotype here that Americans are fat. In truth, 65% of Americans are overweight, while only 24% of the Japanese population is overweight.[6] 32% of Americans are obese, which means a BMI of over 30, and only 3.6% of Japanese are.[7] Unfortunately, the number of overweight Japanese is climbing due to their recent romance with Western cuisine.

Of course, everyone knows that traditional Japanese food is very healthy. It is a diet rich in fish, vegetables, soy and rice. In addition to the healthier diet, they also get more exercise

---

[6] http://www.boston.com/yourlife/health/fitness/articles/2006/02/15/japan_battles_rising_obesity

[7] http://ideas.repec.org/p/ags/umrfwp/14321.html

in daily life than Americans do, walking and riding their bicycles to the train station, school or work. I usually walk or ride my bike to school, which only takes 10 minutes. It seems to me now, after living here for more than ten years, that driving is silly for such a short distance. However, when I was in graduate school in the U.S., my home was maybe 15 minutes from school, and yet I rarely thought about walking or riding my bike. It is such a car culture that I chose instead to spend twice the time looking for a parking space on campus. It is funny how one's perception of "far" and "close" can change over time, and how it varies from country to country. When I visited China and my hosts said we were going to walk somewhere "close," it took almost an hour!

That being said, I do think the Japanese have their skinny genes to thank for their skinny jeans. I have friends who eat much more than I do, and who are skin and bones. Japanese women are much more petite, and men much smaller boned than their American counterparts. Almost all the women I know, and many men, too, weigh less than I do, although I am considered skinny by American standards. College students here eat a ton of junk food like instant noodles and packaged bread, as well as go drinking regularly. Older busy folks eat a lot more fried and greasy foods than they used to, and for some it is starting to show on the scale, but for the many metabolically-gifted Japanese, it isn't. So, while American food culture is wrought with problems, and there is definitely some serious overeating going on, the American stereotype that the Japanese are always eating healthy food is just not true either. They do eat better than we do on most occasions, but they can eat crap with the best of them.

One area I think is killing the American waistline is drinks. Americans drink an average of 450 calories a day, or 37% of total calorie intake[8]. Soft drinks and sugary coffee drinks are the biggest offenders. Health conscious Americans will drink a lot of water, but the drinks of choice are still soft drinks for many. The Japanese, on the other hand, although they will splurge on an occasional Starbucks Frappuccino, consume mainly non-calorie barley tea, oolong tea, and green tea. I love watching my Japanese students visiting the U.S. horrified by the colorful American soft drinks like red Hawaiian Punch and green Mountain Dew. I enjoy watching their reaction after mistakenly ordering sweet tea, and their subsequent urge to spit it out. They just aren't used to color or calories in their beverages like we are. My husband and I were amused at the Diet Green Tea we found last summer at a store in the U.S. If you have to make green tea diet, which is a naturally calorie-free drink, something is wrong.

I have lost over twenty pounds since coming to Japan. Riz seems to have found it. It is interesting how my taste buds have changed to prefer Japanese food to Western food if given a choice. Riz prefers it, too, but probably is much less active than he used to be, plus he likes a lot of the more high calorie modern Japanese fare. He is also a drinker, not of alcohol but of

---

[8] http://www.sparkpeople.com/resource/nutrition_articles.asp?id=1556

calories. The Japanese have copied the West and figured out a way to put calories in tea, too, and he and my kids, love that kind of stuff.

While the Japanese can eat too much with the best of them, I must admit, that the Japanese stereotype about America is somewhat true: many Americans are gluttons with little self-control. Of course, just as my home country has extremes in almost every area, there are also many fitness nuts out there, and people very conscious about what they eat. You don't find much of that extreme in Japan. There are not that many fat people, and there are not that many people extremely careful with diet and exercise either. Every time I go back to the U.S, I am amazed at the portion sizes of the dishes in restaurants. It seems like nobody can finish their meal anymore, and needing a take out box is a given.

Up until recently in Japan, asking for a takeout box was bad manners, and some places will still not give one to you. It is not that big a deal, though, because rarely will you have enough food from the small portions to need to take home. In fact, the other day we asked for a takeout box in a family restaurant, and we were given aluminum foil and a plastic bag. That was all they had. The portions in America are legendary here. I would love to take a Japanese friend to an American buffet, where the mostly obese customers are stacking their plates high with greasy, fried food, topping it off with another plate of sugary desserts. I bet she would eat with glee feeling like she had entered the gates of heaven, only to be doubled over with diarrhea and stomach pains later that night, regretting the day she first heard the words "Golden Corral."

Which brings me to another area that makes Americans fat and Japanese people skinny: dessert. Ask a Japanese kid what his favorite dessert is, and he is likely to say an apple or orange. Ask the same question to an American kid, and he would be likely to say chocolate ice cream topped with whipped cream, hot fudge sauce and nuts. The most popular Japanese desserts are jello, light puddings, or fruits. American-style desserts are extremely sweet, and many Japanese are unable to eat them. Costco Japan was even forced to change the icing on the birthday cakes they sold because American icing was too sweet for the Japanese.

So, when my students talk about Americans being overweight, I acknowledge that it is true, but challenge them to not lump the whole country together. After all, I am American and I am not fat. I am very careful about what I eat, and very disciplined about exercise. Many of my friends are like me, too. I challenge them to really think about their stereotypes, and get to know real Americans to find out if they are true or not. I challenge them to go to America and see for themselves. While they will certainly see their fair share of obese people, massive hamburgers, and red and blue drinks, they will also see a subculture of health nuts--runners, vegetarians, and ordinary folks like me just trying to keep myself and my family healthy by making wise choices. So not all Americans are fat after all, just like all Japanese people are not healthy and skinny. There is nothing like actually living somewhere to help you figure out the truth from the fiction. I never would have thought before coming here that the Japanese eat as much crap as they do. After all, just because you are skinny, doesn't mean you are healthy, right?

#76 Ruled By Rules

Last Sunday, we visited some American friends, and their daughters did lots of girly stuff with mine, like playing dress up and trying out different colors of nail polish. Since I am not a girly girl at all, it is hard for me to understand the joy that doing their nails brought to my girls, but it did. We got home late that night, and went straight to bed. When we got up the next morning, I realized two things. First, we did not have any nail polish remover; second, nail polish is a huge rule violation in Japanese schools. Just like most every other expression of individuality, nail polish is a big no-no in Japanese public schools.

I wrote a note to Mia's teacher the next day, apologizing profusely for my stupidity and lack of foresight. Mia, however, forgot to show it to her and was busted by some of her classmates, who ratted her out to her teacher. She came home crying that night about the persecution, telling us that she spent most of the day trying to hide her nails from everyone, hoping her rebellious behavior would not be made known to the world. I found myself at first irritated with Mia for not showing her teacher the note; much of the trauma would have been avoided had she just showed it to her teacher. But I also found myself annoyed with the ridiculous importance put on squashing such a seemingly harmless childhood pleasure. It reminded me of the equally ridiculous experience we had last year upon returning to Japan after getting our girls' ears pierced in the States. You would have thought they (or their parents) had committed some heinous crime by the reaction to those pierced ears. While there are no official school rules against pierced ears or nail polish, it is understood that neither are welcome in Japanese schools.

And wait until they get to high school. There are rules about what color socks they can wear and how high they should be. There are rules about the length of a girl's skirt and a boy's hair. There are rules about how you come to school (getting a lift from parents is out of the question). You cannot dye your hair. You cannot even bring your cell phone to school. You cannot wear makeup. Students must wear the same uniforms and carry the same bags. Rules. Rules. Rules. Now, don't get me wrong--I am all for rules when they are necessary. Without rules you would have a disordered society and an out-of-control home. But rules for me are made to protect and guide those who follow them, bringing about order and safety, whether for a family, school, company or society. I do not like rules meant purely to subjugate others, rob individuality or exercise power. These kinds of rules are often found in Japanese schools, especially the ones trying to suffocate individuality. Having pierced ears has no bearing on whether or not a student will learn well or not; having on purple nail polish at age seven does not mean my child is a rebellious wild child who will rebel on every other issue in class.

What are the rules for? To promote obedience? To keep other kids from wanting to do the same thing? My American friend allowed her daughter to get her ears pierced in the States, and she refused to back down from the school's pressure to take out the earrings. And while the principal said it was going to make all the other kids want to get their ears pierced, too, my friend found this wasn't the case at all. The kids didn't care one way or the other. I have a sneaking suspicion that is was more about the adults enforcing the rules than about worrying about what the other kids would think.

We live here, and as long as we do, we will try to fit into Japanese culture and respect it the best we can. So for now, nail polish will be a weekend treat, and I will make sure that I always have a supply of nail polish remover on hand. The beautiful earrings in the bathroom closet that have been there since my girls were forced to let their holes close up last fall will have to stay there for the time being. I don't like these rules, but it is not worth the energy fighting them. But at home, and on the weekends, we are going to encourage our kids to be themselves as much as we possibly can, to express their individuality and not be ashamed of it. In four more years when Mia is out of elementary school, and we are either homeschooling her or sending her to an international school, she can paint her nails everyday of the week for all I care. What matters is not the color of her nails or how many holes she has in her ears, but the attitude of her heart. As long as she respects others and lives with integrity, she can dye her hair pink as far as I am concerned.

#77 Reflections on the Tohoku Disasters

Between the two of us, my husband and I have been up to northern Japan five times to help with the relief and restoration efforts needed after the devastating earthquake and tsunami of 2011. The first time I went, I volunteered with Operation Blessing, a Christian relief organization based in Virginia Beach, VA. I helped with a clinic that traveled to different shelters and community centers providing free glasses to those victims who had lost theirs in the tsunami. The second time I went one year later, I cleaned houses damaged on the coast of Sendai with Samaritan's Purse, the organization run by Billy Graham's son, Franklin. Both of these experiences impacted me deeply, and I learned a lot from my time up there.

1. I learned how incredibly resilient the Japanese people are. Despite such enormous tragedy, they bonded together to help each other out. People all over Japan joined to do what they could. Why was there a restriction on how many diapers I could buy, as well as a flashlight shortage in my town of Kitakyushu, over 1000 miles away from Tohoku? Because people here were buying up everything and sending it up there. Musicians wrote songs about the area; famous people visited the shelters to cheer people up; and many volunteers, especially students spent part of their breaks volunteering their time to help out.

2. I learned how slow the Japanese work and how fast Americans do. When the mayor of Shiogama said he needed generators, or the fishermen of a nearby island asked for boats, Operation Blessing ordered them that day. The Japanese were totally shocked at the efficiency and speed with which American and other foreign relief agencies work. Japanese agencies tend to do things slower, thinking things through and getting consensus from various places. Many Japanese organizations, from universities to churches to businesses, tend to bring new meaning to the term "pending." I don't know how many meetings I have attended and, after discussing something for hours, the end result was, "Let's think about it and bring it up again at the next meeting." This cautious approach may work well for businesses, but can be detrimental in the aftermath of a tragedy. The Japanese were moved by the fast-moving foreign aid, and somewhat annoyed when the Japanese government dragged their feet.

3. I learned how much the infrastructure of an entire country can be disrupted by tragedy. Even in areas undamaged by the earthquake and tsunami, trains were not running, supermarkets and restaurants had no food, convenience stores were closed, and people waited hours in line for gasoline. There were massive food shortages in Tokyo, one of the richest and most modern cities in the world. Wide areas had no water, electricity or gas for weeks. Transportation was disrupted all over the country. And farmers and small business owners in Fukushima saw their livelihoods shattered forever. Who wants to eat vegetables that may be tainted with radiation? Who can relax at a hot spring if they are worried about whether or not there is radiation in the water or air? It took months for these areas to return to any semblance of normalcy, but normalcy doesn't mean now what it used to.

4. I learned how much joy a pair of glasses could bring. Kudos to Operation Blessing for recognizing this small, but very significant need. At a time when people were hungry and freezing, not many people gave much thought to the thousands of people who lost their glasses in the tsunami and had been unable to see well for weeks. That glasses clinic brought smiles to faces and joy to hearts that had not known much since the tsunami.

5. I learned not to take food for granted. My husband, who went up ten days after the tragedy to photograph the area at the request of a Christian aid group, lived for a week on rice, miso

soup and Power Bars. I visited a shelter where meals consisted mostly of donated bread and canned fruits. One meal was a six pack of dinner rolls and a small orange. Maybe you think you could live on this, and I guess most people probably could, but could you for weeks? And what if you were like most of the shelter residents--elderly Japanese used to eating rice everyday, but now eating processed bread because that was all that was available? This dietary stress, coupled with emotional stress can be both physically and mentally damaging. I did not experience any hunger while I was there, but I saw the suffering the shelter victims were going through, and the amazing joy one simple hot meal of noodles provided by volunteers gave them.

6. I learned how devastating nature could be. One year after the tsunami, we stood on the shore of Kesennuma at the very spot the tsunami devastated an entire neighborhood, much like the suburban one in which we live in Kitakyushu now. It was hard to imagine that if we had been standing there one year earlier we would be dead, like so many of that neighborhood's former residents. We drove around Kesennuma amazed at the destruction. Everything was just leveled. All the debris was cleared and piled up like huge mountains all over town. The sparkling new convenience stores on the coast provided a huge contrast to the devastation all around--and a glimmer of hope that restoration was coming.

7. I learned that the swath of destruction was so much bigger than I had imagined. The tsunami destroyed a huge part of the

coast of Miyagi, Fukushima and Iwate Prefectures. I would say you could drive about six hours or so along the coast and see devastation everywhere.

8. Most of all, I learned that life is so fragile, so fleeting, and therefore, so precious. We don't know how much time we have left on this earth. The 20,000 people who lost their lives that day probably thought they had all the time in the world, not knowing that that day was their last. What should we do then? Be depressed and think there is no meaning or reason to go about daily life if we are just going to die anyway? On the contrary, quite the opposite. We should live each day as if it is our last, with no fears and no regrets. We should tell people we love them every chance we get, and let them know how much they mean to us. And we should live our lives full of substance and meaning, helping those around us and pleasing the God who made us.

At the end of our lives, I doubt we will have wished we had worked harder for our companies or had a cleaner house, but we will probably wish we had spent more time with those we love. Last year, the day I returned home from Tohoku, I saw a second-grade girl trapped under a car after being hit by a driver who had run a red light. Even now if I close my eyes, I can still see her light blue backpack and her motionless little hand sticking out from under the truck. I shielded my daughter Mia's eyes because I didn't want that image etched into her mind like it would be in mine. I found out later the little girl didn't make it. I doubt when she said goodbye to her mommy in the morning that her mother thought she may never see her again. Being a mother myself, I cannot imagine what that little girl's mommy must have been feeling, what she is still feeling even now. I went home that night and hugged my kids a little harder. Some days, when I say goodbye to my kids in the morning, I wonder if it may be the last time. I am reminded to live my life, and to love my kids with the the knowledge of that reality always before me.

I am so glad that I decided to take these trips up to Tohoku. I think tragedies like that remind us that what is really important in life is people. We don't need another pair of shoes, the latest iPhone, or a new car. These trips helped me to realize anew that happiness is found in relationships. Of course, the key is to not let this fade from my mind, and get sucked into the materialistic morass that is modern society. How am I doing, one year later? I don't know. Maybe I still clean the house when I should be cuddling with my kids. And did I really need those clothes I bought recently? It's something to think about, and I never want to stop thinking about it.

#78 If I Only Had a Healthy Colon...

Hey, that title sounds like the new country hit! "If I only had a healthy colon, I'd eat all the tacos I like after a good ride on my dirt bike..." Anyway, the other day I was thinking about all the things I would probably eat if I did have a healthy colon. I would indulge my love of spicy food everyday, and the entire shelf devoted to Tabasco sauce in my refrigerator would have to be replenished far more often that it is now. I would drink way more coffee than I should. I would probably eat more greasy foods and more vegetables. Vegetables, you say? You would think all the fiber in vegetables would be great for you, but when your colon is sick, well, all those veggies can wreak havoc. I am sure that I already eat lots of stuff I shouldn't be eating like caffeine, nuts, and cabbage. If I had a healthy colon, I wouldn't have to take medicine every day like I have since I was 19; I wouldn't be tickled pink by a good bowel movement; and I wouldn't have to have a torturous colonoscopy every two years. But, I don't have a healthy colon, so well, enough of that.

I have had ulcerative colitis, a disease in which small ulcers form on the inside of the colon, for half my life. When I was first diagnosed with this disease when I was a college freshman, it was devastating. College kids think they are invincible, so being told I have an incurable disease was not fun. Throughout my college days I struggled with terrible stomach pain and diarrhea, sometimes for months before my doctor put me on an additional steroid medication to clear it up. This disease can be in remission for months or even years at a time in which I have no symptoms, but then it can flare up out of the blue with no warning. While it doesn't really interfere with my daily life, it is always there, and I know that it could flare up at any time. I have never really been able to figure out what causes flare ups even after all these years. Is it a certain food? Is it stress? I still have no idea.

After coming to Japan, partly thanks to the National Health Care system, doctors would give me steroids much earlier in my flare ups, causing me to be more comfortable. For the last ten years I have been enrolled in the Special Chronic Disease Program, which provides all the medication for my colitis for free, and also caps the amount I have to pay for any outpatient and inpatient hospital visits related to my disease. To be honest, my husband and I have thought of returning to the U.S. many times, but fear over how crazy expensive it might be to treat my colitis is one of the reasons we are hesitating. Here, the care is constant, treatment cheap, and medication free. Plus, my colitis has been in remission longer than it ever was in the States. The special program for chronic diseases like my Ulcerative Colitis, Crohn's Disease, Parkinson's and many others enables sufferers of chronic diseases to be free of financial worry, and allows them to focus on getting well instead of how much the medication is going to cost.

Still, I hate having a diseased colon. I hate not being able to eat what I want to. I hate more than anything having to have a colonoscopy every two years. More so than for other people, colonoscopies are torturous for me. The liquid to cleanse the bowels doesn't work on me, so I have to drink like 4 liters of the stuff. I am not kidding. Four liters. While the newly developed lemony taste has made drinking it a little more bearable, it is still gross. Even four liters doesn't work that well. In addition, in Japan, they do not use anesthesia. So not only does the procedure hurt, but I also usually puke afterwards because I am so nauseous from drinking all that nasty liquid. I usually spend the day of the test sulking and feeling sorry for myself, giving dirty looks to all the people having the test done that finish their prep in less than two hours when it takes me at least twenty. And it seems that in the test prep room where everyone is together drinking their lovely concoction, there are ALWAYS cooking shows on the TV with the participants smiling and shouting OISHII (SO YUMMY!!) every time they put food in their mouths. This country is crazy about food, and it is manifested in the endless cooking shows, the last things you want to see when you haven't eaten in forever with no hope of eating anytime soon.

I hate having a diseased colon, but I usually have a good attitude about it except when I am having a colonoscopy. You see, I realize there are a lot more people out there who have it way worse than I do. There are people struggling with colon cancer or other diseases; there are poor people in Bangladesh who lose their entire families to a cyclone; there are parents who lose children and children who lose parents. I, despite having a malfunctioning colon, am able to go on with my daily life unhindered. I have a husband and three girls who love me. I have a good job, good food to eat (even if almost everything makes my stomach hurt), a place to sleep and good friends. I have nothing to complain about. Sure, I wish that I had a healthy colon and didn't have to go through the tests I go through every couple years. But all people have things that they struggle with and challenges in their lives.

Maybe if I had a healthy colon I would take things for granted more than I do. Maybe I wouldn't be able to relate to other people who are sick with chronic diseases and be able to encourage their spirits. Maybe I wouldn't have been able to encourage a friend last year diagnosed with Crohn's Disease. As a Christian, I do believe that there is a reason for everything, and that God can work all things together for the good of those who love him. And I love him, so that verse applies to me and to my ulcerative colitis.

And what better place to have colitis than in Japan? I mean, if you have to suffer from a chronic disease, this is the place to be. My disease will never send me into bankruptcy like it might if I lived in the States. Of course, I sure would appreciate it if my doctor could figure out a way to keep me from suffering so much from the colonoscopies. Oh, and a little more anesthesia would be nice, too. But, I guess you can't have it all. I am happy to be in Japan, and happy with the life that I have been blessed with. The fact is, I don't have a healthy colon, and unless God heals me I never will. But that doesn't mean that I cannot be thankful for the blessed life I do have.

If I only had a healthy colon. You could substitute anything else you may be longing for in for the healthy colon part. If I only had more money. Or a better job. Or less tummy fat. Or better behaved kids. Or a more helpful husband (not something I wish for, since mine is already very helpful). This list could go on and on. Everyone always wants stuff they don't have or can't have. That is part of human nature. But I think it is better to be satisfied with what we have, instead of always wanting something we don't. Sure, I would love to be able to eat Taco Bell and Nacho Cheese Doritos every day. But I can't, and that is okay. We don't have a Taco Bell here in Japan anyway.

#79 What a Bunch of Garbage!

I remember when I was a kid going out with Dad on Saturday morning to collect aluminum cans. We would scour my town's back roads for hours for that shiny metal, and then take our haul to the local recycling center for a few extra bucks. My Dad used to always be amazed at my eagle eye; I seemed to be able to spot a can hiding under a tree, 90% buried under rock and dirt, but poking out enough for my eagle eye to spot. Those days of collecting cans, along with looking for forgotten baseballs at our town's minor league baseball field, are some of my most vivid memories of childhood. I probably made less than 50 bucks from those cans my whole childhood. As for the baseballs, we found over a hundred of them along with three cases of poison ivy, which was covering the baseballs we found behind the fence. But no value can be placed on the memories I made with my Dad.

My parents always taught me to save money whenever you could, and while for many of my friends recycling was probably a pain in the neck, for me it meant extra bucks and more bonding time with Dad. Recycling, though, while seen at that time as a good thing to do for the environment was by no means mandatory. As far as I remember, most people just threw everything away together on the weekly garbage day.

When I came to Japan, I was surprised at how environmentally-conscious everyone was. Recycling was encouraged, and cans and bottles were picked up on a separate day from regular kitchen garbage. Buses would turn off their engines at stoplights; many people carried around their reusable shopping eco bags to reduce plastic bag usage; many people were driving hybrid cars. Apparently, my city of Kitakyushu was really dirty 40 to 50 years ago due to the massive air pollution caused by the manufacturing plants driving the city's economy. The city has made a huge push in recent years to clean up the environment and improve the reputation of Kitakyushu, and has been largely successful. Kitakyushu is now regarded as one of the most environmentally-conscious cities in Japan. One of the new measures to clean up the environment dealt with garbage separation.

Seven or eight years ago, the city of Kitakyushu decided to institute strict garbage separation rules in an effort to decrease waste and increase recycling. Burnable kitchen garbage was collected twice a week; plastics were collected once a week; aluminum cans and plastic bottles were collected once and week; finally, cardboard boxes, newspapers, comics and other paper recyclables were collected once a month. I guess the city figured it was going to take people a while to get used to the new measures, and, a lot of lazy people were probably not going to pay attention to the new rules. So many places, including the public housing complex in which we lived, placed volunteers at the trash stations for about a week or two monitoring everyone's garbage disposal. My husband and I called them the "garbage police," and they made me really nervous. They were checking everyone's garbage, and if someone was throwing away something improperly, they were told to take it back and try again. It was a little stressful everyday going down and hoping not to get stopped by the garbage police.

Luckily, I didn't. However, there have been times I have thrown things away improperly, and when I passed the garbage station later that day I saw my bag of garbage still there with a big "X" on it. Apparently, if you get busted for bad garbage behavior the city won't pick it up; you have to take it back and put it in the proper bag and try again. Now, they don't bust you for EVERYTHING. For example, the garbage collectors are not going to look for every misplaced can or bottle and refuse to pick it up. But if you blatantly disregard the rules by using the wrong bags or putting out last night's chicken bones in the plastics garbage, there is a good chance of being busted.

Speaking of the proper bag, official city garbage bags are sold around the city, and you must use these designated bags if you want your garbage picked up. In an effort to try to encourage people to recycle more, the city sells bags for plastics, cans, and bottles for dirt cheap, around 10 yen (10 cents) a bag or less. However, bags for food and paper garbage are anywhere between 30 and 50 yen (30 to 50 cents) per bag. That is a lot of money for something you are just going to throw away! But I am guessing that the city is aware of that.

I don't usually intentionally throw stuff away improperly, although there may be times it is too gross to be a stickler for the law, like when there is melted chewing gum stuck all over an aluminum can. Most of the time I just have no idea what goes into what category. I try to figure it out the best I can, but I have been wrong a few times. For the big stuff, like old suitcases, bikes, TVs etc, you have to pay extra, and wait for a designated day that only comes once or twice a month. Since this is such a pain in the neck, most people do one of two things--they call a junk yard to come get it for free or for a cheaper price (and much sooner!), or they tape a garbage bag on it and hope against all hope that the city will take it away. A lot of the time, this works for stuff like suitcases, old carpets or blankets, but you cannot get away with this for the really big stuff.

Many Japanese who are much more environmentally-friendly than I am also recycle milk cartons, lightbulbs, and styrofoam trays. I am ashamed to admit that these things are too much of a pain in the neck for me. In addition to having to haul it all down to the collection center at the local supermarket, preparing this stuff, especially the milk cartons, for recycling is a hassle. You first have to rinse it out, then cut it up so it lies flat, and finally, you have to dry it before taking it to recycling. I wish I had more patience for this, but I don't. Of course, hauling it down to the supermarket is a bit of hyperbole, considering I go to the supermarket almost everyday anyway. Yep, I am just lazy.

I used to get irritated by all the garbage separation rules, but I now see it is really good for the environment. Since many people are probably lazy like me, setting up a basic separation system and requiring everyone to follow it is a good idea. After living here a while, I now look back at the lack of garbage separation in my hometown with amazement; after all, anyone can separate garbage. All it requires is an extra trash can or two. I may not be as diligent as I should be, but living here in Kitakyushu has definitely made me more environmentally aware than I have ever been in my life.

Now if I could only remember to actually take one of the five or so reusable shopping bags I own with me when I go to the supermarket...

#80 Here Comes the Rain Again...

Well, it is the end of May, usually one of the most pleasant times of year. The weather is warm, but not blistering hot and humid like it gets in August. This means that every morning I can indulge my new exercise passion--cycling. I hop on my bike in the mornings and just go wherever I feel like going. I love the quiet mornings in usually hectic Japan--there are few cars on the roads, the birds are chirping, and I am one happy girl.

Was a happy girl. Until yesterday, that is. Because yesterday, you see, the island of Kyushu entered rainy season 11 days earlier than usual. Rainy season is one of my biggest enemies and joy suckers. There is not a time of the year that I hate more than rainy season, a six-week period from the beginning of June to the middle of July. Rainy season steals away my morning bike rides, makes it impossible to dry laundry outside, and causes mold to grow on almost everything. I know that farmers need the rain and all, but part of me is totally selfish and prays anyway for a mild rainy season every year. I probably have Seasonal Affective Disorder, as my moods are so majorly affected by the weather.

Every year it is Anne vs. rainy season. In the laundry department, a couple years ago I started getting the upper hand when I got my first clothes dryer since coming to Japan. Up until then, I just hung my clothes outside like everybody else. Before I got my dryer, rainy season was truly the bane of my existence. I would hang out the clothes on a sunny morning, only to the see the weather change suddenly and drench them all by the time I came home. Or, I would not do laundry because it was rainy when I left, only to see it become a perfectly sunny day by the time I arrived at work. A perfect laundry day wasted. So, the clothes piled up, not getting washed, or when they did, ended up damp and smelly. Hanging them inside didn't really work, either. The humidity in the air made them stink to high heaven. So, you can see why getting a dryer made my rainy season.

Then, two summers ago, my dryer suddenly broke. In Japan, washing and drying are functions on the same machine. Since the washing machine function still worked and I am a cheapskate, I couldn't justify buying a new one. So, until the washing function breaks, too, I figured it was back to the world of damp and dirty clothes during rainy season. Luckily, we had moved to a new house with an overhang over the outside laundry area, so in a light rain the clothes could still dry outside. Plus, for some reason hanging the clothes inside in my new house doesn't lead to them stinking. Of course, a living room full of hanging bras and underwear is not aesthetically pleasing, nor does it lead to an atmosphere conducive for inviting friends over.

Then there is the mold. It gets everywhere. A couple of years ago, I went to get a stroller out of storage at the end of rainy season and found it covered in mold. Really gross. I learned to wrap stuff like that in tarp or plastic to protect it from the rainy season mold. Mold grows all over the shower area, too, little black spots on the wall hard to take off even with the best shower cleaner. Like I said. Gross.

Lastly, rainy season just robs me of being outside. More than anything, I love being outside, and go outside whenever I get the chance. I like to walk and go cycling in the mornings. I like to take my kids to the park after school. And family weekends are almost always spent at parks, riding bikes together or taking walks. Going to indoor play areas is just not the same; it just doesn't bring joy to my heart like being outside.

It doesn't rain nonstop during rainy season. There are some years when it even seems like it is sunny more than it is rainy. The rain, when it does come, is usually unpredictable. It will rain and then the sun will come out. Then it will rain again. Every year is different. I find myself obsessed with checking the weather report during rainy season. I check it everyday, hoping against hope to see that sunny mark and not the umbrella. I find myself counting the days till the middle of July, eagerly anticipating the official announcement of the end of rainy season by the Japan Meteorological Agency. Usually just when I think it is over, there will be another two or three days of heavy rain, and then...blistering, suffocating, smothering HEAT, which is the true sign that rainy season is indeed over. Most people hate this time of year, but not me. I absolutely love it. The hotter, the more humid, the better. Bring it on. I can handle anything better than rain. Rain is the only kind of weather that keeps me inside like a trapped animal. At least in the heat and freezing cold I can still enjoy being outside.

So, rainy season come on! Let's fight it out again this year! Maybe this year, I will employ a new strategy. Maybe I will wash my clothes and ride my bike no matter how hard it is raining. Why not? I am not going to let it get me down this year. So, if my clothes stink a little when I pass you by, sorry. They won't stink for more than another six weeks.

After an unusually dry rainy season, the end of rainy season was announced in Kyushu on July 8, about two weeks earlier than usual. With the exception of a couple of torrential downpours, the rainy season went out with a whimper instead of a roar. As I write this, we are now experiencing an unusual July heatwave, with temperatures soaring into the 90s.

#81 The 240-Minute Load of Laundry

In my previous post, I bemoaned the effect rainy season has on my ability to do laundry. Having three small kids, doing laundry everyday is a must. I had always wanted to buy a dryer, but they were so expensive, and I heard they didn't work very well either. They would take forever and leave your clothes so wrinkled that you would have to iron everything, even t-shirts and shorts. What a pain in the neck, I thought. So, for a while, I just endured hanging my clothes outside in the mornings, and bringing them inside at night after work and folding them and putting them away. You can guess that there were many days that I was exhausted and had absolutely no desire to fold laundry after a long day's work. Often, I would just leave them outside overnight, causing them to get wet again from the morning dew.

Most Japanese people feel that hanging clothes outside is good for the clothes. The fresh air and natural sunlight is the best. When I was a kid, we had a clothesline in our backyard, but really only used it to hang out sheets and towels and stuff like that in summer. But many Japanese still hang out their clothes everyday. Of course, with the Westernization of society, many modern families are buying dryers, hanging out their clothes less and less. Some people are worried about the air pollution drifting over from China making their clothes dirty; others are embarrassed by hanging out their underwear for all to see. Indeed, there have been some cases of perverts in

Japan stealing women's undergarments off the clotheslines. But many families just like the modern convenience of having a dryer. The clothes get dry much faster and oftentimes, smell better. Some new dryers can even dry a pair of jeans without them being wrinkled like a pretzel. But still, few families use dryers exclusively. Most will just dry stuff like underwear, towels and t-shirts. The rest of their clothes they will still hang outside. Why?

Well, maybe it is to save money. Dryers take up a lot of energy, and thus, lead to higher electricity bills. As I mentioned earlier, unlike in the U.S. there are few stand alone dryers in Japan; in most cases the dryer and washer are functions on the same machine. Buying a machine which has both functions in the first place can cost between $500 and $2000 dollars, so you gotta save money wherever you can. Really nice ones that lead to unwrinkled clothes and low electricity bills can cost $2000. But one thing remains--it takes around 3-4 hours to wash and dry one load of laundry in a Japanese washing machine. What??!! Four hours?? Yep, four hours. It is even more ridiculous when you think that the dryers are so small that they only hold about 1/3 of the amount of clothes a Western machine does. So, if you do the math, it will take a Japanese washing machine/dryer about 12 hours to do what it takes around 90 minutes for an American set to do.

About five years ago, one of my friends moved back to the U.S., and he offered us his washer/dryer combo. Yes! Finally

I was getting a dryer! It is funny what kind of things make you happy after you have kids. Not new clothes or shoes anymore. Nope. It's a dryer or refrigerator. But for me, who had been exhausted for years washing, hanging, and folding clothes everyday for my five family members, it was the best gift ever. No more stinky clothes hanging inside during rainy season. No more late nights bringing in clothes. I was finally going back to my American ways.

But you know what? Even with a dryer, I was stuck in my Japanese ways. I still found myself hanging clothes out on sunny days. I would use the dryer sometimes when I was really tired, starting it at night and folding the clothes in the morning. I really love the smell of clothes right out of the dryer. But most days, I found out what many Japanese people already knew-- dryers take forever and cost an arm and a leg to use. Luckily, I had a machine that didn't wrinkle clothes at all, but I still had been so influenced by my years of Japanese laundry culture that I didn't use it all that much.

When the dryer function broke two years ago, I thought it would affect me more than in did, but it didn't. I was so used to not having a dryer, that I just went back to my old ways. The washer still works, but I have a feeling that it is nearing the end. It cannot be normal for it to vibrate so much that it ends up two feet farther from the wall when it is done than it was when it started. But for now, I wash the clothes, push the washer back against the wall, hang the clothes and take them in every night.

The next day, I do the same thing again. Most Americans would see it as a huge pain in the neck, but not me. I am used to it, just like most of the country. Maybe I am turning Japanese. Guess what? I have never had a dishwasher either!

My friend recently told me how her daughter scratched up her face with a towel. Strange as it may seem, the towel was so rough and stiff from hanging outside all day that it injured her youngest daughter. Note to self: beware of line-dried bath towels!

My washing machine has recently mysteriously stopped vibrating uncontrollably and moving away from the wall after years of constant moving.

#82 Sports Day and the *Bento* Scheming Mommy

It is the end of May, one of the best times of the year in Japan. The weather is sunny, the days are warm but not too hot, and it is the time for one of the most anticipated and uniquely Japanese events, Sports Day. The yearly Sports Day, called *undokai* in Japanese, is looked forward to and practiced like crazy for by students all over Japan. That is, of course, unless you are one of the handful of students who hates sports, dancing or exercise. Or a parent who hates making *bentos* as much as I do.

In my city, most elementary school Sports Day events are in May, and preschool, junior high, and high school Sports Days are in October. There are different events at Sports Day, but it seems to me, that it is pretty much the same stuff every year. Sure, the dances will change, but most of the other events, from foot races to ball games to tug of war, are the same. The kids practice learning the dances and prepare for the other events for weeks, most of them wanting more than anything to make their parents and grandparents proud.

Mia's Sports Day was yesterday. She practiced this dance to a cheesy Japanese pop song for weeks at home and at school, and came home everyday telling us she was the fastest in her group at running. She, like most elementary kids, was so excited about Sports Day. It is an all-day affair, starting at 9 am and ending around 3 pm. So, since there is lunchtime in the middle, Japanese moms wake up at the crack of dawn to make extravagant *bentos* for groups which often include grandparents, cousins and friends. Since I hate making *bentos*, this year I hatched an ingenious plan to have a potluck *bento* party with about ten other friends planning on attending. Since I love baking, I was in charge of dessert and snacks. Score!! I had escaped making bunny-shaped rice balls and meatball and cheese skewers!

I must admit that I was a master schemer last week. There were three events in four days which required *bentos*. I have gotten okay at making them, but I still don't enjoy it at all.

The first was an outing at Abby's school. One of my *bento*-making expert mommy friends, Chie, said she was already making one that day for her daughter, so she volunteered to make Abby's too. Thanks, Chie! Abby, of course, loved eating something different than the same old *bentos* I always make. It is interesting, though, that even though I think I am the world's worst cook and *bento* maker, my kids always love my *bentos*, eating every bite of frozen food I prepare for them.

The second event, on Saturday, was a family picnic at the girls' preschool. My wonderful hubby made his famous chicken adobo, so all I had to do was put together the *bentos* with rice, veggies, and adobo, and get fruits ready. So, when I conned (I mean, convinced) my friends that a potluck *bento* party for Sports Day would be fun, it was another score for me! Yes! But you know what, while I felt a little bad for getting off easy just making dessert and bringing snacks, everyone had a blast, and my friend Chie (the one who generously volunteered to make Abby's *bento*) even commented how much more time she had since she only had to prepare fried chicken and hamburgers. She said wants to do it again! She told me that she always barely finishes making the elaborate *bentos* in time, but this time she got done way earlier than usual. So, she made more food. If it had been me, I would have read a book or something. Anyway, the others brought fruits, noodles, rice balls, and veggies. Everyone ate a ton, was very satisfied, and there was almost nothing leftover. Chie told me this would make her kids happy since they hate eating leftover Sports Day food for dinner that night. See, although my original idea may have been slightly selfish, it ended up benefiting everyone involved!

Since the elementary school Mia attends is huge (there are over 1000 kids in six grades), parents began lining up at 5 am to get a good spot to hang out on the field. Parents (almost always dads) line up, and when the gates open at 7 am, sprint to get prime views and more importantly, a spot with shade. Riz got there around 6:30, so he was a little too late to get a prime spot, but ours wasn't too bad. It didn't really matter regarding the view anyway. This year, the school put up tents to shade the students, so anywhere you sat the view was terrible. There was little chance of getting a good view of your kid, or any good pictures.

The rules were abundant this year, too. Some were good--like no drinking or smoking at the Sports Day. I hear in the past, parents would break out the beer and *sake* from 9 am. Seems bizarre to someone like me who comes from a country where drinking in public is illegal. I found it humorous that there were signs up that said, "No drinking. Your kids are watching you." There were numerous other rules. No tents were allowed due to the possibility of them flying away in the ever-present Kitakyushu wind. No parasols when watching events due to the danger of poking others or obstructing views. No ladders to take pictures because you would be in the way. There were so many tents and poles everywhere. I have no idea how anybody got any good pictures.

There were so many kids wearing the same uniforms and hats that I couldn't find Mia during her dance at all. I scanned the group for the entire song and never found her. I guess it is my fault for not asking her where she would be. I saw her practice it so much I could imagine her doing it, but it still stinks that I couldn't find her and take a picture of her. I did get to see her run her race because I knew where she was going to be. She finished second, even though she had won every time in practice. She got tangled up with another girl going around the turn, so I know in my heart that she would have thrashed her had that not happened. But I know she did her best, so I would have been proud whether she had been first or last, whether she was the thrasher or the thrashee. Funny enough, Abby was really upset that Mia didn't win. We tried to tell her that it was okay because she did her best, but she couldn't be comforted. Showed me that even though they fight like cats and dogs, Abby still looks up to her sister and is her biggest fan.

Six hours and 18 or so events after Sports Day started, it came to a close. We left with pride in our hearts at the effort that Mia made; we left with lasting memories of good times with friends; we left with full tummies full of delicious *bento* fare (and my chocolate chip butterscotch cookies); we left covered in dust from the day long high winds blowing dirt all over everything and into our eyes. We left, happy and contented, getting home after 4 pm, taking our filthy clothes off in the entranceway and hopping immediately into the shower. Refreshed, we went and got ice cream at the local supermarket, bought some sandwiches, came home and watched TV a little, and just before 8 pm, crashed. The whole family was in bed before the sun went down. It was an exhausting, but fulfilling day.

I think Sports Day is just as exhausting for parents as it is for the kids. Sports Day coupled with the all-day picnic at preschool the day before made for one pooped set of Crescini parents. I was thinking today that weekends after kids sure are different than they are before kids. But you know what? As exhausting as it is, being with my kids and cheering them on is where I wanted to be. I am glad, though, that there are no more *bento* days on the calendar for a couple of months...

#83 Where's My Kid?

The other day, my children's preschool held a family picnic day in this huge park in my city. I mean, it is huge. There is so much stuff to do, and almost everything is free. This picnic is held every year in the same park, weather permitting. Usually, the school will prepare some games and other activities, and then there will be about two hours of free time for families to eat their packed *bentos* together, and for the kids to have fun on the playground, play catch, soccer, or any of the other millions of things to do at this park.

After we ate lunch at the kid-friendly hour of 11:00, we took the kids to the playground. My oldest daughter, Mia, was also there, even though she had graduated from preschool two years before. No way we were going to leave her home. Anyway, one of her friends who had graduated with her was also there, as her brother and my middle girl Abby are in the same class at preschool. Mia, deciding she was too cool to hang out with the little kids and the folks, asked permission to run off and play with her friend. I was hesitant about letting her go without us, but Riz figured she was getting old enough; plus, the park was within sight of where we were. Turns out she couldn't find her friend right then, so I ended up going with her. Soon after, Riz, Abby and Emmy came, and Mia met up with her friend so she came, too. After a half an hour or so of hard play and lots of sweat, the inevitable, "I'm thirsty" was spoken, so I told the girls I would buy them a shaved ice. Mia's friend wanted one, too, but was short 100 yen, so I told her I would get her one. But then I got to thinking, what if her mom doesn't want her to have one? Or, what if she has a rare shaved ice allergy? That wouldn't be good. I know that I wouldn't want someone I don't know well to give my kids food, so I thought I should look for her mom for permission.

I asked her where her Mom was and she gave me the Japanese head tilt to the right and said she didn't know. So, I bought her a shaved ice anyway. How many kids have shaved ice allergies, right? A few minutes later, her little brother, who is five, comes running up crying because he cannot find mommy and hasn't seen her in a while. While his sister calmed him with shaved ice (works every time on upset kids), I went to look for a preschool teacher to take care of him. I found two, they came over and hung out with us until the kids finished eating, and then they took him back to the main picnic site to wait for his parents.

I must admit that I never cease to be amazed at how easily Japanese parents let their kids run off on their own without supervision. Maybe it stems from the fact that most kids are walking to elementary school on their own at age six, but many Japanese parents I know are much less freaked out about accidents and kidnapping than I am as an American. I have a friend who often leaves her three girls at home alone while she is working. Her oldest is ten and she feels like she can be in charge, but I don't know if I would do that. She also lets them go to the park alone, too, when she is not home. I guess she figures that as long as they are together that no one is going to kidnap three kids at once. They do have one of those kid cell phones for emergencies.

I often see kids younger than my own alone at the park, and parentless kids are always running around stores and supermarkets here. I know that statistically Japan is a much safer place for children than the U.S., but there are still stories in the news about crazy people kidnapping kids on their way home from school or just killing them for no reason at all out of the blue. Events like these seem to be increasing more and more in recent years, and some of my mommy friends are becoming more and more cautious.

I, for one, don't even like to let my kids out of my sight. Even Mia, who is almost eight, is not immune from my constant attention. I remember once I lost sight of Abby for just a few seconds at an electronics store and I felt the panic welling up in my chest. I am sure some of my precaution is cultural; American parents have just seen too many news stories to trust people not to hurt their kids. Plus, my kids may live in Japan, but they are American, and they stick out like a sore thumb, as my mom used to say. I worry that they are easy targets for kidnapping, so I am not going to let up anytime soon.

Just letting Mia walk to and from elementary school alone was a hard decision for us to make. It is the culture here, and walking with her everyday just wouldn't be cool. We did go with her to school the first few days, but then she started walking with friends, and we decided we just had to let go. She often comes home alone, which worries us, but we have taught her about not talking to strangers and she has a cell phone if she needs to call us. So, we are just trusting God to take care of her. But when we are together, especially in crowded places, Riz and I watch all three girls like a hawk. While Mia may be able to take care of herself okay, we definitely don't trust her to keep an eye on her sisters. I know that she loves them and feels responsible enough, but I also know that she gets easily distracted by what she wants to do and takes her eyes off of them. She isn't mature enough yet for that kind of responsibility. We are the parents, and that is our job still.

I found out that the mom at the Saturday picnic had gone to another area of the park with her youngest son, telling her other two kids she would come back for them. I still find it unbelievable to leave a five and seven year old alone playing at a crowded park. It wasn't even that the older one was looking after the younger one; they were doing their own thing. Maybe I am just an old fuddy duddy, but who cares? I have to think about what is best for my family, for my children, and if not letting them go out alone until they are 18 is what I have to do, I will do it (just kidding, girls!) But seriously, I would rather be safe than sorry on this point. I would rather my kids be embarrassed by me than kidnapped by a stranger. So, hang on girls! Your mommy is going to be stuck to you like glue for a long time to come.

#84 No Fun in the Sun

I remember how puzzled I was the first time I saw a young woman using an umbrella on a bright summer day. What the heck, I thought? Why use an umbrella when there is not a cloud in the sky? Little did I know, this experience was the first lesson in my continuing education about the Asian woman's aversion to the sun.

That umbrella, as I now know, was not an umbrella at all. It was a parasol, a word I am not even sure I knew before I moved here. A parasol is used to keep the sun's harmful UV rays away from the smooth, pearly white skin of Japanese women. Rarely do women leave home without one during late spring and summer. And on days that they do, they make sure they have on their absolutely huge brimmed sun hats and arm covers. Arm covers are a convenient little invention. You just slip these cotton or nylon sleeves on your forearms when wearing a short-sleeved shirt outside, and then take them off when you go inside to keep you from getting too hot. Many women buy them to protect their right forearms from getting tanned when driving a car on a sunny day. God forbid my right forearm got a tan.

And don't think men are immune to this obsession. I saw a guy once carrying a parasol, and even men will sometimes wear long sleeve shirts and pants to keep from getting tanned in summer. My student once told me he wears sunscreen just walking from his house to class every morning. This is in stark contrast to my husband Riz, who just this past weekend commented with pride about the nice tan he has going on so early in the summer season.

I often wonder exactly what it is women are trying to prevent. Is it that tanned skin is not attractive? Is it the wrinkles and spots caused by the sun? Is it skin cancer? I have a feeling that it is all of the above, but my humble opinion is that if you asked the average Japanese woman and she were honest in her response, she would admit to being more concerned with her beauty today (white skin and no wrinkles) than her skin of the future (skin cancer).

It is true that what is beautiful is different here than in the West. White skin is beautiful, young and pure, the sign of being refined. Dark skin is unattractive and rough, the sign maybe of a laborer working long hours in the fields. As any American knows, it is exactly the opposite in our culture. While someone might make fun of someone for having a farmer's tan, in general, bronzed skin denotes beauty, health, and vigor. A Japanese would probably be horrified even more than some Americans by the notion of a tanning salon. They spend so much money to keep the sun away from their skin, and we pay money to artificially darken ours.

I used to make fun of all the women paranoid about the sun, and I must admit, I sometimes still do when I think it is over the top. It makes me so hot to just look at how covered up some women are during summer. Growing up, I was a typical fair-skinned American girl who longed to be dark and healthy looking like many of my friends, so I spent my summer days outside, never using sunscreen or hats to protect my skin. Like so many others cursed with my complexion, I never really did tan, just got burnt to a crisp, peeled like crazy, and then was white again (with some extra freckles). I never worried about my skin, until I looked in the mirror one day and saw my mother's face staring back. Now, don't get me wrong. I love my mother and she is beautiful to me, but the wrinkles that she has had as long as I remember are now a part of my own face. Of course, some of this is the inevitable result of aging, but some of the blame must be placed on my irresponsible lack of regard for my skin growing up.

Now, I wear hats when I go outside, and put on sunscreen when I plan on being outside for a long period of time. However, I refuse to let the fear of the sun rob me of my love for summer. I will not stay inside on sunny days because I am afraid of getting burned. I love summer, and I love being active with my kids on summer days. One of my friends doesn't like to go to water parks with her kids because she worries about her skin. I think that is sad. She should just follow the new swimsuit trend I have been witnessing recently in Japan. Moms are wearing this full bodysuit thingy complete with a hood to the beach and water parks. To me, it is cool not because I am afraid of the sun, but because it would cover up my body, especially my thunder thighs. Riz makes fun of those getups, so I will probably never buy one. I know one thing for sure: I will never let my fear of wrinkles keep me from playing with my kids.

So, what to do? I think, just like for everything else in life, moderation is the key. Do your best to protect your skin from the sun, but enjoy life. Who knows? You might spend your whole life hiding from the sun because you don't want skin cancer, but then you eat a healthy apple sprayed with pesticides unknowingly and die anyway. Or, you may get hit by a car driven by a lady distracted by putting on her arm covers. Ultimately, we can do our best to keep ourselves and our families healthy, but our fate and health is in God's hands. So whether it be in skin care, health, eating habits, education or whatever, do the best you can, relax and enjoy life. We only have one, and it is not very long.

#85 189 Pills

I have written a lot about the Japanese medical system. Most of it is highly favorable, because I have benefited greatly from it. But like everything, this system is not perfect. There are many crazy things that I cannot understand. Things like ambulance drivers taking you to the wrong hospital, washing your nose for weeks for a sinus infection, nine visits to complete a root canal, and doctors who seem to have less confidence about treating your disease than you do (all of these things have happened to me, by the way). One thing that has been on my radar lately is the ridiculous amount of medicine prescribed for seemingly minor ailments.

If you go in for a cold, which most Americans rarely do anyway, you can count on getting four or five different kinds of medication. One will probably be an antibiotic. Anitbiotics are overprescribed here just like in the U.S. Many times my kids' doctor will give us antibiotics just in case. You can also count on getting a decongestant, some kind of pain medication, and probably another one or two mysterious medications. I figured out that going to the doctor for a cold in Japan is cheaper than getting over-the-counter medicine, so maybe that is why people here seem to always be going to the doctor for a cold. But I don't bother. Why? Well, first of all, colds will get better on their own, so unless it is a sinus infection, I tough it out. Lately I have even been toughing out sinus infections. Plus, like I wrote earlier, Japanese medicine is like candy for me. Doesn't work at all.

My oldest daugter, Mia, has a wart on her hand. We ignored it for a while, but some friends said it might spread so we should get it checkout out. So we took her in, and the doctor said it is the worst kind of wart, so she has to come in several times over the next few months to get it frozen off. In addition, she has to take some kind of medicine to keep the wart virus from spreading in her body. At least I think that is what is is for. When I was a kid, the doctor just blasted that baby off with subzero frozen liquidy stuff. Yeah, it hurt, but it was done and over with. Why does my kid have to go for months, and take 9 pills a day for 21 days to get rid of a little wart? Maybe there is some medical necessity that I am not understanding, but come on. There has got to be a better way. I am a little uncomfortable with pumping my seven-year old full of 189 pills for a wart. I probably should just get my Mom to send me some of the good old OTC medicine, Compound W.

One of the drawbacks of the cheap medical care here is that people probably tend to rely on it too much, and doctors drag out visits to milk the system for more money. Of course, it is great when you really need it, but I do think there is a tendency to go to the doctor when you could probably deal with it yourself. Something like, torching a wart with Compound W. So, Riz and I need to have a talk about whether Mia really needs to take these 189 pills to kill one wart.

I found out that these pills were harmless Chinese medicine supplements to increase the body's immune system and the spread of warts. However, I still didn't like my kid taking all those pills. It became a moot point when the wart fell off days later. Now, however, Abby has a wart on her foot, the same hideous kind that tends to spread. She was also prescribed 189 pills...

#86 School Lunch Gourmet

I remember the pizza in my high school cafeteria like it was yesterday. It was this rectangular, greasy masterpiece with cheese thicker than my finger. I looked forward to eating it everyday for lunch. Of course, I am sure the pizza was loaded with fat, calories, and lots of other bad stuff, but you know, kids don't care about stuff like that. All they want is what tastes good.

There were other healthy options at my cafeteria, a meal usually consisting of some kind of meat, vegetable and bread. It was supposedly healthier but of course, it tasted terrible and no self-respecting kid in their right mind is going to pick that cardboard tasting stuff over pizza. There was also the option of bringing your own lunch from home which I did sometimes, but the pizza was my first choice.

I don't have much memory of it, but I think the school lunches in elementary school were at least a little healthier. I am pretty sure we didn't get to eat pizza everyday, though it was on the menu sometimes. We could bring our lunches or eat the lunches at school. Like 99% of American kids, my bag lunches consisted of sandwiches, chips and apples.

I have three kids who are all enrolled in some sort of public school in Japan. My oldest is in a public elementary school, and my two youngest are in public preschools. I gotta tell you that I am really impressed with what they are feeding the kids. The daily menus are always healthy, and rarely include sugar or fried foods, Baked or grilled fish is served several times a week. The kids get some kind of vegetable and miso soup at every meal. In preschool, parents are responsible for only sending rice or bread with the kids everyday to supplement their school lunches. Once or twice a year, the preschool has an open house, and parents can eat lunch with the kids for like $1.50. What a deal. Of course, it is not nearly enough to fill up an adult, but it tastes better than anything I have ever made. There is comfort in knowing that my kids are getting healthy Japanese meals everyday at preschool. Plus, as a result of eating it everyday, they are not picky eaters, and absolutely love Japanese food.

The elementary school menu is similar. Of course because the kids are bigger, the portions are bigger, but the taste is comparable, as is the nutrition content. The Japanese government takes pride in the fact that childhood obesity has declined each of the past six years thanks to a dietary education program.[9] The main difference is that kids are not allowed to bring their lunches from home unless there are religious reasons or allergy considerations. The average kid gets no choice, and has to eat what is before him. If he doesn't like it, too bad. As far as I can tell, every kid in Kitakyushu elementary schools eats the same school lunch everyday. I went to a lecture at the school once on school lunches and I was impressed by the thought that goes into planning the lunches. They provide parents every month with a complete nutrutional breakdown of all the lunches, including ingredients, calories and salt content. At the end of the lecture, we got to eat the same thing they were eating for about two bucks. It was *yummo*, as Racheal Ray would say.

In addition, the kids are responsible for serving lunch to each other, as well as cleaning up. They eat everyday in their classroom. I think giving kids this responsibility at such a young

---

[9] http://www.washingtonpost.com/world/on-japans-school-lunch-menu-a-healthy-meal-made-from-scratch/2013/01/26/5f31d208-63a2-11e2-85f5-a8a9228e55e7_story.html

age is good for them, and teaches them to respect their surroundings more. They will not make such a big mess if they know they have to clean it up.

I am not really sure what school lunches are like at junior high and high schools. Up until recently, parents have been responsible for preparing *bentos* everyday, but these schools are gradually moving to a school lunch system. There are many grateful parents that this is happening.

One thing is for sure. There are no vending machines in Japanese schools full of soda, candy, or chips. The only drinks kids can have are the milk served with every lunch, or the tea they bring in their Thermoses from home. I always think it is kinda weird that milk is served with Japanese food; it just doesn't seem to go with it. I think it is a remnant from the American influence after World War II. There are no snacks at school, so when Mia comes home around 4 pm, she is absolutely starving.

I know that some people probably complain that there is no choice, but school lunches are completely in line with the major tenents of Japanese culture. Everybody has to do everything the same way. A Japanese proverb says, "The nail that sticks out will be hammered down." I have many complaints about the Japanese education system, but the school lunch system is not one of them. I love it. I love knowing that Mia is getting healthy, nutritious lunches everyday, and it only costs me

$40 a month. Even if it is a busy day and I end up giving my kids less than nutritious meals at dinner, at least I know they have eaten a good lunch (and breakfast, since they like to eat rice, bread, fruit and yogurt). Plus, it develops in them the ability to eat anything and everything. I have so many Japanese friends who tell me there is nothing that they really don't like. Maybe my kids will grow up to be much better eaters than I am. They have eaten more fish already than I have eaten in my entire life. Not to mention *natto*, miso soup, seaweed and pickles. Emmy is crazy about fermented pickles. When this country girl came to Japan 16 years ago, I never imagined in a million years that my kids would be begging me for seaweed and fermented pickles. My mom might disagree, but it is much better than them nagging everyday for Doritos...

#87 Fill 'Er Up

Okay, most people have never written a chapter in a book, or anything else for that matter, about gas stations. Honestly speaking, if you are American, there is really not that much to write. Most of what I can think of is negative, starting with having to prepay if you are using a credit card due to the dishonest bums driving off without paying. So much for filling her up, because you have no idea how much it is going to actually cost if you prepay. Often gas station food is disgusting, too, but I must say, the coffee is excellent. That is the one thing that I absolutely love about U.S. gas stations. Sheetz? Love. Wawa.

Heaven. I think the best coffee in America is found not at Starbucks, but at gas stations. Many of you may think I am crazy, but what I look forward to the most, along with seeing my family of course, is drinking gas station coffee every morning. Taco Bell comes in a close third.

Japanese gas stations are the bomb, but not because of food or drinks, which are non-existent, but for the service. But I will get to that in a minute. Let me first talk about gas prices. I don't want to hear any more bellyaching from my U.S. friends about high gas prices. We pay two, maybe three times here what you pay there. It just cost me $80 to fill up my minivan. $80!! When I was in college, I could fill up my car in the U.S. for about ten bucks. We don't even really drive all that much, and I feel like we are always dishing out the cash for fuel.

I love the full service stations. They are just a couple yen per liter more than self serve, and the service rocks. First of all, they are running the whole time they are waiting on you. Yesterday when I went to fill up my car, the attendants were constantly wiping their brows, running, wiping, running. They looked so hot, and yet they still kept running. They must lose a pound or two a day during the summer. After you pull in, they start filling up your car, and then proceed to wash all the windows, give you a wet towel to wipe off the dashboard, throw away the garbage for you, and check your oil and tire pressure. It can be a little annoying when they are always telling you this or that needs to be replaced and of course, it cost twice as much if you buy it from them, but I guess it is kind of like suffering through trips to Duty Free Shops on a cheap travel tour. You put up with it because of the benefit it brings you.

After you are all filled up, they then proceed to help you get out into the road, sometimes not only checking to see when it is safe to pull out, but even stopping traffic. From the time you pull in until the time you leave, it is top notch service all the way.

I used to vacuum and wash my car myself until I figured out the gas station will do it all for about twenty bucks. I don't think I have done it again myself since. Maybe you think this is expensive, but if you have three small kids like I do, vacuuming up weeks of Cheerios, broken Crayons, and papers is just not a battle I feel like fighting. I will gladly pay someone else to do it.

#88 A Better Anne Than I Am

A book about my experiences in Japan would not be complete without a section devoted to my grandmother, Annie Gillette. I would not be the person I am today without her, and being separated from her was one of the hardest things for me about living in Japan. I hope this chapter can be a tribute to her, and a testimony to the influence she had on so many.

Born Annie Dunton in rural North Carolina, she decided to ditch "Annie" for "Anne" as an adult. She was married one day before her 17th birthday, had her first child (my mom) at 19, and never went to college. She worked as a beautician, raising three young kids alone while my grandfather was off fighting in Germany during World War II. She was old-school, very traditional, very opinionated, very frugal, and very in love with her family. She loved her kids and grandkids with a passion. My greatest memories of childhood are when we all got together at Grandmother's house for Christmas. I mean, it was a total madhouse at Christmas. Tons of kids, tons of presents and tons of food. My grandmother was a master cook who scoffed at the idea of recipes. She made these incredible buttermilk biscuits from scratch never once using a recipe. As far as I could tell, she just threw a bunch of ingredients in a bowl, mixed them all together, slapped them in the oven, and twenty minutes or so later out came nine rounded pieces of heaven. On special occasions she would shape the dough into our initials or different animals. We used to love that. My mom tried many times to copy her biscuits, but she could never get it right. When she died four years ago, those biscuits and their magical taste died with her.

When I was a kid, I would go and spend the summers with my Grandmother. She had six grandkids, but I was the only girl so she loved me best (just kidding Mike, Greg, Dave, Britt and Jarrette). She loved us all the same, but we did have a special bond. Not only did we share the same name, but we shared so much more. We would go shopping all day long, me struggling to keep up with her pace; we would bake together,

Grandmother teaching me her secret chocolate fudge recipe, which unfortunately I am still unable to copy; we would watch Days of Our Lives together and bemoan the crazy things Marlena, Victor and Stefano were up to again; we would visit the local pizza shop with friends and just hang out. I would earn a few extra bucks by cutting her humungous yard, or letting her cut my hair. She was probably the only stylist to pay her young customers to cut their hair. She loved short hair on me and was always trying to con me into cutting it. After a while, I had to ban her from touching my hair because it always ended up shorter than I wanted it to be.

We were close throughout my childhood, and I would confide in her all the time. I couldn't wait to visit her for holidays, and went to see her whenever I got the chance when I was in college. I took my friends to meet her because I wanted them to see how awesome she was, and she treated them like family. I was so proud to have such a cool Grandmother, and wanted everyone to know about it.

It was really hard on her, and on me, when I moved to Japan. The first time I was in Japan, I lived in Kobe, but only for three years. She could handle it I guess knowing that it was for a limited time. After that time was up, Riz and I didn't really know what we wanted to do or where we wanted to live, so Grandmother let us live with her for a year. It was so fun. Of course, a newly-married couple could have stood for a little more privacy, but all in all, it was a great year. We saved money, and got to hang out with Grandmother and hear her pearls of wisdom everyday. Plus, we could help her out by carrying in the heavy groceries, bringing up wood for the wood stove, and cutting her grass.

I still remember all the crazy things she used to do and say. After washing her bed sheets, she would crawl into the freshly laundered sheets and moan and groan about how wonderful they felt; when she was lying on the couch comfortably, she would ask me if I would go pee for her; she would constantly remind everyone who would listen that you fall in love, get married and have children—IN THAT ORDER!! She would get irritated at slow drivers and say, "Pee or get off the pot!" Whenever I find myself saying something that she used to always say, I find myself smiling and thinking that she is still around after all, if only in my memory.

As she got older, she started slowing down. Now it was she who was not able to keep up with me, getting winded after short walks around the mall. Her hair was graying and her body weakening. It was really hard for me to tell her that Riz and I had decided to move back to Japan, as I knew it would break her heart to not get to see us very much anymore. But, being the awesome Grandmother that she was, she told me that more than anything, she just wanted me to be happy.

During my time in Kitakyushu, she battled and defeated breast cancer, and then, color cancer. I really thought she was going to live forever, as it was really hard for me to admit that this rock of a woman who always seemed to have more energy and spark than anyone else was going to get sick and die just like everyone else. She just seemed to brush everything, whether it was lifelong high cholesterol or cancer, off like an annoying fly. She was irritated at these diseases for trying to rob her of the abundant life that she was busy living, and not ready to stop living anytime soon.

Finally, five years ago, she fell and was hospitalized, and just didn't seem to be able to get better. My mom would give me regular updates, saying she seemed better, but then she would have a relapse. Just when she defeated one thing, something else would knock her down and my mom would get discouraged once again. Mom spent several months making the six-hour drive from my hometown to Grandmother's hospital a couple times a week sometimes. I kept asking Mom if I needed to come home to see her, but Mom said she thought she would make it until I came home on a planned business trip that summer. It became evident that she was not getting better, and she would never be leaving the hospital. I guess that when you are old, being inactive is the worst thing for you, because problems just seem to lead to other problems when you are just lying around.

At the end of August 2008, I was on my way to the airport to fly to the U.S. to accompany my students on a month-long study abroad program. I got a call from my mom that Grandmother had passed away. I couldn't believe that I had been so close to seeing her, and she died one day before that could happen. I couldn't even go to the funeral because I was responsible for the students during a weekend tour of Washington D.C. So, I never got to say goodbye to my beloved Grandmother, my namesake who taught me so much and is still teaching me even today as I remember things she told me when I was young. But that is okay, and I am at peace. I know that she knew how much I loved her and that I was her biggest fan. I know that she loved me, and I know I will see her again in heaven one day.

Every now and then, something will happen to remind me of our childhood times together, like the time Riz went to find some plants to plant in our garden. He took a leaf and gave it to me to smell, and my childhood came rushing back to me. It was the same kind of plant that could be found all over Grandmother's yard, and that I had smelled everyday I spent playing in her yard during my childhood. She made such an impact on me, that I am determined that even if we stay in Japan forever, my kids will know their grandmothers and have special times with them just like I did with mine. Maybe when they are older, they can go spend the summer with them, too. My grandmother was a special lady, and I will never forget her, and she lives on not only in my memory, but in my actions. You see, I often find myself telling slow people to pee or get off the pot too…

#89 Hair You Go

The first time I went to a hair salon in Japan, I spoke very little Japanese. I still remember the entire conversation, which consisted of only one line on my part: *nan demo ii,* which can be translated "whatever." Of course, that is not what I meant, but at the time, it was all I could say. There was definitely a way I wanted my hair cut. It was just that I had no idea how to say it. So, I ended up saying, "Anything is fine." Weird as it is, it actually turned out looking okay. Gestures are definitely underrated. You can have a whole conversation with gestures if necessary.

When I came to Kitakyushu, I decided that I wanted to change my image, and I heard about this cool technology called *shukumou kyousei.* This can be loosely translated 'straight perm,' but oh no, it is much more than that. Apparently, a regular straight perm is for returning naturally straight hair that has been permed back to its straight condition; it doesn't really work all that well on naturally curly or wavy hair like mine. My hair has always been unmanageably thick and wavy, and it was starting to get on my nerves. The *shukumou kyosei* perm is much stronger. It uses special chemicals to tame your natural wave into submission. It costs about $150 dollars and takes about three hours, depending on just how much wave you have. I hear that this perm is available in the U.S., but costs an arm and a leg (around $500). It usually takes four or five hours for me here in Japan because they have to do it twice due to the crazy amount of wave I have.

I love this perm, and I have been getting it for eight years or so. I can guess that it is probably not all that good for my hair to keep putting chemicals on it all the time. In fact, my hair that was once so full of body seems to have given up; even when the perm wears off it doesn't get all that wavy anymore. I have decided not to do it again for a while. I guess there are several reasons. First, I am a cheapskate and I don't feel like paying for it anymore. And, I am tired of the same of the hair style. While it is convenient, maybe it is time for an image change again. After all, I am almost 40.

Japanese hair and American hair are different, and I wonder if stylists here know how to cut Western hair. A few years ago, there was this annoying hair cut called "The Shaggy." It was this ragged-looking cut, totally frizzy and unkempt looking in my opinion. When I would go in for a haircut, no matter what, the stylist would cut my hair in the Shaggy style. It was like it was all they knew, and the default hair style in Japan. I absolutely hated it; I found out that I had to explicitly ask them not to do the Shaggy to protect my hair from that monstrosity. I finally found a stylist who realized how much I hated it, and that wretched style never graced my head again.

The perks at Japanese salons are awesome. They do this 15-20 minute shampoo. They lather you up so many times, scrubbing, massaging, scrubbing, massaging, over and over again. Ahh. Feels so good. Then, they put this hot towel under your neck and do a head massage. Riz tells me that at barber shops, they give you a good shave of the beard and eyebrows, along with a long massage to finish it off.

Since the super straight tame-your-hair-into-submission perm takes so darn long, my salon provides a coffee and snack break. They have a drink menu where you can order what you want for free, and it is served with chocolates and cookies. This kind of snack service can be found almost anywhere; even when I went to cancel my cell phone service, I was served coffee and candy.

I took my kids to get hair cuts yesterday. I can cut bangs (poorly), but it had been almost a year since they had had a real haircut, so I figured it was time. The excitement they showed at being allowed to get a haircut showed me that maybe we should go a little more often. You would have thought we were going to Disneyland. They were perfect little angels, smiling the whole time, not moving a muscle. When they were done and it was my turn, the salon staff put on a kids DVD for them, and they hung out in the awesome kids' play area. When we left, they were given little snack bags with chocolate and cookies. I don't know if they were happier with the haircuts or the goody bags.

I was worried about finding a place that could cut my hair like I want, but that hasn't been a problem. With the exception of the occasional unwanted Shaggy I got, I have found three places that have done a pretty good job with my hair. All of them have given me great service, good conversation (you get to know your stylist pretty well in four hours), and great coffee. I think if I ever move back to the U.S., I am going to miss the free coffee on my first visit to the Hair Cuttery, which is where I will end up for sure since I am such a cheapskate.

Last week, I decided I couldn't stand the wave anymore and went in for a straight perm. I surpassed my personal best (worst?). It took 5 hours, 10 minutes and you know what? It is still a little annoyingly curvy around my face. I was told they had never seen a wave as stubborn as mine.

#90 Above and Beyond

A couple of years ago during the May Golden Week holiday, I got a phone call. I was shocked to hear my pharmacist on the other end. I had forgotten to go pick up my medication before the holiday started, and since it was a four-day holiday, he was worried about me since I didn't have my medication. Actually, I had enough left to last through the holidays so I was going to be okay, but the pharmacist was so worried about me that he brought the medicine to my house, during a national holiday when the pharmacy was closed. I am not easily moved, as all my friends will tell you, but I was moved by this. Yes, he was going above and beyond the call of duty, and this is just another reason that I love this country.

This kind of service is commonplace here. We have a life insurance policy with a Japanese company, and when we change our policy, they always come to our house so we can fill out the paperwork; we have never been to their office. They usually bring with them a calendar or pencil set for the kids or some other goody. When we get our oil changed or car inspected, we usually get a free box or two of tissues. Japanese people don't think much of this kind of service because they are used to it, but it still shocks me after all these years. I am not sure if they provide all this extra service because they think that box of tissues is going to be the tipping point for whether I come back or not, or if they think it is just common courtesy. I would like to think it is the latter.

Customer service in general is just amazing. Even at McDonalds, the staff is rigorously trained about manners and politeness, and 'smile' is even a menu item. It is 0 yen. You will not find the gum chomping, grumpy, rude cashiers that you may encounter in an American McDonalds. One of my Korean students studying in the U.S once asked for ketchup at McDonalds, and the cashier threw it at him.

I remember ordering something once at McDonalds here and having to wait 30 seconds or something. The cashier sprinted out, bowed deeply, and profusely apologized that she had so inconvenienced me by making me wait an unbearably long time. You are kidding me, right?

In Japan, there is a proverb, "The customer is god." This can definitely be seen in the way customers are treated here. Interestingly enough, though, while they are polite, they are not all that friendly. Once when I went back to the States, the cashier at Children's Place commented how cute the kids are, asked me where we lived, and then engaged me in conversation for ten minutes because she was utterly fascinated that we live in Japan. While this kind of interaction happens all the time in the U.S., it has happened to me maybe three times in the thirteen years I have lived in Japan. Because Japanese customer service reps are trained so rigorously from a manual, they tend to be kind of robotic at times, just repeating what they have learned from the manual. They tend to be very polite, but not all that friendly, and have zero flexibility. Don't even think about asking for onion rings instead of fries. Big no-no. That is not in the manual. And my husband, who loves to dip fries in BBQ sauce at McDonalds? Not since we came here, since BBQ sauce is strictly for chicken nuggets. He cannot even get it if he pays for it.

They will however, give you water that you didn't even ask for, and tape down the lids on the cups for kids so they don't spill. And they will refuse to allow you to throw away your own garbage, taking it from you and telling you to leave it all there, that they will take care of it. Can you imagine this happening at

McDonalds in the U.S.? Are you laughing yet? I guess I can put up with fries instead of onion rings, and boring ketchup on my fries if I am going to get this kind of service.

Yes, the Japanese go above and beyond the call of duty when it comes to customer service. So the next time someone in customer service is rude to you, or talking on the phone or chewing gum while they are waiting on you, remember that you can always come to Japan and get a smile for 0 yen at McDonalds.

#91 Bad English

Japan is famous for its bizarre usage of English; from weird stuff on T-shirts, hats, bags and signs, to grammatically questionable national slogans used by major businesses like Hitachi's "Inspire the Next." The next what? You would think a huge company like Hitachi would run a slogan by a native speaker before using it in ad campaigns all over the country.

Not that the Japanese really care if the English is weird. The advertising world uses English because of how it sounds or looks, or because English is cool, and they don't really care how it sounds to native speakers. That is fine and all, but you would think that they would at least be a teeny bit worried if the English was so bad that a native speaker had no idea what they were talking about.

Last weekend, my family visited a hot spring in our city, and in the entranceway I noticed a sign in Japanese, with the English and Chinese translations underneath. I wish I had taken a picture, but the English translation was, "Hello Happy Customer. We would be happy is you talk to desk first" or something like that. Huh? What they wanted to convey was "If you are here to eat at the restaurant and do not plan on using the hot spring facilities, please inform the front desk upon arrival." I would have had no idea what that meant had I not looked at the Japanese. I went to inform the desk not that I wanted to eat at the restaurant, but that their English was insufferably bad. I told them I would be happy to give them a better translation, but I was informed that was not necessary. They would just look it up on the internet! Hello??!! That is what got you that weird English in the first place! Internet translation sites are notoriously bad in Japan; I can bust my internet-translation using students quicker than you can say "lazy slacker." It is so obvious. My students, while their English is chock full of mistakes, are usually able to convey their general meaning to me in their writing. In other words, it is often hard to understand, but I can figure it out. But internet translation is a grammatical mess with no hope of comprehension. It is so bad that as a teacher, I don't even know where to start when correcting it. So I don't. I give it back and tell them to do it again in their own words. The prevalence of "it" is a telltale sign of internet translation usage. Since Japanese doesn't really use subjects, all subjects become "it." For example, "Today, it woke up at 8 am and after it ate breakfast, it to school came tiredly."

Now, if a company is marketing to Japanese people with catchy, but grammatically incorrect English slogans, that is their right. But when a business like a hot spring translates Japanese rules of usage into English *for foreign customers,* and then doesn't care that those foreign customers are going to have no idea what they are talking about, that is wrong. I mean, if a native speaker tells you something posted in the entranceway for all to see is weird and unintelligible, wouldn't you think you would want to fix it? Maybe the guy at the hot spring was embarrassed; maybe he was lazy. Who knows?

Yes, this country has a very strange and complicated relationship with the English language. It doesn't care if it doesn't understand what it is trying to say to it. Oh well, it can't be helped, can it?

#92 It's Summertime...Now Do Your Homework!

Everyone who knows me is aware of my daily struggle with having my kids in the Japanese education system. There are so many things I like and appreciate, especially about the elementary schools. But there are battles, not as much with other people but with cultural ideas, expectations, and myself. I don't like the mandatory volunteerism that is PTA; I don't like sending my kids to school on Saturday, and most of all, I don't like summer homework.

This is the first day of Mia's summer vacation. She is out of school until the end of August, and we ushered in summer today by taking a long bike ride together in the stifling heat during lunchtime. Sounds fun, doesn't it? But as soon as she got home, she had to sit down and start the homework that she must finish by the end of summer vacation.

Now, to be be totally candid, it is not all that much homework, especially when you consider that she has six weeks to do it. I think it is eight handouts or something, and probably a few essays and keeping a summer diary or something. I must admit that I haven't really taken a look yet at what she is supposed to do. She could probably sit down and finish it all in a couple of days if she put her mind to it. I guess I just have a fundamental problem with homework during summer. To me, summer vacation should be magical for kids, fun, and free from the worry of homework and structure. I understand that one reason they have homework is because of the school calendar year; in the U.S. students finish a grade prior to summer break and start a new grade in the fall, but in Japan, summer break comes in the middle of the school year. The teachers give homework so the kids don't forget. And to tell the truth, kids do need to keep practicing the difficult kanji characters. Japanese everywhere, kids and adults alike, are forgetting them at an alarming pace due to reliance on technology like email and the internet.

But still, part of me wants to tell her to blow off her homework and just have fun. But I know that I can't do that, I shouldn't do that, and this is a battle not worth fighting, especially considering how bad Mia is at math (she can thank my genes for that!) So she will do one page a day until she is done, and then she will play, and do English homeschool with Riz. I guess I need to backtrack and say that while of course I want her to play during summer, I also want her to focus a little on her English education. There is not much time for that during the school year, so summer gives her and Riz and chance to get caught up.

Sometimes I think that parents here use summer to cram more info into their kids' heads. During the last few weeks of school, flier after flier came home with Mia advertising some kind of cram school or intensive summer study program or something similar. I tossed them into the garbage barely looking at them. I wonder if kids like to go to those things or if it is their parents? Maybe if their friends are going some kids will want to go too, but we just don't have the time, energy, or excess money for even more busyness in the summer. It is a time to relax together, play together, and be together. Which brings me to the next topic...

Getting up early during summer vacation. What?? Isn't the point of summer being able to sleep late without worrying about rushing around getting ready in the mornings? The last week of school, Mia came home with a pamphlet talking about keeping a healthy life rhythm during summer. Get up early, eat breakfast, don't watch TV, play outside, go to bed early. While most of these are reasonable, and all of them are ideals for the school year, to me the point of summer is being able to relax and do stuff differently than you did during the school year. Why on earth would I wake me kids up early when I don't have to? The neighborhood kids' association is having radio exercises for the kids every morning from 6:45 to 7:00. This is a time-honored Japanese tradition for schools and businesses all over the country. Kids and adults alike do morning calisthenics for ten minutes every morning to get their blood flowing and their muscles loose. But mornings are very special to me, a time I have to myself to exercise, spend time reading my Bible, and go hang out at the bakery and drink coffee. If I were to wake my kids up, I would not be able to do this every morning. Am I being selfish? Maybe. But I don't think it is necessary to wake kids up during summer vacation. My mom never woke us up unless we had to be somewhere or go somewhere.

I guess I just wish that at least during summer kids here could be free from structure and pressure. I know that kids play (after doing their homework); I know that kids take family vacations (for a day or two), and that summer is still fun here for kids despite the homework and waking up at 6:45 to exercise. It just seems to me that kids should be less busy during the summer, not more. I know that mommy sure wants to be less busy...

So, in the spirit of compromise, Mia will do her duty and finish all her homework, but stay in dreamland while her friends are stretching in the middle of the road at 6:45 am. I just have to be careful to avoid the radio exercisers when returning from my morning jaunt to the bakery. I can't be seen as the radio rebel mom...

It turns out that Mia actually had much more homework than we realized. We had failed to read in detail all her summer homework instructions, which was totally our fault. The day before school started, we realized that she should have been keeping a diary all summer, which she hadn't been. She also had to do two art projects and a parent-child book report. Yes, that's right. Riz and I had homework, too. So, for two hours on a Sunday night in early September, the whole family stayed up late doing last-minute summer homework. Mia completed her art projects and her diary, trying hard to remember all that she did during summer. Riz completed his book report, and we all went to bed after ten p.m. As much as we dislike summer homework, we are living in Japan, and as Mia's parents, we are responsible for making sure she does it. So, in other words, we totally dropped the ball. We will be much more careful in the future.

#93 Seven

Well, today is a little different from the kind of stuff I usually write, but I think you might like it anyway. I want to write about books, specifically a book that is impacting me more than any book I have ever read. I am a writer, and all writers would like to think that they have something significant to say that will change people in some meaningful way. Maybe it will make them think about the world differently; maybe it will make them passionate about a cause; maybe it will give them knowledge about a particular topic, or maybe it will just make them laugh, and there is nothing wrong with that. But I am also aware that I have read a lot of books that, while I enjoyed them at the time, didn't impact me in any significant way and I don't even remember what they were about. I would like to think that my books, and my blog, fall into the make people smarter category, or at least into the just make people laugh category, but who knows? Only time will tell.

Before I tell you about this awesome book (gotta build the suspense a little) I have to say, I just love books, and I read every chance I get. I read often. I read happily. I read fast. I can finish a good book in a day or two if I have the time (never), and some times I have five or six books going at the same time. Unlike most people, I have absolutely no preference for either e-books or print books. My husband, although he is a huge techie with a sizable collection of e-books, still prefers the smell of print books and treats them as well as his own children. Just kidding. He loves his children a little more. He respects books and sees them as treasures, which is why I horrify him every time I doggie ear a page. To him, I might as well go draw a mustache on the Mona Lisa, which would be about the same level of cultural desecration as doggie-earring (is that a word?) a book. He has grudgingly accepted my freedom to do as I please with my own books, but he has made it clear that I better not even think of doing so with his.

While I love books, it is the content--not the actual book--that enamors me. While I have been known to read some fiction (love Ted Dekker), I am mostly into non-fiction stuff--personal memoirs, historical stuff, and most importantly, Christian living books, which I hope can make me a better follower of Jesus. The problem with my voracious reading habit is that I live in Japan, and the English language book section at the local library is mainly books about Japan, translated books by Japanese authors, and Japanese cookbooks in English. I love Japan and all (obviously since I am still here after all these years), but I do want to read other stuff, too. There is a little better selection at the local bookstores, but I rarely get to them. When I do, it is a lot of the same stuff as the library, and being only a 1% Christian nation, the odds of getting a Christian living book in English are only slightly better the the Cubs winning the World Series.

So, I have only two options: read one of the hundreds of books on our bookshelves at home that Riz has bought but never read (you know it's true Honey), or download a book from

Kindle or iTunes. While I do both, recently iTunes has been my e-store of choice. My other problem is that I am a cheapskate, so I have a general rule that I will only download books that cost $3.99 or less. While I have found some real gems for that price, I have also gotten my share of lemons as well. With the advent of self-publishing, everybody thinks he's a writer...Oh yeah, I self-published this book.

Now that the suspense is killing you, I will tell you about this awesome book I found. I was browsing new Christian books on iBooks, and I came across this book called "7." The author is Jen Hatmaker, a hilarious lady around my age who, being overwhelmed by all the excess and consumerism in her life, decided to do a radical experiment using the number 7. For seven months, she focused on seven areas of excess in her life, seven areas that she needed to simplify, one month at a time. This is what she did.

Month 1: Food (eat only seven foods)

Month 2: Clothing (wear only seven articles of clothing)

Month 3: Possessions (give away seven things everyday)

Month 4: Media (get rid of seven forms of media in her life)

Month 5: Waste (cultivate seven habits for a greener life)

Month 6: Spending (spend money at only seven locations)

Month 7: Stress (pause and pray seven times a day)

Since I have recently been bothered by excess in my own life—excessive food, excessive possessions, excessive busyness—I felt like this book would be perfect for me. Only it was $9.99, meaning that I would have to break my own rule on excess to buy a book about getting rid of excess. Oh well. I figured it would be worth it.

And was it worth it? I am not finished yet (I am in month six), but I have already given away a whole bag of baby stuff, about 40 articles of clothing, and I am looking for places to donate much, much more. I absolutely cannot wait to look for more stuff to get rid of. I decided that I am going to inventory my clothes to see just how much I have. I don't really think of myself as being a clothes hoarder, but I have a feeling I have a lot more than I think. I do know I have at least 20 pairs of shoes because I cleaned out the shoe cabinet yesterday. I am reminded of a homeless ministry trip I did in New York City in college. This guy asked me if I had any socks. When I looked down at his feet, I saw they were wrapped in paper towels. And I have twenty pairs of shoes.

And I am not even mentioning my kids' shoes. They must have at least twenty pairs each. I am one of those expatriates that goes hog wild every time she return to the U.S. I think, I won't be back again for two years so I have to buy this cute shirt. If I don't, my kids will have to wear a drab navy blue shirt from a Japanese kids store that says, "Let's you playing elephant together." I have never met a sale rack I didn't like. My kids have way more shoes and clothes than I do.

Which brings me to my desire to get my kids and husband on my get-rid-of-excess bandwagon. I want my whole family to desire simplicity, and for our excess to bless someone who may really need it. Of course, Japan is a terrible place to live if you are looking for someone who really needs it. Finding an outreach to the poor or a collection center for used clothing is almost as hard as adopting a baby (we have been trying the latter for seven years). One night last week, the kids were trying to give away the whole toy room. Abby was especially enthusiastic, but Mia didn't like it all that much when Abby tried to give away her stuff.

Anyway, the other day my kids were fighting for the thousandth time over who got to use the pink cup at breakfast. Apparently, I am unaware that milk tastes better in a pink cup. Well, I lost it and decided to get rid of all the pink eating utensils. I promptly went through the cabinets, finding three pink IKEA cups to give away (I wasn't thinking straight because I gave them to a friend with a baby boy), and I threw away the pink plates, forks, and knives because they were a little too ratty to give away. As I was on my rampage, I realized that I have like 15 kids plates, 10 bowls, 10 forks, and a huge collection of sippy cups, Thermoses, chopsticks, forks, spoons and knives. I thought, "Hmm. I have 15 kids plates and only three kids. That is a little (lot) excessive." Using this as a teaching moment, I told my kids that the little girl we support in Africa (for some reason I always use Africa at times like this) may not even have one cup or plate. After I was satisfied they understood, I commenced my assault on that cabinet.

My husband is always afraid of me reading new books. It seems that when I do, I decide we need to go gluten-free, or vegetarian, or give away all our stuff or stop using social media or travel to Ethiopia to see our sponsored child (he likes that one). I guess I do have quite a mercurial personality, but in truth, like everyone else, I just want to be significant, and to leave a legacy. I want to be remembered for doing something valuable, something significant. When I die, I cannot take any of my stuff with me; I don't care about the stuff I leave behind, but I do care about the legacy I leave behind. Were lives made better because I lived on this earth? Are my children growing up into godly women who respect others and have compassion on the needy? Are people going to remember me as someone who loved God and her family? Maybe the reason I am always searching for a healthier and simpler lifestyle is because I want to be healthy and strong so I can live a long enough life to make a lasting impact. Like all people, I want to be significant.

Who knows how the rest of this book is going to influence me. Maybe it will be a while before I write my next blog post because after reading the Media chapter I may cancel my Facebook account and not go online for a month. All I know is that God is doing something really significant in me through this book. And I like it.

I finished reading Seven, and liked it so much, I am reading it again. It has forever changed how I see the world, and my place in in. For the first time in my life, I am recycling milk cartons and food trays. But don't expect me to do composting. I am not there yet.

#94 You say fuu-TAAN, I say fu-TONE

Well, summer is here again, and with it the blistering heat and suffocating humidity. Usually, the suffocating humidity doesn't come until the end of rainy season, but since there has not been much rain this rainy season, the humidity seems to have joined us a little earlier than usual. Because a lack of central heating also means a lack of central air, I have been hot, hot, hot. I took three showers on Monday. Part of me keeps the air off because I am a cheapskate and want to save money, but part of me keeps it off because there are lots of people all over the world suffering without air, so why shouldn't I?

Anyway, we have four air conditioning units in our house, all little wall units that only cool off the room we are in. These do a horrible job of heating a room, but cool it off rather nicely. There is one in our bedroom, one in the kids' bedroom, one in the toy room (God forbid the toys get hot), and one in the living room. Recently, we have been opening the windows in the living room instead of turning on the air. Of course, only the ones that still have intact screens, as the kids have busted holes in some of the others. Opening these windows would of course be an open invitation to the entire mosquito population of Kitakyushu to come on in and feast.

Last year, we had the air on in the living room for what seemed like 24-hours a day, and the ones in the kids' room and our bedroom on all night. Sorry, toys. However, this summer in an effort to save money, we have decided to all sleep in the kids' room on this giant futon on the floor. The kids, of course, are thrilled as they are always begging to sleep with Mommy and Daddy. But alas, with three kids and only one mommy (who has only one right side and one left side), there is always fighting as to who gets to sleep next to mommy. Sometimes they even try to climb up and sleep on top of me, which makes me feel loved but suffocated and hot...

Japanese people used to always sleep on futons. Now, I am not talking about the 50-pound monstrosities called "fuu-taans" in the U.S. There are no frames for Japanese fu-TONES. They are lightweight, meant to be slept on at night, and then put away during the day in a closet. They are hung outside to air out on sunny days. A good Japanese will hang them out at least once a week, and many will hang them out everyday if the weather is nice. Me? Usually when someone pees on it, or I decide to vacuum the room once a _____ (You fill in the blank). Hmm. I wonder if that is why we keep getting bitten by mites and fleas...Hmm...

Anyway, the lightweight futon helps utilize space better in small Japanese living quarters. Since you can put away a futon during the day, it means that room can be used for other stuff without a bulky bed getting in the way. Many families will sleep together on futons lined up side by side, and then after the futons are put away in the morning, will turn that room into a living room.

While many people still use futons, these days, younger Japanese are being enticed away from traditional culture by the Western bed. Many of my friends now have beds, and keep futons for when guests come for a visit. We slept on a futon for our first nine years in Japan, getting our first bed a little over four years ago. While I love futons, they are not very friendly to heavily pregnant women who must get up four times a night to pee. It is a very long way from lying on the futon to a standing position. So, finally, when I was pregnant with my third daughter Emmy, we happily bought a big American size bed from some friends who were returning to the U.S. It looked way out of place in our first house; it must have taken up half of our bedroom. However, when we moved to our new house three years ago, our new bedroom was spacious and suited our bed just fine.

So, which do I prefer? I actually like both and can sleep well on either one. My mom had severe back pain from sleeping on a futon during her first visit to Japan, so she had to sleep in our bed when she came the next time. I have never thought that one was more comfortable than the other. Of course, the bed is better during pregnancy, but that stage of my life is possibly over (never say never), and the futon actually has some advantages. Have you ever heard of a kid falling out of a futon? Of course not, because that would mean falling about one inch. On the other hand, there have been many mornings when I am downstairs and I hear the familiar thump of one of my kids falling out of our bed. They tend to come in during the night to cuddle or after having a nightmare, and until recently, they had trouble staying in the bed. I started putting pillows on the floor just in case. Riz even fell out of the bed once. I think he was having this vivid dream about falling out of a bed or something. I am not sure, but he cracked his head on the bookcase beside our bed. So, the futon is probably a little safer.

There is something comforting about the futon. It just seems so simple, so comfortable and so conducive to cuddling with the kids. I love my bed and will probably never give it up, but I am planning on enjoying this summer of snuggling with the girls while they are still young enough to snuggle...

#95 Peanut Butter Girl

After months of meaningful, enlightening writing, I have decided to let my hair down and write an entire post about peanut butter. But come to think of it, writing about peanut butter can be very meaningful, especially to someone who relies on it for her very existence, someone, say, like me.

I mentioned earlier how the Japanese have this new Japanese English way of referring to stuff that is yours that you carry around with you, something you own and don't have to borrow, buy or rent. They just add 'my' to the item in question. For example, the environmentally-conscious carry around 'my bag,' and 'my *hashi*,' meaning their own reusable shopping bag and chopsticks, respectively. They also have 'my racquet' for their tennis racket, and 'my glove' for their baseball glove. I have taken liberties with the language and decided to refer to my own small jar of peanut butter as, you guessed it, 'my peanut butter.' You see, up until recently, I carried around my own peanut butter in my bag just in case. You never know when you will need peanut butter, right? I mean, what if there is a zombie apocalypse? (Yes, I watch The Walking Dead). I have recently put an end to this disturbing habit, but I still love me some peanut butter and eat it almost everyday.

So what does peanut butter have to do with a collection of writings on Japan? Well, first of all, the Japanese are newcomers to peanut butter. Many have never eaten it, although many of those who have become just as crazy about it as I am. One of my friends gained ten pounds in the U.S. and blames it entirely on peanut butter. There is a peanut cream spread here which has many fewer calories (and in my opinion, much less taste) than good old American peanut butter. This peanut cream is sometimes included in the school lunches. I am horrified that my daughter Mia likes this impostor better than Skippy.

Anyway, the Japanese have this unfair stereotype against peanut butter. They think it will make you fat. Maybe it is not just the Japanese. A lot of Americans think that, too. The world is being deceived into thinking it is better to eat processed "diet" cookies with a list of ingredients a mile long than peanut butter on a banana. Anyway, of course, if you eat peanut butter by the spoonful (which my Japanese friend who got fat did) you are likely to pack on the pounds, but in moderation, peanut butter is a perfect food.

Unless you are one of the growing number of Americans with a peanut allergy. Now it is estimated that 1% of the population is allergic to peanuts, and they can be deadly to some. Peanut allergies are almost unheard of in Japan. I do have one Japanese friend whose daughter has a peanut allergy, and it is so rare that everyone is surprised by it. She is so worried about it that she pretty much doesn't let her daughter have anything that may possibly have peanuts in it. That knocks out one of her favorite foods, curry, since most curry sauces contain peanuts.

It seems that people in any given country develop allergies based on what kinds of foods they consume the most often. Americans eat peanuts and bread like crazy, so peanut and gluten allergies are on the rise. While neither of these allergies is common in Japan, a soba noodle allergy is, and it can be deadly, too. Since Americans don't eat soba, soba allergies are almost unheard of.

What would I do if one of my kids had a peanut allergy? Well, of course I would give up peanut butter and banish it from my house, because as much as I love peanut butter, it is nowhere near the love I have for my kids. Thankfully, though, they do not have peanut allergies, and while none of them have developed the passionate affection for peanut butter that their mommy has, they all like to eat it. But since they were born in Japan, if given a choice between a peanut butter and jelly sandwich and a fish rice ball, they will pick the rice ball every time.

I am on a mission to spread the love of peanut butter to the Japanese people. Just the other day, my friend was telling me her son didn't like meat, so she was worried about him getting enough protein. Of course I saw my chance for peanut butter propaganda, and promptly recommended the protein rich savory delight to my friend. The next time I saw her at our church's cafe, I had the staff prepare her son a piece of Texas Toast smothered in peanut butter (they also put butter on it, which is weird, but when in Rome...) He absolutely loved it, so I had one of my earliest and most successful peanut butter converts. I am also on a mission to inform everyone around me just how well peanut butter goes with chocolate. While people in Belgium scoffed at me for asking for chocolate with peanut butter inside ("That's an American invention," they said with disdain), my students who try it for the first time love it.

It's funny how ideas of what is healthy vary from country to country. Americans see tofu as a genetically modified tasteless monster food and avoid it like the plague, while the Japanese see it as the ultimate health food and try to find ways to add it to various dishes. So I find it weird they avoid peanut butter, but fill up on tofu, white bread and other highly processed junk food. If it is the last thing I do, I am going to rescue peanut butter's tarnished reputation from the pit that it is in, and get this island country's 126 million people on the peanut butter bandwagon.

Just don't try to contextualize peanut butter and put it on white rice like I did once. Like I said earlier, even I thought that was nasty.

#96 Socialize Me

Well, it's that time of year. I spend my days filling out mountains (okay, maybe only hills) of paperwork in order to get a lot of free stuff from the Japanese government. You see, I may get more benefits from the Japanese social welfare system than any other foreigner in Japan. I know, I said the 'S' word, the word that leads many upper-middle class independent Americans to boo and hiss like a snake—'social.' This of course is the adjective form of perhaps the most hated word in America —'socialism,' the fear of the American masses.

Maybe before I came to Japan I was like many middle to upper class Americans. Keep the government out of my business as much as possible, work hard, reap the benefits and not feel sorry for those not as lucky or blessed as me. The U.S. really is a dog-eat-dog survival of the fittest kind of place. Sure, many Americans are giving and donating to the poor and needy, but they want to do it on their own terms. They do not want the government to take their taxes to pay for it. Of course, the government just takes their taxes instead to pay for wars and guns. But, hey, that is another topic for another day.

Japan is not a truly socialized state like, say, England or many countries in Northern Europe. When I was hospitalized in Northern Ireland during a backpacking adventure in 2000, they didn't know what to do with me since no one ever paid for anything. I hear in Scandinavian countries that, not only is health care free, but so is all education. Of course, taxes are through the roof, but if I didn't have to worry about health care or education, I don't think I would care. The Japanese system is partially subsidized by the government, partiailly subsidized by the employer (like the U.S. system), and the rest is paid for by the insured. I pay about $300 a month for health care for my entire family, but then each time we visit the doctor we have to pay 30% of all out-of-pocket expenses. This may seem like a lot, but since the government runs the system, there is no price inflation. Most doctor visits are under $10, and very often under $5. So, I would like to describe it as somewhere in between the true social welfare systems of Europe and the price gouging, I-hope-I-don't-get-cancer-because-I-will-go-bankruptsystem of the U.S.

The medication to treat my colitis is expensive, and if not for the special program for chronic diseases that I am enrolled in, I would be paying around $50 a month out-of-pocket for my monthly medication. That is around $6000 I have not had to pay since coming to Kitakyushu ten years ago. That is not even including the ridiculously expensive steroid medications that I get for free, too, when I have flare-ups of the disease. Or the very little I paid the one time I was hospitalized for it. Criticize a socialized system all you want, but it has helped people like me tremendously.

Another reason I love the social system is the Childcare Allowance system. In an effort to help parents offset child raising costs and encourage more women to bear more children in a time of population decline, the Japanese government gives families a stipend three times a year based on their income and number of children in their family. I usually get about $1400 three times a year. It is amazing how this money always comes in right when we need it. Always. Just when the funds are low, there it is, magically appearing in my account. I am as happy as a child on Christmas morning. The amount that we receive is always changing due the revolving door government that is Japan, but it is always around the same, and we are always very thankful.

I could go on an on about the way we benefit from the social welfare system. I could talk about the free health care for kids until elementary school, the free immunizations, the cheap preschool fees, or the excellent maternity leave system. I could, but I won't because it might make my U.S. readers a little jealous.

I think that it is easy to have an opinion about something until you see things from the other side. I wonder if many Americans who are railing against a social welfare state would feel the same way if they benefited the way I do here. I wonder if they would turn down the cheap medical care because it goes against their beliefs. I doubt it. Seeing your own country through the eyes of another is not only enlightening, but necessary in order to have informed debate. You should see the confusion on people's faces here every time there is another shooting at an American school. They just don't get it. I know the problems in

U.S. society are deep and the issues complex, but sometimes the naive response of my friends here makes me wonder if they really need to be. Of course, no system, no country is perfect, and there are numerous problems with the various social programs in Japan, namely the aging population that seems to live forever. Hundreds of thousands of seniors paying two bucks a couple times a week at the hospital doesn't bode well for the future of socialized medicine in Japan. But for now, it is working, and it is benefiting a nation.

So, I may grumble and complain about the endless paperwork, but in the end, I recognize that the possible carpal tunnel syndrome I may get from filling out all the forms is worth it. I get not only a lot of free stuff from the government, but more importantly, the peace of mind that comes with it. So, give me a coffee, pass me a pen, and let me get to work.

#97 Your Phone is Smarter than You

Recently, I have really been into cycling. I love going out in the mornings and riding around for exercise, but I also like using my bike to get where I am going whenever I can. I realized that while many Japanese ride their bikes out of necessity to get somewhere, it is weird to me when they call riding their bikes from their houses to school "cycling." That, to me, is well, riding your bike to school.

Anyway, cycling (or riding your bike for that matter) is good exercise, good for the environment, and I thought good for my overall health, but I am starting to wonder these days. I went out to buy a helmet a couple weeks after I started riding after almost getting into an accident almost every single day. The straw that broke the camel's back was the danger I felt trying to avoid texting cyclists (I mean, bike riders). I am not kidding. I passed at least two or three students on bicycles texting while I was riding about 30 minutes to a private lesson one day. Most people talk about the dangers of texting while driving, but you never hear about texting while cycling. While talking on the phone while riding a bike is challenging but doable, I just cannot fathom how people can maneuver a bike while writing an email, checking Facebook, or the internet, or doing any of the other million functions a smart phone is capable of.

Smart phones have generally taken over the world, and can be found attached 24-hours a day to the hands of most people under the age of 40. I am at times just as guilty as the next guy. Everywhere I go, it seems that people are more connected to those little devices than to actual humans. Parents sit on the bench texting while their kids play at the park; families eat together but each member is doing his or her own thing on their phones; friends are hanging out with their friends but not really--in reality they are ignoring them to text still another friend. I remember not too long ago when I was a kid, if I wanted to talk to my friend I used the landline in my house (they still make those things?), and if I wanted to search for some information I used an encyclopedia (they still make those things?) Now, it seems that since everything can be done on a smart phone, they are becoming more and more indispensable to life. How many times have you panicked when you are out for the day and your phone dies? You frantically find yourself looking for a coffee shop with a plug. Come on. Be honest. I know that I have done this on numerous occasions. What am I going to do now that I cannot learn on Facebook what my elementary school classmate who I haven't seen in twenty years had for dinner last night? Tragic! Or, how am I going to get directions to that restaurant? I haven't used a map in years! (they still make those?) I am way too dependent on my smart phone, and I know that I use it much less than most people.

Anyway, Internet access can be both a blessing and a curse. I never used to know or care about random celebrity news, but now my smart phone and computer constantly give me updates about Kim Kardashian and her poor, directionally-named child. I don't give a hoot, yet I still spend my limited hours in the day clicking on the latest drama. My kids, whenever they have a question, just tell me to look it up on the Internet. Of course, this instant info can help entertain and quickly educate the little ones, but it is more than a little disturbing that they think the Internet knows everything. Abby once asked me who the loudest person in China is. I wonder if they think that the Internet knows that, too. My student just did a speech about wanting to visit The Netherlands because the people there are kind. When a classmate asked him how he knew that, he responded, of course "The Internet said so." Well, then. That settles it. It is almost as if the Internet has taken on a personality of its own, and an omniscient one at that.

I used to be able to bust my students in class for using their cell phone (they still make those?) in class. It was easy to see when they were playing around because the only functions were games, email and phone. Now, however, when I bust them, they can say, "But I was using the dictionary to look up a word," or "But I was searching for information to use for my presentation." It is not so easy now. It seems half the class is using their phones, and the other half charging them out of panic that they (the phones, not the students) may die sometime during the course of the day, leaving them unable to function or to learn anything new. Maybe they forget they are at school and should be learning from that person called a teacher (they still make those?)

But I am not totally bashing the smart phone. The usually correct GPS navigation has kept us from buying an expensive in-car navigation system. Having access to Facebook and mail instantly makes communication much easier. But I wonder, is it really going to be the end of the world if I don't learn something until I get home that night? If something is really important, can't I just call a friend instead of texting them or Facebooking them (I am surprised that "Facebooking" is not yet an English word; it is still getting underlined in red on Microsoft Word.) I, for one, am disturbed by my reliance on the smart phone. I know that comparing today's technology to that of my childhood is useless. We now live in a different world and are not going back. It is just that I think there is a need for us to put the brakes on, and to evaluate what we are really using them for. Do we really need to check Facebook every five minutes? I am sure that my kids for one, would love it if I kept my phone in my bag and played tag at the park instead (I hate tag. Maybe that is a bad example). I am thinking of trying a technology fast sometime to unplug my life, and hopefully recharge my heart. I want to get to the point where the first thing I do when I wake up is not grab my phone, but my Bible or my husband or something or someone way more significant than my phone. I think I will be a better person for it.

#98 You Shoes, You Lose

Last weekend, my family took a mostly unplanned, spontaneous vacation around the island of Kyushu. Riz and I are like that; we figure something will work out, we will find somewhere to stay, and somehow we will stay safe. When we travelled to Europe backpacking in 2000, we made zero hotel reservations and had only a rough plan of where we would go. So, when we fell asleep on an overnight train and ended up in Frankfurt rather than Munich, we thought, "Oh well. No biggie."

So, we just hopped back on the train and arrived in Munich four hours later.

Normally, though, we give great thought to our gear. We want to make sure that we are taking rugged enough stuff to support our roughing it kind of outlook on travel. As we left for our trip around Kyushu, I made sure I had on my hiking sandals, but in the rush to get out the door, I forgot to check my kids' choice of footwear. Everyone who has kids knows that they never wear appropriate shoes for the occasion; you know, boots in summer; flip flops in winter; Sunday dress shoes when going to the park. Well, for our trek around Kyushu, Mia picked Crocs-like shoes (not bad); Emmy had on dressier Crocs-like shoes (not great, but acceptable traction); and Abby chose worn out flip flops with no traction at all. We were driving, not taking the train, but we were still planning on walking a lot, so these were not the best footwear choices, especially since I had just bought them all hiking sandals FOR THE PURPOSE OF THIS VERY TRIP!! AHHH! Speaking of shoes bought for this trip, Riz forgot his, too. He had only my favorite black flip flops which he often steals, uh, I mean borrows, and his zero traction flip flops.

We found Abby some cheap replacement shoes which subsequently gave her blisters. Riz made due with my flip flops, and Abby and Mia managed to hike around Mt. Aso without falling down and breaking their necks. My obsession with inappropriate footwear continued as we visited the Takachiho

Gorge in Miyazaki Prefecture, an absolutely stunning place, with beautiful scenery and stifling humidity. Not hardcore trekking, but there was a good amount of walking up and down slopes required. I mean, it was a gorge after all. I was compelled to look at the feet of all the other tourists and was appalled at the inappropriate footwear on Japanese women. Platform shoes, flats, dress sandals, heels. Did they think they were going to a party or something? The guys were almost always wearing the right kind of shoes for walking and hiking, but the feet of probably half the women I saw were inappropriately attired, and I am not even going to get into what many of them were wearing. Then again, maybe, just maybe, they were all like my kids. They rushed out the door with the wrong shoes on their feet. But considering there were so many of them, I kind of doubt it.

Mia, Abby and I played a game in which we counted how many women were wearing inappropriate shoes for walking. We counted ten in just a few minutes. When we go sightseeing around Japan, I am really made aware of the cultural differences regarding fashion. Whereas most American women on vacation, especially doing something that involves a lot of walking would be dressed in shorts, t-shirt and tennis shoes or Teva sandals, many Japanese women just wear the same stuff they wear everyday. I guess it is fine if they are comfortable, but I just cannot imagine that platform shoes and a skirt are as comfortable as tennis shoes and shorts when walking around a gorge on a blistering hot day.

Maybe it is just because I am such a tomboy that I think this way. I have never in my life put fashion about comfort, probably to the degree that I look like a slob a lot of times. My summer footwear every year is a pair of ten dollar flip flops from Uniqlo and, um, that is about it. I wear them 90% of the time. The other ten percent can be divided between my hiking sandals ($17 knockoffs I bought in Korea), and brown flip flops (5 bucks).

Anyway, there you go. A whole chapter on shoes. Today, I made my kids wear their hiking sandals to school. Gotta get my money's worth, even if they were only 11 bucks...

#99 Costs an Arm and a Backpack

Most people are aware of the rapidly decreasing birthrate in Japan. It is estimated that the Japanese population will be down by 30% in the next 50 years, and if you ask people to give you the biggest reason for this decline, the answer will be MONEY nine times out of ten. It got me thinking, why are the bottom dwellers in the birthrate department rich Asian countries (Japan, South Korea, Taiwan, Macau)? Why is it that the richest countries in the world say they have no money for more than one or two kids, and the poorest countries in the world have five or six? I think it can be boiled down to what kind of standard of living that families wish to maintain, and for Japanese families it is a pretty high one.

The Japanese standard, the way I see it, is that they want to give their kids the best--the best opportunities, the best education, the best food, the best access to success. Of course, all parents all over the world want this, it is just that many Japanese couples won't have kids unless they think they can give it to them. Almost all parents here pay not only for college, but also for the rent, utilities, spending money, food, etc. that comes along with university students living alone in a society where having a roommate is unheard of and dormitories rare. So, if parents don't think they can pay for all this 18 years down the line, well, maybe they shouldn't have a kid then. Not only do they have to pay for tuition and room and board, but also thousands of dollars in entrance fees to college. Not to mention the thousands of dollars paid for public schooling up to college and the many times that for children who attend private schools. Then of course, there is cram school, school uniforms, and the various other after school activities that suck up not only money but time.

Elementary school students need leather backpacks that can cost hundreds of dollars. Do you have to buy one? Well, technically, no, if you want your kid to be the only child in the entire 1009 student body not to have one. My friend bought her kid a $520 backpack made out of materials manufactured by NASA. Uh yeah, I think that will will make it six years, even if used by a rowdy elementary school boy. My oldest Mia's was a middle range backpack, but it still cost $300, and I was crying all the way to the register.

Then there are the $800 desks, hundreds of dollars spent on uniforms, at least that much and maybe more on after school activities every month. Yes, kids are expensive. But wait a minute. Are they? Let's think about it for a moment.

What do you really need when you bring that bundle of joy home from the hospital? Well, a car seat (not necessarily if you are Japanese, but don't get me started on this because it is my pet peeve issue) which will run you a couple hundred bucks, especially if you get those car seat/stroller combos that are so popular in the U.S.; you need diapers, which cost about $50 bucks a month; you need a few clothes, for which you can be frugal and buy at consignment shops (totally love Once Upon a Child), or get as hand-me-downs; you need formula (about $100 a month) if you are not nursing; and maybe a baby carrier, and well, that is about it. Do you really need a crib, baby bouncer, bottle sterilizer, wipe warmer, twenty pacifiers, four strollers, a doorway bouncy thingy, a color coordinated nursery complete with glider rocker, diaper changing table and armoire, fifty bibs, and thirty pairs of socks which the baby will just kick off anyway?

I am making fun of myself because, in my naivety, I had all this stuff (except the armoire and diaper changing table). I had a jogging stroller, car seat combo stroller, portable stroller and double stroller. I even had a bike trailer. I used all this stuff, but did I really need it all? I have many regrets about my over shopping in the early days. I bet my kids had more than twenty pairs of shoes when they couldn't even really walk all that well yet. Do babies need a lot of toys? Everyone knows that they prefer to bang on a pot with a spoon or play with a rumpled piece of plastic to expensive toys. I have found with my own kids that the more stuff they have, the less they play with any of it. It is almost like they are overloaded by the choices and have no idea what to play with.

It is nice to send the kids to soccer, piano, abacus, calligraphy, Kumon, drums, swimming school, ballet, baseball, etc, etc, etc, but is it really necessary? Do you have to spend $1000 a month on this kind of stuff like my friend does? I find half the time my kids don't really even want to go anyway. So why do we send them? Of course I think it is good to spend time doing activities which stimulate the mind and train the body, and these out-of-the-house activities are way better than the kids watching TV or playing computer games (I really hate computer games), but there are plenty of free ways to get mental and physical exercise: playing in the park, riding a bicycle, playing board games, etc.

So, does it really cost hundreds of thousands of dollars to to raise a child from infancy to age 18? I can see how it would, especially living here in Japan. Parents naturally want to give their kids whatever they can to help them get ahead, be happy and send them on their way to success in adulthood. I admit that I often spend money on things my kids don't need when in reality they just want time with me. And about education, which is the number one money worry for parents in Japan BY FAR, well, my kids can pay their own way to college if necessary (insert horrified gasp!) Of course, I will pay for it if I can, but I am not about the let that worry so far in the future determine the number of kids I have. My kids will not go to cram school or own $500 backpacks. In fact, I just bought a used one for Abby for $10.00, and she likes it just fine; not only are we saving a ton of money, but also recycling resources. Why buy something new if old stuff still works just fine?

So anyway, what I am trying to say is that, yes, kids are expensive, and you will have a lot less money if you have them than if you don't. That is a no brainer. But I think that sometimes we make child raising way more complicated, busy, and expensive than it has to be. As I was teaching the topic of the declining birthrate in Japan in my classes, I noticed that in most cases, the more money people have, the more likely they are to think it isn't enough. Here, in one of the richest nations in the world, people are just not having kids. However, the pressure to conform is such that I doubt that this fact is going to change anytime soon. Maybe one day Japanese parents will follow my lead and buy used backpacks and shun the $800 desk, having their kids study at the kitchen table instead. I am realizing more and more as I raise my own kids that they don't really want that stuff anyway.

#100 I Love It Here But...

My husband and I have been in Japan for 13 years. There are plenty of things that irritate me about this place, and there have been numerous times over the years that I have felt like throwing in the towel and moving back to the States, where people say what they mean and mean what they say (even if it is extremely abrasive and rude). But the frustration passes, something great will happen to make me forget it all, and I stay another year. Our original plan to stay five years has turned into thirteen. So, obviously, there has gotta be something I love about Japan. No one would voluntarily stay here that long if it didn't have a hold on his or her heart.

I could talk forever about why Japan is a great place for me and my family, but I will try to keep it to one paragraph. For starters, it is a great place to raise children. The preschools and elementary schools are top-notch, medical care is free until age 7, and the government gives me a whole lot of money to help raise my kids ($6000 a year to be exact). Salaries are much higher here than in the U.S, and I am pretty sure I make at least twice as much as I would doing the same job in the U.S. Medical care is cheap, reliable and accessible; food is delicious and healthy; and best of all, the people are the nicest you will ever find. This country has been very good to me, and despite the minor irritations, I am very happy here.

But I would be lying if I said it was always easy. Although the number of things that I really miss continues to go down as I get more and more assimilated into Japanese culture, there are a few things about living here that are hard, really hard. Actually, there are more than a few, but I will just tell you about five of them here.

1. **Separation from family**.

By far the hardest thing about living in Japan is being so far away from family. I have always been close to my parents and two brothers, and getting to see them only once every two years is not cool. Yeah, we talk on Skype often, and I am very thankful for the new technology, but it is not the same. My kids rarely get to see their nine cousins; they love them like crazy and play together until they are worn out when they are together. Yet, the other day when I asked Abby and Emmy to name them all, the couldn't. My parents are sad that they cannot see their grandkids, and my Dad is missing out on playing catch with them like he always did with me when I was a kid. And you know what? It is hard on me, too. I am 39 years old, but I still love my mommy and sometimes need her just as much as when I was three. I hate not being able to see her more. What is more, what do we do when family members pass away? It costs $7000 for all of us to fly home to the U.S. The reality is, if someone dies, we just cannot all hop on the plane and head off to the funeral. And what if the timing is not good, and there is absolutely no way to get away? I am thinking about this more and more as I get older and so does everyone else around me, and I know some tough decisions are going to have to be made in the near future.

2. **My Kids' Weird English**

My children are completely bilingual, fully capable of carrying on an English conversation. Well, maybe not fully. While they can have conversations easily and understand what is being said to them, they are often unable to express their thoughts, opinions or anything remotely abstract in nature. At least once a day I cannot understand what one of my kids is trying to tell me. Just yesterday, four-year old Emmy said, (pointing to her skinned knee) "Mommy, what's this for?" To be honest, I had no idea what she meant. "Umm. I knee is for bending and walking and..." Turns out what she meant was, "Mommy, how did I hurt my knee?" Yeah. Not even close. These kind of conversations are routine in the Crescini house.

3. Holidays

Holidays in Japan are hard. I miss my parents, my brothers, my nieces, nephews, and cousins. It is hard to talk to my family on Skype and see them all gathered for Thanksgiving dinner while we eat a Costco chicken. It is hard to be here in Japan with their counterfeit Christmas. My parents can never attend my kids' birthday parties, and real 4th of July BBQs are only held in the my dreams.

In addition, Japanese holidays, which are so magical to the Japanese, are not so magical for me. The love that I have for Christmas, they have for New Years. But for me, it is just a day to relax and go shopping for good bargains. *Obon* and Golden Week are nothing but days off from work to spend time with my family. But honestly, nothing is as hard as being in Japan on Thanksgiving and Christmas. Thankfully, God has given me a wonderful family here, as well as awesome friends to make it a little easier.

4. Taco Bell

I know. Many of my Texas and California friends with access to authentic Mexican cuisine scoff at my passion for Taco Bell, but it is the best you are gonna get in the mountains of Virginia. I am absolutely crazy about Taco Bell. When we return to the States, I eat at Taco Bell every other day. I can feed my entire family for about ten bucks, and they all love it, although not quite as much as I do. I turned green with envy when I found out from a friend that neighboring Korea recently got their first Taco Bell. I still cannot figure out why it isn't in Japan. I heard that it was here once and failed. I cannot imagine how it could have failed, but it had to have been terrible business practices because most of my Japanese friends who visit the States love Taco Bell, too. The only Taco Bells in Japan are on the military bases, and I, unfortunately, don't have access to them. Being a huge Doritos lover, I bet if I lived in the U.S. I would eat that Doritos Locos Taco everyday and gain 10 pounds in a month.

5. **Access to Exercise Programs**

I am an exercise addict, and I am dying to try kickboxing. While it would be easy to find a class in the States, it isn't here. I have never seen one advertised in my city. I love rock climbing, but the nearest wall is 30 minutes away by car, open only when it is hard for me to go, and very expensive. I would like to try Spinning, P90X, and inline skating. But I can't, so everyday I try to keep from getting bored with running on the treadmill, letting Jillian Michaels and Billy Blanks whip my butt into shape on home DVDs, and riding my bike. Sometimes it gets old, so every now and then I head to the rock climbing wall as a splurge.

So, yes, it is hard sometimes to live here, but totally worth it. We are where we are supposed to be, doing what God wants us to do, having experiences that others could only dream of. We are both lucky and blessed to live in Japan. Plus, when we do get to go back every two years, it is such a treat and excitement for us all that we appreciate time with family and the experiences that we have all the more. We don't take much for granted while we are there. I am hoping to go home this summer by myself for a couple of weeks. I should notify Taco Bell to get ready for my arrival…

And finally...

As I was proofreading this book, I realized two things. FIrst, I cannot believe that after all the experiences and observations about Japanese culture that I put into my first book that I able able to fill this one with 371 pages of almost entirely new information. Second, I realized that my writings were heavily influenced by the seasons and time of year, which is very fitting for a book about Japan. Much more so than in my home country of the United States, Japanese life changes with the seasons: food, clothing, holidays, attitudes. Everything is in harmony with the time of year. I remember being annoyed that some of my favorite foods were only available during a certain time of year. But I realized that the fact that foods are not available all the time, the fact that they were limited, was what made that food so special to the Japanese. I realized that it took me not quite a year to write this book, and I feel like it is a trip through a year in the life of the Japanese people.

I feel like I have written my heart out in this book. But I am pretty sure that as soon as I submit it for publishing, I will think about the stuff that I didn't include in this one, and I will soon start on book number three. My goal in writing this book is the same as it was for my first--for you to know and love Japan as I do.

I am sure that you will both question and disagree with some of the things I have written, and I welcome any feedback, comments, or criticism about anything in this book. This is a book about life in Japan, but it is my take on Japan and my experiences, and everything that I have written has been influenced by both my experiences and my worldview. This book is just the opinion of one American girl who has sometimes hated but mostly loved this mysterious place, and I am sure that other foreigners here have had completely different experiences and hold different opinions. Feel free to send your comments to me, and be sure to check out my weekly blog post on Japan. Thanks for taking the time to explore Japanese culture with me.

Contact Me

Anne Crescini

annechan01@hotmail.com

Thanks....

Again to my wonderful hubby Riz for being the kind of husband who helps so much that I can work full-time, raise three beautiful daughters, and write books. I couldn't do it without you.

To my girls for being patient with me.

To Jim Xavier, for the cover design and website help. I am very glad for more reasons than you know that God has called you and your family to Japan.

To Sophie Xavier, talented and wise beyond her years, for designing the awesome caricature of me for the book cover.

To my students, who inspire me everyday.

Answers to #69 Japanese English Quiz

1. ending note=living will

2. running machine=treadmill

3. cunning=cheating

4. doctor stop=stop doing something on doctor's orders

5. idling stop=to turn off your engine while stopped at a light

6. soft cream=soft serve ice cream

7. short cut=short hair cut

8. cooler box=a drink cooler

9. best ten=top ten

10. ice candy=popsicle

11. salaryman=businessman

12. mother bag=diaper bag

13. child seat=car seat

14. skinship=bonding, particularly between mother and child

15. nighter= night baseball game

16. silver seat=seat reserved for the elderly

17. one piece=dress

18. trainer=sweatshirt

19. don't mind=don't worry about it

20. blind touch=touch typing